By Grace Alone

Stories of the Reformed Church in America

Donald J. Bruggink and Kim N. Baker

All volumes of the Historical Series of the Reformed Church in America are published by William B. Eerdmans Publishing Company and available from the RCA Distribution Center in Grand Rapids, Michigan. Special thanks to the Archives of the Reformed Church in America, the Joint Archives of Holland, and the *Church Herald*.

The Historical Series of the Reformed Church in America, No. 44

By GraceAlone

Stories of the Reformed Church in America

Donald J. Bruggink and Kim N. Baker

Wm. B. Eerdmans Publishing Company
Grand Rapids, Michigan / Cambridge, U.K.

Wm. B. Eerdmans Publishing Co.
255 Jefferson Ave. S.E., Grand Rapids, Michigan 49503
P.O. Box 163, Cambridge CB3 9PU U.K.

Printed in the United States of America

Library of Congress Cataloging-in-publication Data

Bruggink, Donald J. & Baker, Kim N.
    By Grace Alone, Stories of the Reformed Church in America / Donald J. Bruggink & Kim N. Baker.
    p. cm. - (Historical Series of the Reformed Church in America, no. 44)
    Includes bibliographic references and index.
    ISBN 0-8028-2691-1
1. Reformed Church in America, History. 2. Reformed Church in America, Colonial period to 2004. 3. Reformed Church in America, Biographical and Anecdotal Material. 4. Reformed Church in America, World Missions.

Dedicated to all those herein who have served
and to those who continue to serve.

The Historical Series of the Reformed Church in America

The series was inaugurated in 1968 by the General Synod of the Reformed Church in American acting through the Commission on History to communicate the church's heritage and collective memory and to reflect on our identity and mission, encouraging historical scholarship which informs both church and academy.

General Editor
        The Reverend Donald J. Bruggink, Ph.D.
        Western Theological Seminary

Commission on History
        James Hart Brumm, M.Div., Blooming Grove, New York
        Lynn Japinga, Ph.D., Hope College, Holland, Michigan
        Scott M. Manetsch, Ph.D., Trinity Seminary, Deerfield, Illinois
        Melody Meeter, M.Div., Brooklyn, New York
        Jesus Serrano, B.A., Norwalk, California
        Robert Terwilliger, M.Div., Kalamazoo, Michigan

Table of Contents

Marble Collegiate Church

Preface ix

Introduction Reformed from What? 1

Chapter 1 Modest Beginnings 19

Chapter 2 The Limitations of Language 29

Chapter 3 The Problems of Polity 37

Chapter 4 Big Conflicts for a Little Church 47

Chapter 5 Indian and Dutch 59

Chapter 6 Slave and Free 71

Chapter 7 Freed to Grow 81

Chapter 8 Tai-Hoey for Amoy 89

Chapter 9 Black and White 101

Chapter 10 How We've Worshiped 111

Chapter 11 An Irascible Spirit 119

Chapter 12 The Reluctant Seceder 125

Chapter 13 Room for Everyone—Almost 135

Chapter 14 The Rightful Role of Women 143

Chapter 15 Justice on Earth 155

Chapter 16 Two Nations, One Church 167

Chapter 17 Westward Ho 179

Chapter 18 Limitations of Doing It "Right" 189

Chapter 19 Limitations of Being Christian 197

Chapter 20 What's Next? 207

Index 219

Preface

The purpose of *By Grace Alone* is to share the stories of the Reformed Church in America that many may rejoice in the grace God has shown to the people of this communion. It is an exciting and grace-filled story, and the attempt has been made to tell it in a way that will engage the reader.

To that end, a word of explanation concerning the format: The twenty essays that comprise the book are set in larger type on a white background. Alongside this text, and sometimes occupying more than a page, are sidebars, set in slightly smaller type on a colored background. Readers are encouraged to follow their own styles, reading the essay from beginning to end of a chapter, stopping to read sidebars as they appear, or reading the sidebars first and the essays last, or not at all.

While the essays are intended to respond to the larger issues of our experience as a denomination, the sidebars are intended to provide supplemental information, often in the form of institutional or personal vignettes. When used for group enjoyment, while the essays may raise questions for the leader to clarify, it is hoped that the sidebars will stimulate members of the group to share their memories and experiences for mutual enrichment.

Each chapter includes a timeline, to help orient the reader in history. Major persons and events treated in the chapter are found below the timeline, while a variety of historical benchmarks are found above, varying from battles to Bach.

A glossary has also been provided in each chapter to amplify terms of particular importance to readers' understanding. No offence is intended to those for whom the terms are familiar.

It is to be hoped that many of the essays and sidebars will stimulate a curiosity for fuller investigation. Accordingly, at the end of each chapter a list of resources has been provided for further reading.

Initially the book was conceived as a matter of my authorship, with Kim N. Baker as editor. In the course of preparation, I found that my former student had become a very apt historian in his own right, and Baker must certainly be credited with coauthorship.

Functioning as editor, he shortened and enlivened my essays, as well as being responsible for format. As author he provided many of the sidebars.

Many persons and institutions must be thanked for their contributions to this volume: to Russell L. Gasero, Reformed Church archivist, for invaluable assistance with text and illustrations; to Carl Meinke and Maria Orr for the format and layout of the book; to Laurie Z. Baron, our competent copy editor; to the pastors and church members who supplied information and photos for sidebars concerning their churches; to the *Church Herald* for allowing me to use some of my earlier published work; and to the Joint Archives of Hope College and Western Theological Seminary and the A.C. Van Raalte Institute.

Every writer of history hopes that it will be a helpful guide for the present. At the very least, the story of the individuals who have ministered in the Reformed Church in America should often be an inspiration to us. While considering our frailties, we should give thanks to God for the grace which has allowed the church to continue to serve with the good news of Jesus Christ our Lord. Our help is in the name of the Lord who made heaven and earth.

Donald J. Bruggink

Introduction

Reformed From What?

Christ the Good Shepherd was the most common Christian representation in places of Christian burial during the period of persecution. A loving, caring God was at the heart of the Christian message.

Donald J. Bruggink

"**R**eformed from what?" is a question frequently asked by people unfamiliar with the Reformed Church in America. While the names of Luther, Zwingli, and Calvin are household words to some of us, to those raised in churches of American origin they may not be familiar. To answer "Reformed from what?" will take us, by way of the Reformers, back to the early church.

The great Reformers, Martin Luther, Ulrich Zwingli, and John

Calvin, did not wish to start new churches, but only to reform what was bad in the church that had continued since the time of the apostles. To be fair to the Reformers, we must spend time telling what had happened to the church that confessed to be "one, holy, catholic, and apostolic," and yet was in need of reform.

TIMELINE—Pre-Reformation
Events referenced in the chapter are below the line. Other historical events are above the line.

527-565
Reign of Justinian

410
Sack of Rome by Huns

1380
Gerhard Groote founds
Brethren of the Common Life

711-715
Muslim conquest of Spain

1453
Ottoman Turks capture
Constantinople

325
Council of Nicea

570-632
Mohammed

1096-99
First Crusade

1348
Black Death

312
Constantine victorious over
persecuting emperor Maxentius

635-637
Muslims invade Iraq

1054
Great Schism between
Latins & Greeks

1204
Latins pillage
Constantinople

1529
Turks besiege
Vienna

300	600	900	1200	1500

313
Constantine brings
peace to the church

800
Charlemagne crowned
Holy Roman Emperor

1294-1303
Boniface VIII

1471 d.
Thomas à Kempis,
Imitation of Christ

537
Justinian dedicates Hagia Sophia

1073-85
Gregory VII

1309-76
Babylonian Captivity

381
Nicene-Constinopolitan Creed

1198-1216
Innocent III

392
Theodosius proscribes
pagan worship

1378-1417
Great Schism

1379-1449
Conciliar period

TIMELINE—Reformation
Events referenced in the chapter are below the line. Other historical events are above the line.

1519
Cortez discovers Mexico

1520
Magellan sails round the world

1540
Jesuits approved

1555
Peace of Augsburg

1500
Portugal establishes secure
trade routes to India

1527
Sack of Rome
by Charles V

1545
Council of
Trent begins

1562
Huguenot wars begin

1500	1525	1550	1575

1502
Luther's B.A.

1531
Zwingli dies at Cappell

1546
Death of Luther

1564
Death of Calvin

1512
Luther's Th.D.

1541
Calvin back in Geneva

1517
Luther's 95 theses

1536
Calvin's Institutes,
Calvin at Geneva

1519
Zwingli begins ministry at Zurich

1538
Calvin at Strassbourg

The Pre-Reformation Church

For three centuries following Pentecost the Christian church never had civil legitimacy. Persecution was sporadic, and in the third century there were several widespread attempts to wipe out the church. All failed, and the church only grew stronger. During that time the church saw itself as one in unity, as holy, set apart from the world as it sought to live in obedience to Christ, catholic in that it embraced all Christians throughout the known world, and apostolic in that it followed the teachings of Christ's apostles. Centuries later, the Reformers continued to confess that belief.

With the emperor Constantine, peace came to the church in 313 AD. Favors to the church soon followed. Constantine moved his capital from Rome to

Constantine built the pilgrimage church of St. Peter's, here represented in a seventeenth century fresco prior to its destruction to make way for the present St. Peter's.

Donald J. Bruggink

Constantine—Peacemaker, Church Builder

The emperor Constantine is remembered for having brought peace to the persecuted church through the Edict of Milan in 313, which gave Christianity full legal status in the Roman Empire.

Constantine was able to do this because of his victory over the persecuting emperor, Maxentius, in the battle of the Milvian Bridge outside Rome. Before this battle Constantine had his famous vision of the symbol of Christ, the Latin letters chi and rho, and he heard the words, "In this sign conquer." The symbol was painted on helmets and shields, and the battle was won.

But Constantine should also be remembered as a church builder. His first church building project was a great basilica (meaning literally, house of the king), St. John in Lateran, on his estates on the edge of Rome. The church was built on his land at his expense, and it is the cathedral church of Rome today. During the Renaissance, Borromini gave it a new façade and redecorated the interior, but except for an enlargement of the apse, the size of the church is today what it was in Constantine's time.

In quick succession followed the building of the great pilgrimage church of St. Peter over the apostle's grave. This church was torn down in the sixteenth century to make room for the present St. Peter's.

Having built a pilgrimage church to honor St. Peter, Constantine also began a church to honor St.

Paul on the site of his burial. Serious building was begun in 384 by Valentinian II and Theodosius the Great. The church's appearance is very much as St. John Lateran would have appeared before it was cosmetically altered by Borromini.

Constantine was also occupied with building projects elsewhere. In Jerusalem he built the Church of the Holy Sepulchre, spanning the distance between Golgotha and the tomb of Joseph of Arimathea. Much of the church still remains, although its ancient splendor is sorely diminished. During the last decade of his reign, Constantine also built the present Church of the Nativity in Bethlehem.

In moving the capital of the Roman Empire to Byzantium, Constantine determined to make it a Christian city, a city of churches rather than pagan temples. Constantine's cathedral church, the first Hagia Sophia, was dedicated in 360. Little is known of it. Constantine also built the Church of the Apostles, about which the fourth-century historian, Eusebius, has left a rather complete record. The ceilings were gilded, the walls covered with marble. The church was cross-shaped, with the central part covered by a conical roof. The altar where the Lord's Supper was celebrated was located there, as was the tomb of Constantine, which was surrounded by piers inscribed to the twelve apostles—a consummate architectural declaration of Christian commitment.

Byzantium and named it Constantinople. By 470 the emperor Theodosius had declared Christianity the only legal religion in the Roman Empire. In the early sixth century, Justinian was the last emperor to reassert Roman control throughout the Mediterranean basin. The same Justinian built the great church of Holy Wisdom—in Greek, *Hagia Sophia* (another name for Christ).

Justinian's tenuous control on the western part of the empire soon slipped away as barbarian tribes surged through western Europe, invading even the city of Rome. The Dark Ages of the breakdown of centralized government, law and order, and educational institutions created a power vacuum in the West. The only source of centralized influence was the church, with the bishop of Rome as its leader. The priority of the bishop of Rome was the result of the fact that the apostles Peter and Paul had lived and taught the Christian faith in Rome and had both been martyred for that faith. Cities that had experienced the personal teaching of an apostle were seen as sources of faithful Christian teaching. Rome was able to claim these two apostles, plus their martyrdom—preeminence appropriate to a city that had long been the capital of the great Roman Empire.

But while the western empire was falling apart, the church continued to expand. Most of the growth took place where the empire had been strongest, in what is now Italy, North Africa, France, and Spain, and, almost independently, in Ireland. From there it spread to Scotland and down to England, where it met Christian monks from Rome. It was during this period that the institution of feudalism began to develop—important for its impact on the development of the church. The feudal system created order in the absence of centralized government. Each local squire or lord or duke swore to protect the peasants who worked his fields if they would help defend his interests. The more land one controlled, the more power one had. These local centers of power in turn swore allegiance to local kings, where again more land meant more power.

At the beginning of the ninth century there was a bright spot in the Dark Ages with the emperor Charlemagne. By gaining the allegiance of minor kings and lords, Charlemagne established nominal control of what is now France, Germany, Switzerland, and northern Italy—with lesser control in parts of what is now Poland, Austria, and the Czech Republic.

Donald J. Bruggink

The Emperor Charlemagne

Charlemagne was a friend of the church and a friend of scholars (all of whom were churchmen). Charlemagne not only saw himself as a friend of the church, but as appointed by God to protect the church. His chief scholar, Alcuin, compared his kingdom to the city of God as defined by the great fifth century scholar, Augustine of Hippo. Alcuin also compared Charlemagne to David of the Old Testament as a leader of the New Israel, the Church. In consolidating his rule, Charlemagne established bishoprics, with feudal lands, in order that the power of the bishops might act as a counterbalance to that of the local lords. Charlemagne was crowned Holy Roman Emperor in Rome in 800 AD. (The Holy Roman Emperor in Constantinople did not look kindly upon this usurpation of title and, by implication, of power— another action contributing to the division between the eastern and western church.)

After Charlemagne's death, his vast empire disintegrated, and feudal relationships grew more powerful. Because land represented wealth and power, whether in the hands of barons or bishops, it was in the interest of the civil power to control the power of the church. Therefore it became important who would appoint (invest) the clergy to their offices. At the very least, rulers wanted to approve clergy friendly to themselves, and often nobles tried to place their younger sons in positions of churchly power. Needless to say, such clergy did not often have spiritual values as their primary concern. Many of the terrible instances of abuse in the medieval church are the result of such appointments. Even the papacy became a prize for which the powerful families of Rome competed. Within the Holy Roman Empire, emperors and kings insisted on appointing the important clerics of their lands to serve the interests of state.

Many within the church were appalled by such appointments and began to take steps to enable the church to regain the right to invest its own candidates for church offices. Largely through the power of large, spiritually committed monastic groups, monks began to gain ascendancy in the hierarchy of the church, ultimately gaining even the papacy in the person of Gregory VII. Ultimately, the investiture conflict was won by the church, at least temporarily, and it became possible for the church to place in office those it thought most fit. The papacy reached its pinnacle of power in the person of Innocent III in the early thirteenth century.

However, to exercise the control of appointments in a far-flung church required an increasingly large bureaucracy, which in turn required more funds. This need for more money brought about another conflict between church and state. In response to the demands of Pope Boniface VIII for funds from the churches of France, Phillip the Fair forbade the export of gold from the country. Boniface responded by excommunicating

Investiture conflict: The dispute as to who (church or secular power) should "invest" or determine who should be priest or bishop, thus controlling the church.

Innocent III

Donald J. Bruggink

The papal palace at Avignon

Great Schism: The great division in Christendom when there was simultaneously more than one pope (1378-1417).

Conciliarism: The concept that councils composed of the heads of church and state most fully represented the church, the body of believers (1379-1449).

Phillip, who then took the pope prisoner. Boniface died shortly thereafter, whether from abuse or embarrassment has never been proven. The rising power of the nation state had proven more powerful than an incompetent papacy. Phillip, not wishing a continuing conflict with the papacy, arranged to have the next pope come to live in Avignon in French territory. This strange arrangement, with the pope of Rome residing in Avignon, was a scandal in the church that went on for almost seventy years, and it became known as the Babylonian Captivity of the church—a reference to the seventy years that the Jews were captives in Babylon.

The other nations of Europe did not look kindly on this French nationalizing of the papacy, with resulting political as well as ecclesial and moral pressure to return to Rome. After the death of Pope Gregory XI at Avignon, there was an election in Rome of an Italian pope, Urban VI, the result of considerable pressure by the Roman populace. This did not please the

French king, and when the cardinals (who elected the pope) returned to Avignon, they were pressured to elect a pope favorable to the French (Clement VII) and depose their earlier Italian choice. However, Urban refused to step down. In this event, known as the Great Schism, Europe was confronted by the impossible—two claimants for the sole headship of the church, each with his national supporters, each claiming full legitimacy and the revenues of the church, and each hurling anathemas at the other.

Conciliarism, the view that the church was best represented in councils by bishops and the emperor (the pope being the chief executive between councils), seemed to be the answer to this Great Schism. A council met in Pisa in 1409 and deposed the two existing popes and elected another. Since neither of the first two popes would resign, Christendom now had three popes. Another council was called, this time at Constance (1414-18), where all three popes

Donald J. Bruggink

The tower and cathedral of Pisa

were deposed, this time successfully, and a new pope elected. Another council at Basel (1431) attempted to reform the church. Unfortunately, many reforms simply transferred power (and the opportunity for abuse) from the papacy to the bishops.

One abuse was a frequent lack of clerical fitness and education. The method of training for the priesthood is what would today be called the teaching church. A priest in training attached himself to a church and acted as an intern or apprentice, learning what should be done, until the supervising priest recommended him for ordination. When he was apprenticed to a good and wise priest, the method was excellent. When apprenticed to a scoundrel, the results were frequently bad. The teaching-church system of priestly preparation had few safeguards, especially considering that the final test for appointment was usually simony, the payment of money for a parish—or a bishopric.

A poorly trained priesthood often resulted in poorly educated laity. The universal use of Latin in the western church, intended to preserve the faithful apostolic witness to the truth of the gospel, had the unfortunate result of keeping the content of worship from the laity. Since worship could no longer educate people, super-stition abounded. Then as now, plenty of religious charlatans played upon the religiously gullible. Saints and martyrs, who were to be regarded as examples of faithful and valiant Christian living, became themselves the subjects of venera-tion, worship, and superstition.

The church also abused its power to raise money. It took a lot of money to support the large bureaucracies. One money-raising device for the papacy was the annates, whereby a new bishop turned over the first year's revenues of his diocese in exchange for his appointment. A century before the Reformation, some contended there was hardly a priest or bishop in Christendom who had not been required to buy his office.

There were even less reputable means for exacting money. Those who could afford multiple bishoprics paid extra for the privilege. When Albert of Brandenberg, bishop of Halberstadt and Magdeburg, also wished to become archbishop of Mainz (further increasing his revenues), he was required to pay ten thousand ducats. The sum had to be borrowed at a very high rate of interest. For prompt payment, the papacy allowed a special sale of pardons for sins, with half of the proceeds to go to the archbishop of Mainz to pay his debt, and the other half to go directly to the papacy. It was this very sale of indulgences that triggered Luther's protests— even though he

> ### *Come Down, O Love Divine*
>
> *Come down, O Love divine, seek thou this soul of mine, and visit it with thine own ardor glowing; O Comforter, draw near, within my heart appear, and kindle it, thy holy flame bestowing.*
>
> *O let it freely burn, till earthly passions turn to dust and ashes in its heat consuming, and let thy glorious light shine ever on my sight and clothe me round, the while my path illuming.*
>
> *And so the yearning strong with which the soul will long shall far outpass the power of human telling, for none can guess its grace, till he become the place wherein the Holy Spirit makes his dwelling.*
>
> Bianco of Siena, d. 1434

knew nothing of the seamy financial dealings behind the sale.

It's important to remember that many faithful Christians lived lives of holiness and devotion in these centuries prior to the Reformation. While many used the church for power and gain, others committed their lives to loving service. St. Francis gave all in his service. Bianco of Sienna, in the fourteenth century, wrote poetry celebrating the love of Christ (cf. *Rejoice in the Lord*, "Come Down, O Love Divine"), even as he established a halfway house for prostitutes in Sienna. During these centuries, Thomas á Kempis wrote *The Imitation of Christ*, and northern Europe enjoyed a resurgence of lay piety and devotion. The very disparity between the spiritual earnestness among many of the laity and the failure of the institutional church to reform its abuses helped

The Reformation of Worship

Worship is not entertainment or even edification; it is the joyful work of giving glory to God in recognition of God's worth.

During the Middle Ages in Western Europe, the entire service of worship was in Latin. Everything in the liturgy, including the prayers and the music, was fixed from Sunday to Sunday. This was thought to be necessary to protect the apostolic truth of the church. In a time when few could read or write, the comfort of the church was found primarily in the

The Basel Grossmunster where Zwingli would first have heard a Swiss-German insertion in the Latin Mass.

Donald J. Bruggink

assurance of the sacraments. As learning gradually increased in the late Middle Ages, some priests and bishops began to insert into the Latin mass (which was always said in its entirety) a service called a *prone*, which was in the language of the people.

Ulrich Zwingli's childhood was spent high in the Swiss Alps, where the priest in the local church said mass only in Latin. When Zwingli went to the University of Basel, he would have found the same Latin mass being said in every church in the city. However, in the church of the people's priest, Ulrich Surgant, a service in Zwingli's own Swiss German would have been inserted after the reading of the Gospel in Latin. Then in German they would have heard the Gospel, the Our Father and Ave Maria, sermon, bidding prayer, Our Father and Ave Maria (repeated), Apostles' Creed, Decalogue, confession, and absolution. At that point, the Latin mass would continue.

Later, when Zwingli began reforming the church at Zurich, his service of the Word was little more than the medieval *prone* with a greatly expanded reading of Scripture and sermon. He ultimately abolished most of the Latin mass, and the Lord's Supper was celebrated only four times a year. Zwingli banned organs and choirs from the church service because the music had become so complicated that the congregation could neither participate nor understand its message.

As Zwinglian reforms spread from Zurich to Bern, Geneva, Neuchatel, and Basel, Zwingli's simple service became normative.

Outside of the Swiss cities, however, a different

fuel the Reformation. If there is a moral to the story, it is not that the medieval church was entirely bad but that, in every age, we must be concerned to give valid expression to the claim that the church is one, *holy*, catholic, and apostolic.

The Reformation

The church was reformed from the abuses of the late medieval period, and it was reformed according to the Word of God. Martin Luther's nailing ninety-five theses against the abuse of indulgences to the door of the castle church of Wittenburg on October 31, 1517, is the event often labeled as the Reformation's beginning. Martin Luther was a monk of the Augustinian order who was deeply troubled by the question of how he could be

Indulgences: Luther preached against indulgences that were given under papal authority and were perceived as granting forgiveness of sin and reducing the time spent in purgatory.

type of reformation of worship was taking place. In the city of Strasbourg in 1524, priest Diebold Schwarz translated and said the entire mass in German. A year later an ex-Dominican, Martin Bucer, began a simplification of worship. The term "mass" gave way to "Lord's Supper." The "altar" became the "table," and the priest was described as a "minister." In time, Bucer experimented with free prayers to be said by the congregation, but services became so disorderly that he soon retreated to a set order of worship with set prayers. Bucer, however, maintained the traditional shape of the liturgy that had been common from New Testament times—a service of Word and sacrament. Also in accord with the early church, the Lord's Supper was celebrated every Sunday, at least at the cathedral church, and once a month in the other churches of the city. All Christians were expected to partake. This was a radical change from pre-Reformation times, when the people seldom participated more than once a year, even though the priest said mass daily.

During these years, a brilliant young Frenchman had completed his studies in law and humanities. By early in 1536 that young man, John Calvin, had published a volume called *Institutes of the Christian Religion*. In it he argued forcefully that Christians should celebrate the Lord's Supper each Lord's Day.

Guilleume Farel had reformed Geneva some years earlier. As a follower of Zwingli, he had used the liturgy of Zurich, which had quickly become the

Calvin's church: Sant Pierre, Geneva

Donald J. Bruggink

norm. With both the medieval and Zurich's precedent for infrequent Communion, the city council was not about to be convinced by Calvin to commune weekly.

Three years later, in Strasbourg, ministering to French refugees, Calvin was able to celebrate the Lord's Supper on at least a monthly basis. There, Calvin published a liturgy very similar to that of Bucer, which he titled, *The Form of Prayers According to the Custom of the Ancient Church*. When he was called back to Geneva in 1542, he published the same with slight variations. Because the form of this service is remarkably like the current liturgy of the Reformed Church in America, it is important to ask if his liturgy was truly based on the Bible. While the New Testament does not describe a sequence of worship, it does give us enough insight into the worship of the early church that we know what elements were included, and they are the ones found in Calvin's—and our— liturgy: salutation, praise in psalms or hymns, confession, assurance of pardon, law, prayer, Scripture, sermon, creed, words of institution, Communion, benediction. For a full diet of Christian worship, these constitutive elements of our service to God were there to nourish the New Testament church, even as they are a part of our liturgy to nourish our lives as Christians.

Apostolic church: The church that follows the teaching of the apostles of Jesus.

assured of his salvation when faced by the demands of a righteous God.

The namesake of Luther's order, the fifth-century theologian Augustine of Hippo, has been described as the "doctor of grace." Augustine emphasized the biblical truth that people are saved by the grace of Christ and not by works. Augustine emphasized this sovereign grace of God so strongly that, when asked why some received that grace and some did not, he affirmed, with the apostle Paul, that it was God's own decision.

For Augustine, receiving God's grace meant receiving forgiveness and living a life of faith, hope, and love. For Luther, as he examined his life, the question was whether his life of faith, hope, and love could withstand the demands of a righteous God. Between the fifth and the fifteenth centuries, the understanding of how God's grace produced in a person a life of faith, hope, and love had fallen into an imbalance between the free grace of God and the good works of the Christian.

The church struggled with how to communicate the relationship between the forgiveness of Christ and the good works expected of the Christian. By the fifteenth century, most people perceived the theology of forgiveness and good works as follows: the grace of Christ was given at baptism for the forgiveness of original and all pre-baptismal sins. That grace also enabled the person to live a life of obedience, but when he or she sinned, doing penance was necessary. Penance included contrition, confession to a priest, the penance itself (an act that expressed sorrow for the sin), and absolution. Thus the grace of Christ was extended through the church by the priest. People believed being present at or partaking of the sacrament of Holy Communion also bestowed the grace of Christ for forgiveness and strength to lead a life of faith, hope, and love. Indulgences fit into this theology because people believed they were an extension of the grace (merits) of Christ bestowed by the church. This scheme's failure, however, was that it regarded God's grace in Christ as a thing, a measurable something, rather than as a personal relation with Christ.

Luther's problem with the theology of penance and indulgences was that he did not believe that he—or any person— could lead a life that would satisfy the demands of a righteous God.

Martin Luther, by Lucas Cranach the Elder, 1530

Selling indulgences

How could the penitent ever be sure that the proper contrition for sin existed? How could the penitent be sure that all sin had been recognized and confessed? How could one be sure that the penance the priest prescribed was adequate? Luther could not answer any of these questions in a way that would leave him certain of his salvation. And while Luther found the penitential system comfortless, the sale of indulgences was to him a total outrage, for it implied that the purchase of an indulgence granted forgiveness and made penance unnecessary.

Luther's confessor, the head of his monastery, prescribed for Luther the study of Scripture, and then the teaching of Scripture in the little University of Wittenburg. In this study of Scripture Luther found the answer to his anxious searching: "The just shall live by faith." The righteousness of God declared the sinner justified in Jesus Christ. Luther discovered that in God's grace the sinner did not depend upon his or her own righteousness, only upon Christ's righteousness.

Like Augustine, Luther saw that salvation was solely by God's grace. Unlike Augustine, Luther distinguished between justification and sanctification. For Luther, identifying justification with the Christian life of good works confused the issue and implied that forgiveness was partly due to God's grace and partly due to good works. Instead, Luther insisted that justification was totally of God. Humans could not do enough good works to deserve forgiveness. Good works did follow forgiveness, but they were done out of gratitude. Luther insisted that the Bible's mention of the reward or merit of good works was also the result of God's grace.

Luther's view of justification by faith alone was totally incompatible with the sale of indulgences. Luther challenged the practice of indulgences, selling from a treasury supposedly full of merits, by insisting that the gospel was the treasure of the church and was to be given freely. Rome refused to take Luther seriously, because he was an unknown German monk and because indulgences were a highly profitable source of church income. Rome's response to Luther's challenge was to have him tried and condemned before the German Diet at Worms, and then to condemn and excommunicate him. But by this time Luther's ideas had become too popular to be stopped. Luther's success lay in his theology, which offered certainty of salvation

Donald J. Bruggink

The Grossmunster in Zurich, where Zwingli became people's priest in 1519.

popularity throughout what is now Germany and Scandinavia, Ulrich Zwingli began a reformation of the church in Zurich. Zwingli's reforms, like Luther's, had their origins in the Bible. His first steps abolished fast days and clerical celibacy. Then he reformed worship, putting a heavy emphasis upon the preaching of Holy Scripture. It was the Swiss reformers who claimed the phrase, "Reformed according to the Word of God." Whereas Luther was willing to continue to use in worship and practice everything not excluded by Scripture, the Swiss tended to use only those things specifically included in Scripture. While Luther continued to respect the crucifix in churches, Zwingli excluded it, as well as all art and images. While Luther wrote hymns, Zwingli took out the organs and eliminated all music from the church. Whereas Luther continued a weekly celebration of the Eucharist, Zwingli or the city

through the free grace of God. Associated with that central idea was the concept of the priesthood of all believers—the person of faith could come directly before God.

Two years after Luther nailed his theses to the church door in Wittenburg, and as his ideas gained

Zwingli—Activist and Scholar

Born in 1484, the son of the local bailiff in Wildhaus, Switzerland, Ulrich Zwingli was a social activist and scholar, as well as a reformer.

Social Activist: Zwingli's first parish was in the town of Glarus, whose primary export was mercenaries—Swiss men who fought other people's wars for money. Zwingli was first asked to be chaplain to the mercenaries of Glarus when they fought for the pope against the French. The "battle" was of the Renaissance kind where armies positioned themselves, maneuvered, maintained a standoff, and negotiated a settlement without much shedding of blood. For his services Zwingli received a papal medal and a small stipend. The following year, however, Zwingli witnessed a

different scene. The French, together with their hired Swiss mercenaries from other cities, joined in a real battle with the pope's outnumbered mercenaries, including the men of Glarus. Sickened by the number of maimed and dying, Zwingli returned to Glarus and began writing pamphlets against mercenary service. He was sufficiently effective to earn the hostility of the military and was thrown out of his parish.

Scholar: Zwingli read voraciously. He had a standing order with Froben, the book publisher in Basel, for every new book that came from their presses. He devoured Erasmus's edition of the Greek New Testament and memorized all of the Epistles of Paul in Greek.

council limited the celebration to four times a year and made the weekly Sunday service a service of the Word only.

From Zurich, the Swiss reformation spread to the city of Bern and ultimately to Geneva. Guilleme Farel was the initial reformer of Geneva, but he was no administrator, and the reformed city of Geneva needed organization. At this point a young scholar, who had just published the *Institutes of the Christian Religion*, stopped in Geneva on his way to Strassbourg. Farel implored John Calvin to remain in Geneva to organize the church there. The organization used by the Roman Catholic church had

John Calvin, by Rene Boyvin.

IOHANNES · CALVINVS ·
ANNO · ÆTATIS · 53 ·
· B. ·

been set aside. Geneva had rejected the authority of the bishop and pope along with the canon law of the church. With the rejection of penance— with its requirement of confession and absolution as a sacrament—the church no longer had any formal means of discipline. The civil government assumed control of the church, its functions, and its properties. If the church was to have any independence from the whim of the city councils, it had to be organized.

Calvin agreed to Farel's demand and remained in Geneva. The year was 1536—the same year the

Justification: Luther preached from the Book of Romans that individuals are made just before God by grace alone through the redemption of Jesus Christ through faith.

Sanctification: To be sanctified, to be made holy.

Excommunication: To be cut off from the Lord's Supper and thus excluded from the church.

The Calvin You May Not Know

Most people know John Calvin the theologian, administrator, liturgist, and hymnologist. He was also a workaholic, father, social activist, feminist, and entertainer.

Workaholic: Calvin produced not only eight editions of the *Institutes of the Christian Religion*, but also commentaries on the entire Bible with the exception of Revelation, not to mention volumes of personal correspondence.

Father: Calvin had a single son, over whose crib he would "babble" as parents do with an infant. Calvin used the same word to describe how God in his Word communicates with us in a language we can understand. Calvin's son died in infancy.

Social Activist: Children would occasionally fall to their deaths from balconies and windows.

Calvin insisted that the city council pass and enforce a law requiring adequate railings to prevent such deaths.

Feminist: Geneva, like most cities, had a death penalty for adultery; however, women were usually the only ones put to death. Calvin insisted that, if the death penalty was to be observed, the adulterer as well as the adulteress be put to death. With this insistence, the death penalty ceased to be enforced during Calvin's time.

Entertainer: To entice Calvin back to Geneva after his Strassbourg stay, in addition to his salary, his annual remuneration included two hundred eighty gallons of wine. This was in recognition that Calvin on an almost daily basis entertained up to twelve people at his table.

people had voted for the reform of the church and obligatory public education. Calvin was asked to draw up a book of church order. In his ordinances, he proposed the office of elder to oversee discipline in the church, and the office of deacon to carry out acts of welfare. Both offices were to be held by appointed laypeople. To this the city council agreed, but it decreed that elders were to be nominated and elected by and from the membership of the city councils.

What We Believe

The Church of the Holy Spirit, Heidelberg.

Donald J. Bruggink

Q. What is your only comfort in life and in death?

A. That I am not my own, but belong body and soul, in life and in death to my faithful Savior, Jesus Christ. Christ has fully paid for all my sins with his precious blood, and has set me free from all the power of the devil. He also watches over me in such a way that not a hair can fall from my head without the will of my Father in heaven; in fact, all things must work together for my salvation. Because I belong to him, Christ, by his Holy Spirit assures me of eternal life and makes me wholeheartedly willing and ready from now on to live for him.

—Lord's Day 1, The Heidelberg Catechism

Our Creeds

The Reformed Church in America believes what all Christians believe. First and foremost, we believe the affirmation, "Jesus is Lord" (1 Cor.12:3), the earliest of New Testament creeds.

The first ecumenical or church-wide creed is that of Nicea in 325; it affirms the full divinity of Christ. A few years later, in 381, at Constantinople, the creed was strengthened by affirming the full personhood of the Holy Spirit. That creed is what we find in our hymnals, liturgies, and doctrinal standards as the Nicene Creed. It is believed and confessed by Protestant, Roman Catholic, and Orthodox Christians.

The most commonly used statement of faith in the medieval Roman church was the Apostles' Creed. The Reformed churches all insisted that they stood in continuity with the apostolic church and therefore affirmed the Apostles' Creed as their faith. Remember, the Reformers were reforming the church, not starting a new faith.

A third creed, the Athanasian Creed, also marks our continuity with the early church. In fourth-century Egypt, Athanasius was the principal theologian in the conflict with Arius, who saw Christ as ultimately human. Athanasius saw clearly that Christ had to be fully God if humans were to be saved. While Athanasius did not himself write the creed, which arose out of church-wide councils from Nicea in 325 to Chalcedon in 451, the Athanasian Creed states with precision his doctrine of the Trinity and the two natures of Christ, fully human and fully divine. The Reformed Church in America includes the Athanasian Creed among its confessions.

Our Doctrinal Standards

In addition to these ecumenical confessions, a number of "standards of faith" were written during the Reformation to further define beliefs. These standards sought to declare the Reformed faith as a continuation of the apostolic church, and to distinguish it from the Roman Catholic church, primarily through a positive emphasis upon Reformed beliefs.

The Belgic Confession, first affirmed by the

Furthermore, the council said, any discipline recommended by the elders of the church had to be approved by the city council. Calvin further proposed that, unlike the church in Zurich, in Geneva the Lord's Supper be celebrated every Sunday. This stood in marked contrast not only to Zurich but to Roman Catholic practice. While Mass was celebrated every day, most people partook of the Lord's Supper only once a year. For many, partaking so rarely was an act of

Reformed churches in the Netherlands, was written by Guido de Bres in 1561 as a testimony to Spanish authorities that the Reformed faith stood in continuity with the ancient church, and that its followers were law-abiding Christians. It affirmed Scripture as the only rule of faith and salvation in Christ alone. The Belgic Confession was soon adopted by the synods of Antwerp (1566), of Wesel (1568), and of Dort (1619).

The Synod of Dort also produced another of our doctrinal standards, the Canons of Dort. The Dutch in America often remember the canons with the acronym TULIP, standing for Total depravity, Unconditional election, Limited atonement, Irresistible grace, and the Perseverance of the saints. All of these affirmations

The National Synod of Dordrecht, 1618-19.

were meant to articulate a doctrine of God's grace as totally unmerited. God alone saves. Humankind is unable to save itself. This was all the more important in an age of great human scientific accomplishment and confidence in human reason. The canons attribute saving power to God and God alone.

The most familiar of the Reformed standards is the Heidelberg Catechism. It was written in 1563 at the direction of the prince, and the resulting product was one of genius. In it the staples of Christian instruction from the Middle Ages—the Apostles' Creed, the sacraments, the Ten Commandments, and the Lord's Prayer—are explained in a question and answer format that structures their content in a distinctively Reformed way.

The catechism is organized into three parts: guilt, grace, and gratitude. Its first and shortest section defines human sin in severe terms that would satisfy the apostle Paul; the greatest of catholic theologians, Augustine; and the greatest of Reformed theologians, Calvin.

Its second section, on God's grace, is by far the longest. It opens with the question of how we are saved from sin, and it answers: by faith in what God has done for us in Jesus Christ. In describing the content of that personal faith, the catechism uses the same Apostles' Creed that had been used for centuries.

Also included in the section on grace are the sacraments, but in the Heidelberg Catechism the number of sacraments is reduced to two—baptism and the Lord's Supper. In the catechism, baptism and the Lord's Supper, along with the preached Word, are seen as means of grace, a teaching consistent with that of the Roman church. But here the sacraments are defined not as a "things" or "commodities" that one obtains to buy salvation, but as signs and seals of the presence of Christ to whom we are joined by the Holy Spirit, and in whom alone we have our salvation.

Finally, the catechism describes how we are to show gratitude to God through obedience (the Ten Commandments) and prayer (the Lord's Prayer). The catechism has a distinctively Reformed emphasis: good works are to be done out of gratitude. Faith in God's grace results in salvation. God's free salvation is the cause for our gratitude, our obedience, and our prayer.

Church of the Holy Spirit, where a dispute over baptism prompted the writing of the Heidelberg Catechism.

Donald J. Bruggink

Belhar

Liturgy: Literally, the work of the people. Liturgy usually refers to the order and content of worship.

Votum: Latin, meaning desire. It is the desire to live with our help in the name of the Lord who made heaven and earth.

piety, for they felt they were unworthy. Others abstained because they feared the penance that might be required of them, for one could not partake of the sacrament without having gone to confession and performed the penance given by the priest. Calvin's suggestion of weekly Communion seemed so radical that the city council rejected it. Calvin compromised on frequency, but when a member of the city council,

a known adulterer, proposed coming to the Lord's Table without any change in life, Calvin said this person would not be given the sacrament. The city council, jealous of its authority, expelled all three reforming ministers from the city—including Farel and Calvin.

Calvin then went to Strassbourg, where he took a position as minister to the French Reformed refugees. From the principal reformer of Strassbourg, Martin Bucer, Calvin

A Seal for All Seasons

The Reformed Church seal, or crest, is displayed in many Reformed churches. For those encountering it for the first time, it looks very European and old fashioned, like a medieval crest or royal coat of arms. That impression is correct on every count, for it is very much like the coat of arms of Prince William of Orange, also known as William the Silent.

Discovering the reason why the church adopted this crest as an act of gratitude to William the Silent will also provide glimpses into the origins of the Reformed Church in the Netherlands, into the wars of religion of the sixteenth and seventeenth centuries, the attendant sufferings of the people on both sides, and the resulting antipathy between Roman Catholics and Protestants.

Philip II, Holy Roman Emperor, had been born and brought up in Spain. Of all countries, Spain was the most fervently Roman Catholic, for it was only in the previous century that Islam had been driven out, after centuries of conflict. In Spain Philip exercised centralized political and religious control and hoped to do the same elsewhere in his territories, which included the Low Countries. Philip took away rights and privileges from the nobility, and the religious persecution he initiated hurt trade, as well as those persecuted, and drove workers to emigrate.

The Seal of the Reformed Church in America

Opposition soon organized behind three prominent nobles, William Prince of Orange, Egmont, and Horn. They presented a petition of protest in 1566, gaining for them the nickname of "beggars." The populace prematurely thought the tide of oppression had turned; Protestants began to preach openly, and extremist Protestant elements incited iconoclastic riots, wrecking hundreds of churches.

Philip II saw this as open rebellion and sent the Duke of Alva to restore law and order. Alva executed hundreds, including Egmont and Horn. William escaped to mount a military expedition, but Alva defeated him. William then commissioned the "Sea-Beggars," essentially privateers, to prey on Spanish shipping. Operating out of English ports, in 1572 they captured Brill. The northern provinces rose in revolt. William put himself at the head of the movement and was recognized by the leading towns of Holland, Zeeland, Friesland, and Utrecht.

For a sense of the conflict, consider the siege of Haarlem the next year, 1573. Alva put 30,000 troops into the siege of that city, of which some 12,000 were lost in battle or to disease. During the seven-month siege, the city sustained 10,256 canon salvos, but the greatest

The *Halve Maen*

This authentic replica of the *Halve Maen* was built in 1989.

In 1609 Henry Hudson, an Englishman in the employ of the Dutch East Indies Company, set sail to discover a new route to the Orient by way of the northeast. His ship was the *Halve Maen* (the *Half Moon*), and it measured a mere sixty-five feet in length.

Hudson made it as far north as the eastern end of the Barents Sea before arctic ice and frigid temperatures forced the small crew of ten to fifteen to turn back. After taking on provisions at the Faroe Islands, Hudson headed west, disobeying orders to satisfy his own curiosity.

When Hudson reached the North American continent he sailed the coastline, exploring bays and inlets in search of a waterway that would lead him to Asia. Eventually, he entered the bay now known as New York Harbor. For several days Hudson explored the bay and the river that now bears his name. He ventured as far upriver as what is now Albany, before returning home to report the abundance of beavers and the richness of the land.

in that same year the Classis of Amsterdam called to the attention of the company directors that they were making no provision for religious services. That might seem a bit strange, but in the Netherlands the state was responsible for the support of the church. When the state granted a charter for a company to colonize in another part of the world, the state also mandated that the company be responsible for religious services.

In response the company sent a lay chaplain, Bastiaen Janszoon Krol, age twenty-eight, as a *krankenboesoezker*, or a comforter of the sick. Comforters of the sick, while they could read the liturgy and sermons from books approved by the authorities, could not perform marriages, baptize, or offer the Lord's Supper. Because of these limitations, it was still necessary for the company to provide a minister, and in 1628 it found one who was willing to go to New Netherland, Dominie Jonas Michaelius.

The population of New Netherland grew slowly. By 1643 the colony—which stretched from Albany in the north to the Delaware River in the south and was centered at the southern tip of Manhattan—numbered only about three thousand. That same year, the Indian War

Classis: From the Latin, meaning fleet. A classis is a "fleet" of churches. In the Reformed Church it is the judicatory between the consistory of the congregation and the regional and general synods. It is composed of the ministers and elder delegates of those churches.

Dominie: From the Latin *dominus*, meaning lord or master. It was the common form of address for clergy in the Dutch church.

Walloons: People of what is now southeastern Belgium and parts of France, who spoke a French dialect. Many Walloons became Protestant and fled to the Netherlands to escape persecution.

The Purchase of Manhattes

t' Fort nieuw Amsterdam op de Manhatans

High and Mighty Lords:

Yesterday, arrived here the Ship the Arms of Amsterdam, which sailed from New Netherland, out of the River Mauritius, on the 23rd September. They report that our people are in good heart and live in peace there; the women also have borne some children there. They have purchased the Island Manhattes from the Indians for the value of 60 guilders; 'tis 11,000 morgens in size. They had all their grain sowed by the middle of May, and reaped by the middle of August. They send thence samples of summer grain; such as wheat, rye, barley, oats, buckwheat, canary seed, beans and flax.

The cargo of the aforesaid ship is: 7,246 beaver skins, 178 half otter skins. 675 otter skins, 48 minck skins, 36 wild cat skins, 33 mincks, 34 rat skins. Considerable Oak timber and Hickory.

Herewith, High and Mighty Lords, be commended to the mercy of the Almighty.

In Amersterdam, the 5th November, A 1626.
Received 7th November, 1626

Your High Mightinesses' obedient,
P. Schagen

From *Documents Related to the Colonial History of the State of New-York Procured in Holland, England, and France*, by John Romeyn Brodhead, Esq., vol. 1, 1856. Holland Documents: I. 37-38.

Comforters of the Sick

Before the arrival of the first minister in 1628, Bastiaen Krol and Jan Huygens conducted worship services in New Netherland and cared for the spiritual need of the settlers. They were known as comforters of the sick, a lay office of the Dutch church.

Comforters of the sick generally had little education or theological training. They were expected to show a good understanding of the Bible, be able to read and write, and demonstrate compassion for the sick and dying. While they were not allowed to administer the Lord's Supper, comforters of the sick could read prayers, Scripture, and approved sermons.

Krol, a fabric worker by trade, was twenty-eight years old when the Consistory of Amsterdam approved him for service as a comforter of the sick. He left for New Netherland early in 1624. After only a few months in the colony, he returned to Amsterdam reporting that there were pregnant women there and arrangements would have to be made to baptize their children. Reluctant to send a minister for so few families, church officials authorized him to baptize and perform marriages.

Krol worked alone for two years, ministering in New Amsterdam and 160 miles north at Fort Orange. In 1626 the Consistory of Amsterdam sent a second comforter of the sick, Jan Huygens, an elder in the Dutch Reformed Church in the Netherlands and brother-in-law to Peter Minuit, the director general of New Netherland.

After serving as comforters of the sick, both men returned to secular employment. Krol took the position of company agent at Fort Orange. Huygens became company storekeeper in New Amsterdam.

Island of Hills

The Mohawk called it *Ganono*, meaning reeds, because of the marshes that surrounded it. The Delaware called it *Manahata*, or island of hills. It's that name that stuck.

It's hard to imagine Manhattan as anything other than the fast-paced financial capital it has become. But before steel and concrete there were deer and fox, bear and beaver making their homes among the island's ponds and streams.

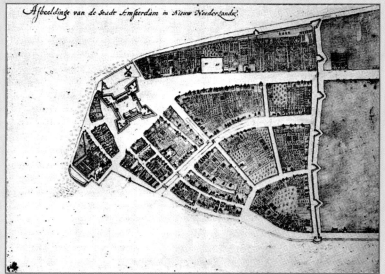

The Dutch built a fort on the southern end of the island. As the colony grew, streets radiated north from the fort—streets with familiar names like Beaver, Pearl, Mill, and Maiden Lane. Bridges, similar to those in the Netherlands, were built over a natural inlet that cut through the settlement. When the canal became badly polluted, it was filled with dirt to form Broad Street.

New Amsterdam's one thousand residents spoke eighteen languages. Nearly half were Dutch; among the others were German, English, African, Scandinavian, French, and Jews.

In the 1650s, as tensions with the English escalated, the Dutch made needed repairs to the fort and constructed a wall made of logs eighteen inches in diameter and twelve to thirteen feet high. It spanned the island from the Hudson River to the East River. The wall proved unnecessary, as the English never invaded. The street that ran along it, Wall Street, remains today.

reduced the population to about one thousand. Two years later the new governor, Peter Stuyvesant, claimed about two thousand people for his colony, although these numbers are estimates, not census counts. The passenger lists, which supposedly give the names of all parties arriving between 1657 and 1664, list an influx of only 1,032 people. If accurate, these indicate that the 1664 estimate of seven to ten thousand people is probably very high.

This figure is important because in the same year, 1664, the British seized New Netherland and changed its name to New York. By this time, 235,000 English settlers lived in New England and Virginia. The English to the north and to the south of the thinly populated Dutch colony outnumbered the Dutch by about twenty-five to one. The British takeover marked the end of Dutch control in the colony and the end of what little Dutch immigration there had been.

Even these figures fail to capture the true numerical disadvantage of the Dutch Reformed Church, since only a portion of the seven to ten thousand colonists in New Netherland were Dutch (Eighteen languages were spoken in New Netherland.). And of those who were Dutch, not all were Reformed. Dominie Megapolensis wrote in

Michaelius—A Modest Minister for Modest Beginnings

Dominie Jonas Michaelius was the first ordained minister of the Dutch Reformed Church to come to New Netherland. Born in 1577, he enrolled at the University of Leiden at age fourteen, and he studied there for six years. Most of his early ministry was spent in the little village of Hem in northern Holland. But in 1624 he went to San Salvador, then a year later to Guinea to minister at the fort there. Michaelius returned to Holland in 1627, and on January 24 the following year, already over fifty years old, he embarked for New Netherland with his wife, who was pregnant and died seven weeks after their arrival. Two daughters accompanied them; his son, Joannes, remained behind.

The voyage lasted rather long and was difficult and perilous, especially about the Bermudas and the rough coasts of this country. Our treatment on board was rather severe and mean, through the fault of a very wicked and ungodly cook, and of our skipper Evert Croeger, with whom, prior to this I had made long voyages, but never before knew him well.

—From a letter addressed August 8, 1628, to Joannes van Foreest, secretary of the Executive Council of the States of North Holland and West Friesland[1]

Michaelius arrived in New Netherland April 7, 1628. He organized a church almost immediately.

At the first administration of the Lord's Supper which was observed, not without great joy and comfort to many we had fully fifty communicants, Walloons and Dutch, a number of whom made their first confession of faith before us, and others exhibited their church certificates. Others had forgotten to bring their certificates with them, not thinking that a church would be formed and established here; and some who brought them had lost them, but they were admitted upon the satisfactory testimony of others to whom this was known, and also upon their daily good deportment, since one cannot observe strictly all the usual formalities in making a beginning under such circumstances.

1655, "We have here papists, Mennonites, and Lutherans among the Dutch; many Puritans and Independents, also atheists and other servants of Baal among the English."

Only thirteen Dutch Reformed churches or preaching stations served a colony that stretched for two hundred miles. And in the fifty years between the first settlement in 1614 and the British seizure in 1664, death or discouragement had limited the total years of ministerial service at these churches to a mere eighty-seven. Of that total, all pastorates were limited to New Amsterdam, Brooklyn, and Rensselaerwyck (Albany), with the exception of a two-year pastorate on the Delaware and four years invested in Esopus (Kingston), New York.

Furthermore, the church in New Amsterdam received the bulk and the best of ministerial attention. New Amsterdam was the largest settlement of the Dutch colony, and its pastor, Dominie Megapolensis, was perhaps the most gifted and dedicated of all of the ministers who had served the Dutch church in New Netherland. By the time of the English conquest, Megapolensis (who had also served in Rensselaerwyck from 1642-49) accounted for twenty-two of the total eighty-seven years of service

We administer the Holy Supper of the Lord once in four months, provisionally, until a larger number of people shall necessitate a change. The Walloons and French have no service on Sundays otherwise than in the Dutch language, for those who understand no Dutch are very few. Nevertheless, the Lord's Supper is administered to them in the French language, and according to the French mode, with a sermon preceding, which I have before me in writing, so long as I cannot trust myself extemporaneously.

Food here is scanty and poor. Supplies of butter and milk are difficult to obtain, owing to the large number of people and the small number of cattle and farmers. All these articles are dear, and, moreover, those endeavoring to secure them are jealous of one another. We need nothing so much as horses and cows, and industrious workers for the building of houses and forts, and to make our farming more profitable, in order that we may have sufficient dairy produce and crops. For to be fed continually from the Fatherland is difficult, expensive, and hazardous, as on the way any ship may be wrecked.

The promise of the Lords Masters to grant me 6 or 7 morgens of land to support myself, in place of free board, which otherwise would be my perquisite, is worth nothing. For their Honours themselves knew perfectly well, that neither horses nor cows nor laborers are to be had here for money. Thus we lead a hard and sober existence like poor people.

—From a letter addressed August 11, 1628, to Dominie Adrianus Smoutius, a minister in Amsterdam[2]

New Amsterdam was barely three years old when Michaelius came, and little is known about his ministry in the colony. It lasted only three years; a dispute with the director general and one of his elders sent him back to the Netherlands. In 1637 he volunteered for a second tour of duty in New Netherland but was rejected by the West India Company. The place and date of his death are not known.

---
[1] A. Eerkhof, *Jonas Michaelius: Father of the Church in New Netherland* (Lyden: A.W. Sijthoff's, 1926), 107.
[2] Ibid., 28.

The Church in the Fort

The first place of worship for the colonists in New Netherland was the loft over a horsemill. Within five years the mill stopped being used for church services, and a small plain wooden building was built near what is now Broad St. between Pearl and Bridge.

This church must not have been an architectural gem, for in 1642 Captain David Pieterszoon De Vries recorded in his notes a conversation he had while dining with Director-General Kieft: "I replied that…there was great want of a church, and that it was a great scandal to us when the English passed there, and saw only a mean barn in which we preached; that the first thing which the English in New England built, after their dwellings, was a fine church, and we ought to do so, too."[1]

Kieft must have taken the remarks to heart, for in that same year a stone church was built within the fort. While it officially bore the name, St. Nicholas, it was commonly known as the Church in the Fort. It was a substantial structure, seventy-two by fifty feet, and it was used for almost a century until it was destroyed by fire in 1741.

Funds for the construction of the Church in the Fort were obtained at the wedding of Sara Roeloff, Domine Bogardus's step-daughter, to Hans Kierstedt, a young doctor. "This was considered a favorable opportunity for raising the required subscriptions. So when the wedding party was in the height of good humor, and mellow with the host's good cheer, the Director General called on the guests to subscribe. The disposition to be generous was not wanting at such a time. Each guest emulated his neighbor, and a handsome list was made out. When the morning came, a few were found desirous of reconsidering the transactions of the wedding feast. But Director Kieft would allow no such second thought. They must all pay without exception."[2]

---

[1] Arie R. Brouwer, *Reformed Church Roots: Thirty-Five Formative Events* (New York: Reformed Church Press, 1977), 39.
[2] Hugh Hastings, *Ecclesiastical Records of the State of New York*, vol. 1 (Albany: J. B. Lyon, 1901), 164.

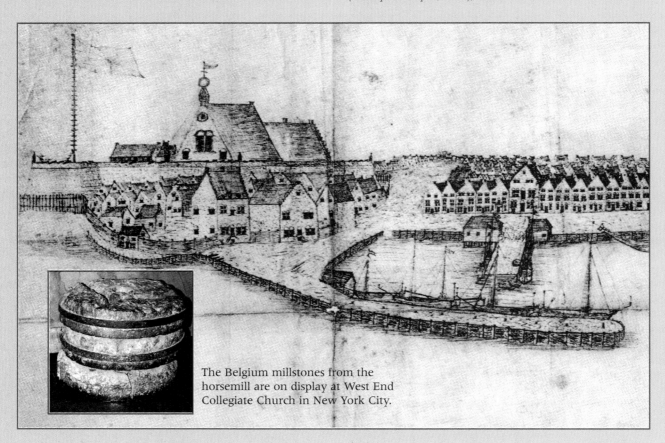

The Belgium millstones from the horsemill are on display at West End Collegiate Church in New York City.

by ministers in the Dutch colony. By 1670, after serving the church in New Amsterdam for twenty years, Megapolensis could count only 170 members as the fruits of his labor. This was the largest church in the largest settlement with the longest period of ministerial service; one can only imagine the condition of the other churches in the colony.

Considering the limited immigration to New Netherland, the limited number of Dutch among the immigrants, the limited number of Reformed among the Dutch, the limited pastoral care given the colonists, and the limited fruits of those labors measured in communicants, the wonder is not that the Reformed Church in America was so small but that it continued to exist at all. Surely it lived by grace alone!

Resources for Further Study

The Dutch Reformed Church in the American Colonies, by Gerald F. De Jong. The Historical Series of the Reformed Church in America. Grand Rapids: Eerdmans, 1978.

Gathered from Many Nations: The Early Years of the Reformed Church in America, 1628-1776, by Christopher Moore and Kim Baker. New York: Reformed Church in America, video, 2000.

RCA Historical Highlights, http://www.rca.org/aboutus/archives/outline.php

The *Princess*

This painting depicts Dominie Everardus Bogardus (second from left in the rowboat) and other colonists being ferried to the ill-fated *Princess*, which stands at anchor in the East River (out of the picture). The date was August 17, 1647.

The relationship between Bogardus and the colony's governors was stormy at best. On this occasion Bogardus was traveling to the Netherlands to bring charges against former Director General Kieft and, in turn, answer charges by Kieft of drunkenness and insubordination. Kieft would also be on board the *Princess* for this fateful journey.

The *Princess* never made its destination. On September 27 the ship went down in gale-force winds off the coast of Wales. Bogardus and Kieft, along with seventy-nine others, lost their lives.

The rare oil painting—believed to be the work of Augustine Herrman (1621-1686)—was discovered in 1952 in the estate of Anne Wilson, hidden in the cluttered attic of her Hudson River Valley house.

What makes this story truly interesting is the fact that Anne Wilson was a direct descendant of Anneke Jans, who married Dominie Bogardus in 1638 after being widowed at an early age.

Twice widowed with the sinking of the *Princess*, Anneke remained on her sixty-two-acre farm in lower Manhattan raising her eight children (four from her previous marriage). She died in Albany in 1663.

Rensselaerswyck

After a few attempts to colonize Fort Orange failed, the directors of the Dutch West India Company came up with an ingenious plan to populate the area and at the same time enhance their own wealth. A director would underwrite the costs of establishing a colony, and the settlers would become bound by contract to work for the director for a specified number of years. The settlers would get land, a place to live, and farm equipment; the patron or "patroon" would receive a third of the harvested crops, earning profit on his investment.

Kiliaen Van Rensselaer, a wealthy pearl and diamond merchant from Amsterdam, subscribed to the patroonship near Fort Orange. He named the area Rensselaerswyck and set out to attract settlers willing to start life over in the area now known as Albany, New York.

A description of how a patroonship was to operate is found in *Albany's First Church* by church historian Robert Alexander. The words are those of Van Rensselaer himself in a letter to Johannes Megapolensis, whom he was trying to recruit as the colony's first minister.

Each farmer must take with him at least two servants and one boy who understands farming and equip them himself. The Patroon, on his part, provides their board till they arrive in New Netherland at the island of Manhattans and on their arrival in the colony causes them to be provided, upon condition of repayment, with grain for eating and sowing and with a suitable site on which to establish their farm. The Patroon will have built for them a good house, a hay barrack and a barn, which according to the custom of that country are usually placed near the river, the waters of which flow by clear and

fresh and full of fish. The Patroon causes them also to be provided once with a wagon and plow and what else is needed for farming; he will further assign them some land in the interior consisting of beautiful woods filled with excellent game such as deer, turkeys, and all sorts of nourishing fowl. He also turns over to them from the surplus of animals in the colony four horses and four cows, of which they are to have half the offspring, the other half to be paid to the Patroon in money or in kind. Each farmer there can, with little capital or advance of money, establish himself as pleasantly and as fully as the best noblemen in this country. As to the rent which the Patroon derives from all this, he reserves to himself in the first place the right of the tithes for the support of the political and ecclesiastical persons and whomever he shall see fit; then every third sheaf of the remaining crop, the other two thirds being for the farmer for the wages of the servants and other expense, and finally the right to sell surplus animals.

Establishing Rensselaerswyck, though, proved to be anything but easy. It wasn't long before those directors who acquired patroonships were seen as taking advantage of the company and disqualified from serving as directors. Bitter disputes ensued among them. Acquiring enough animals and settlers also proved challenging. When colonists bound for Rensselaerswyck arrived at New Netherlands and heard of the hard life waiting for them up river, they disregarded their obligations and settled in and around New Amsterdam. Through it all Van Rensselaer continued to invest money to sustain the colony, and among the patroonships of the company, Rensselaerswyck had the greatest success.

2

The Limitations of Language

In 1664 a fleet of British warships entered the harbor at New Amsterdam and demanded the surrender of the little fort located in what is now Battery Park on the tip of Manhattan. The batteries of the Dutch were no match for British warships, and the Dutch soldiers were vastly outnumbered. It is questionable whether the powder for the Dutch cannon was still sufficiently dry even to fire a cannonball. And yet, the redoubtable Governor Stuyvesant wanted to fight. Fortunately for all concerned, someone in New Amsterdam recognized that the limited numbers of Dutch colonists and their modest defenses could not withstand an all-out attack. Dominie Megapolensis and his persuasive words helped Stuyvesant see the situation for what it really was, and the governor sensibly surrendered.

With that surrender, New Netherland became the English colony of New York. Nonetheless, one hundred years passed before even the most urban, sophisticated, and cosmopolitan Dutch congregation in the colonies began to worship God in English.

Consider the condition of the Dutch Reformed Church in the American colonies when New Netherland became New York. Thirteen Dutch churches, most of which had never been able to install a pastor, were surrounded by more than 235,000 English-speaking colonists. Two years after the English conquest, the total number of ministers serving all of the Dutch congregations was reduced by half—to two. We have no way of knowing the total number of Dutch church members. We do know that within the only large city in the colony, New York, the largest Dutch church—and the one that had enjoyed the most years of pastoral service—had only grown to 170 members. Yet for one hundred more years, this and all other Dutch Reformed congregations continued to worship in Dutch.

Even though military and governmental affairs were in English hands, the Dutch population in New York remained the majority for many years, and at first there was little pressure to change even the language of daily communication—not to mention the language in which one worshiped God. In rural areas settled by the Dutch, villages continued to use Dutch right up to the Revolutionary War. In New York City, where the use of Dutch

Events referenced in the chapter are below the line. Other historical events are above the line.

1696
Wm. & Mary grant charter to Dutch church in New York

1741
Handel's Messiah

1689
William III (of the Netherlands) & Mary (daughter of James II) proclaimed joint rulers of England

1667
Treaty of Breda, Dutch give up claims to New Netherland in return for Surinam

1760
George III becomes king of England

1703
Birth of John Wesley

1660	1680	1700	1720	1740	1760

1663
Catarina DuBois, Kingston

1696
The Charter of the Reformed Protestant Dutch Church granted by the English Crown

1717
Six Mile Run

1743
Synod of South Holland (Netherlands) suggests union of Dutch, German, and Scots Calvinists

1664
British seize New Netherland and rename it New York

1702
Trial of Nicholas Bayard

1764
Laidlie, first English service in Dutch church

1665
Old Stone Church

What's in a Name?

1628: For well over one hundred years, the Reformed churches in the Dutch colony in North America had no name of their own. They were congregations of the Classis of Amsterdam of the Reformed Church of the Netherlands.

1747: When the Coetus was formed, minutes were kept as *Records of the Coetus of the Low Dutch Reformed Preachers and Elders.*

1767: Twenty years later a somewhat modest assertion of independence was evident: *Proceedings of the Rev. Assembly of Ministers and Elders under the Rev. Classis of Amsterdam.*

1774: The minutes referred to the *Reformed Dutch Churches of the Two Provinces of New York and New Jersey,* but consistency was not a hallmark of the records. In 1784 the minutes were of the *Dutch Reformed Churches,* while in 1787 the minutes of May and October used each of the titles. In 1792 the term Dutch was officially adopted.

1803: The title used for the minutes of the General Synod was the *Reformed Protestant Dutch Church in North America*—albeit the "in North America" is usually dropped in references and "Protestant" wasn't recognized as a part of the corporate title by the New York Legislature until 1819.

1867: In June it was resolved that "in the year 1867 the Reformed Dutch Church . . . drop from its ecclesiastical name the word 'Dutch'... and add the words 'in America.'" Since this was a constitutional change, the matter was sent to the classes for approval. In November the vote was in: 25 yes, 6 no, with Arcot (India) not reporting. Since then we've been the *Reformed Church in America.*

---

faded most rapidly, the trial of Nicholas Bayard in 1702 was to be conducted in English. The defense counsel objected to the composition of the twelve-man jury on the basis that those selected understood and spoke English so poorly that scarcely one could even say the Lord's Prayer in that language. In the Hudson Valley, Long Island, and even New York City, the dominant Dutch language sometimes overpowered similar tongues, such as German. In the Lutheran church in New York, with a predominantly German congregation, the language of worship was also Dutch.

Clustered in ethnic groups around a pastor trained in the Netherlands, and with children educated in schools taught in Dutch, Dutch families did not readily see that the sheer numbers of English to the north and south would soon make the use of English a necessity. Sixty-two years after the English conquest, the consistory of the Dutch Reformed Church in New York finally indicated an awareness of the inevitability of English. The consistory insisted that "the true doctrine of comfort in life and in death is preached in the clearest and most powerful manner in the Dutch tongue," and its members urged support of the Dutch school for religious reasons. Yet they admitted that English was also needed "in order properly to carry on one's temporal calling."

Some others among the Dutch were acutely aware of

Consistory: A consistory is the governing body of a local church. Its members are the installed minister/s, elders, and deacons.

Synod: The Reformed Church in America has regional synods composed of the classes in a given area, and the General Synod, the highest governing body of the church. Both are composed of ministers and elders in equal numbers.

The Deacon's Account Books

Wheat, corn, peas, and bread. Thick woolen cloth to make a winter coat. A barrel of bacon, a pair of shoes, windows for the poorhouse—all of these appear on the ledger of the *Deacons' Account Books* of the church in Beverwijck (later known as First Reformed Church in Albany, New York).

Deacons of the Dutch Reformed Church were responsible for collecting gifts of charity to assist the poor and to maintain church property. Poor boxes—strategically placed around a village—along with church offerings, provided the funds. The meticulous, monthly accounts of the deacons provide a unique view into a community's life and social conscious. Here's a sample.

Done in Beverwijck anno[1] 1658 in June
The disbursements of the deaconry

15 [June] ditto paid to Kesie Wouters for two days' work in the poorhouse	f 6.-
18 ditto paid to Evert Noldingh for brandy and beer drunk by the carpenters while building the baptistery	f 11.12
29 ditto to the *matres*[2] wages for stringing the sewant[3] of the poor	f 40.-

Done in Beverwijck anno 1658
Disbursements of the deaconry in July

1 [July] ditto paid to the carpenters 13 ? beavers, amounting in sewant to	f 175.10
5 ditto paid to Abram for lime to whitewash the church	f 6.-
5 ditto paid to Dominie Schaets for hardware he received from Jan Hendricksen van Bael for the poorhouse	f 8.-
Ditto to mother Schaets for goods she gave to the child kept by Marrijtie Klaesen	f 14.-
6 ditto paid to Meester Adriean, school master, for school money for the child kept by Marijtie Klaesen	f 17.8
8 ditto I paid in beavers to mother Megapolensius for a pair of hinges used at the door of the gate of the poor farm	f 9.-
21 ditto to Jan *den Paep*[4] for wine used at the Holy Communion	f 16.-
25 ditto to Marytie Claesen boarding money for the child kept by her	f 25.-
	f 270.18

---

[1] In the year.
[2] The mother. There are no sources revealing who she was or what her function was.
[3] Small strung beads of polished shell used by Indians as currency.
[4] A Roman Catholic.

From Janny Venema, ed. and trans., *Deacons' Accounts 1652-1674, First Dutch Reformed Church of Beverwyck/Albany, New York*, Historical Series of the Reformed Church in America (Grand Rapids: Eerdmans, 1998).

Early Dutch Church Architecture

Artists' renditions of Old Stone Church, Six Mile Run Church, and the French Church at New Paltz provide a glimpse into early church architecture.

Construction of Old Stone Church began in the winter of 1665 on Church Lane (now the corner of New York City's Fifth Avenue and 125th Street). It was a square structure with a cock as its weathervane. The church was destroyed during the Revolutionary War; its bell resides with Harlem's Elmendorf congregation.

Old Bushwick Church (built in 1711 in

Archives of the Reformed Church in America

Old Stone Church

Brooklyn, New York) and Six Mile Run Church (built in 1717 in Franklyn Park, New Jersey) were octagonal—patterned after the first Protestant churches in the Netherlands.

Six Mile Run

Domine Theodorus Jacobus Frelinghuysen preached at Six Mile Run when he came to New Jersey's Raritan Valley in 1720.

In 1677 twelve families of French-speaking Protestant refugees purchased a tract of land between the Shawungun Mountains and the Hudson River from the Esopus Indians and built six stone houses that remain today. In 1717 they erected a stone church with a cupola from which a blown horn or conch shell announced the call to worship. In 1794 the congregation joined the Dutch Reformed Church.

French Church, New Paltz

the changing language situation, and they had been petitioning the consistory of the Dutch Reformed Church in New York for worship in English. The consistory long resisted, but in 1763 it sent a formal request to its ecclesiastical superiors, the Classis of Amsterdam, asking for a minister qualified to preach and catechize in English who was also in full communion with, and ordained by, the Reformed Church in the Netherlands. Archibald Laidlie, a Scotsman who was serving an English church in the Netherlands, was ordained by the Classis of Amsterdam, sent to New York, and in 1764 began to preach in English, one hundred years after the English conquest.

It would be a mistake to imagine that these Dutch forbears resisted using English because they were not very perceptive. Dutch was still the language of daily communication in many rural areas when the church in New York introduced English. The affection that many people retain for the Elizabethan English of the Bible's King James Version indicates the important emotional role that language plays in worship.

However, maintaining the Dutch language did play a part in limiting the size of the denomination. Granted, in a few locations the Dutch language was so predominant that it gained ascendancy over the similar tongue of German settlers, but the increasingly dominant language was English. As a result, the church was cut off from growth within the English-speaking population for a century.

The colony of New Netherland had been founded for commercial purposes, and the West India Company had found it extremely difficult to attract adequate numbers of settlers. Thus, when the English ended Dutch commercial opportunities, immigration from the Netherlands all but ceased. From 1664 the Dutch church would only grow within America rather than through immigration. Because the language of worship continued to be Dutch, church growth would have to be biological

Archibald Laidlie

"Ah! Dominie, we offered up many an earnest prayer in Dutch for your coming among us, and truly the Lord has heard us in English, and has sent you to us." These words were spoken to the Reverend Archibald Laidlie by a member of the Middle Dutch Church on the day of its first English service, April 15, 1764.[1]

Laidlie was born in 1727 in Kelso, Scotland, and received his education at the University of Edinburgh. He served the English congregation in Flushing, the Netherlands, from 1759-63. When the Classis of Amsterdam received a blank call from the church in New York requesting an English-speaking pastor, the classis inserted the name of Laidlie, who accepted and preached the first sermon in English in a Dutch church one hundred years after the British conquest. In 1770 he translated the Heidelberg Catechism into English. At the time of the Revolutionary War, Laidlie was on the side of the patriots and had to flee New York when it fell to the British. He died of tuberculosis in 1779 while in exile in Red Hook, New Jersey.

---

[1] Arie R. Brouwer, *Reformed Church Roots: Thirty-Five Formative Events* (New York: Reformed Church Press, 1977), 44.

among the Dutch. But such growth was not assured. People of Dutch ancestry who lived on the periphery, either geographically or socially, of Dutch-speaking communities were easily attracted by English-speaking churches.

Nonetheless, the enduring power of the Dutch language within centers of ethnic concentration is illustrated by the response to a proposal made in 1743 by the Synod of South Holland (in the Netherlands). The synod proposed that in America the Dutch and German Reformed unite with the Presbyterians to make one large, strong, Calvinistic church. The American churches rejected the proposal, not because of doctrine but because the affection for their native languages still separated those Dutch, German, and Presbyterian churches.

The position of the Dutch is difficult to understand today. The events of the nineteenth century, with its great emphasis upon evangelism and missions, have changed the way we comprehend the church. But for 136 years, from 1628 to 1764, the Dutch Reformed Church in America existed to meet the needs of Dutch-speaking worshipers. In the twenty-first century, as churches compete for members and pastors in order to keep their churches alive, it is almost impossible for us to comprehend the outlook of the historical church that prevailed in most of Europe, including the Netherlands. In these countries a state church provided services for all who wished to avail themselves of worship. Pastors preached; they were not expected to evangelize. Everyone in the community was baptized into the state church unless he or she consciously decided to be Anabaptist, Lutheran, or Roman Catholic. When the church was transported to America, it brought along basically the same mindset. Pastors were to provide the Word and sacrament for those of their own nation and language who wished to avail themselves of those means of grace.

However, in spite of the small

Singing the Psalms

The Dutch were already singing metrical psalms in 1539, when Wiliam Nieuwveldt set psalms to secular melodies intended for young people rather than for worship. Two other metrical versions preceded the Genevan Psalter that was translated by Peter Datheen in 1566 and made mandatory in all churches by the Synod of Wesel in 1568. It was this version that the Dutch brought to America.

Tradition has it that Catarina Du Bois of Kingston, New York, a Huguenot refugee captured by Indians in 1663, sang psalms as she stood bound to the stake, bewildering her captives and delaying her execution until rescuers arrived.

number of Dutch who immigrated to New Netherland and the few pastors who came to serve, and regardless of the limitations on growth imposed by the retention of the Dutch language within a colony overtaken by the English, the church continued to grow. During the one hundred years from the beginning of English rule to 1764 (when the first Reformed Church services were held in English), the number of congregations grew almost ten-fold.

Resources for Further Study

The Collegiate Reformed Protestant Dutch Church (History of the Collegiate Church), http://www.collegiatechurch.org/history.html

Deacons' Accounts: 1652-1674, First Dutch Reformed Church of Beverwijck / Albany, trans. and ed. Janny Venema. The Historical Series of the Reformed Church in America. Grand Rapids: Eerdmans, 1998.

A Dutch Family in the Middle Colonies, 1660-1800, by Firth Haring Fabend. New Brunswick: Rutgers Univ. Press, 1991.

Forerunner of the Great Awakening: Sermons by Theodorus Jacobus Frelinghuysen (1691-1747), ed. Joel R. Beeke. The Historical Series of the Reformed Church in America. Grand Rapids: Eerdmans, 2000.

Singing the Lord's Song: A History of the English Language Hymnals of the Reformed Church in America, by James L. H. Brumm, http://www.rca.org/images/aboutus/archives/singing.pdf

The Collegiate Church

In 1664 Dutch rule ended and the English took control of the colony. Even though New Amsterdam gave way to New York, worship continued in the fort for nearly thirty years, until a new church, Garden Street Church, was built about one hundred yards away in an area now called Exchange Place.

As new churches were built and more ministers were called, the collegiate system developed. Following the custom of churches in the Netherlands, one consistory in a city built and maintained church buildings when and where needed and hired as many pastors as necessary to rotate among the various congregations.

In 1696 King William III of England (a Dutchman) granted a full charter to the Collegiate Church, establishing the church as the first corporation in colonial North America (then an English colony). The charter, pictured here, allowed the Collegiate Church the right to exist as a legal entity alongside the Church of England, the only established church under law. The charter gave the Collegiate Church the right to own its churches, parsonages, and other church property, and also the right to receive legacies of real or personal property and other donations for the benefit of the church. Since 1628 worship has been conducted in twenty-two Manhattan locations.

Archives of the Reformed Church in America

3

Problems of Polity

First Reformed Dutch Church of Fishkill
Organized 1716 ★ Building Erected 1751
~Provincial Convention Met Here 1776
Used As A Military Prison During The Revolution
Enlarged 1786
Interior Remodeled 1806·1820·1824·1882

Archives of the Reformed Church in America

The Reformation churches in Europe were concerned that the Word be faithfully preached and the sacraments rightly administered. Those concerns followed the Dutch to these shores. Church order, the liturgy, and the theology of the Dutch Reformed Church had all been carefully spelled out at the Synod of Dort (1618-19), just a decade before the founding of the Dutch church in North America.

When the Dutch government chartered the West India Company to colonize the New World, it also gave the company the responsibility to govern, and governance included the nurture and protection of the Reformed Church. Accordingly, the West India Company was responsible for ministry in the new colony—in relationship to the Classis of Amsterdam, which had a special executive committee to consider the needs of the church in foreign lands. It was, in fact, the Classis of Amsterdam that first reminded the West India Company of its obligation for ministry in the new world. In theory, the company was to pay for the ministry. In fact, under its terms of governance, it sought to place much of the financial burden upon the people themselves and often arranged for an assessment of the citizens to meet such needs. In addition to finances, the church needed to be provided with ministers.

In Reformed Church polity (the way the church structures life together), it is not the congregation but the classis that examines, licenses to preach, and ordains to the ministry. That is exactly what the Classis of Amsterdam did for the Dutch Reformed Church in the new colony from 1628-1792. For 164 years, ministers were examined and ordained across the Atlantic in the Netherlands.

The concern for the right preaching of the Word and for ministers of ability and integrity was commendable, but the implications of ensuring these traits by requiring overseas ordination were serious for church growth in America. Initially, recruitment was handled by the West India Company and the classis, and at times their interests conflicted. When Classis Amsterdam recommended on three occasions that Dominie Michaelius (the first minister to the Dutch Reformed Church in New Netherland) be given another pastorate in the colony, the company refused

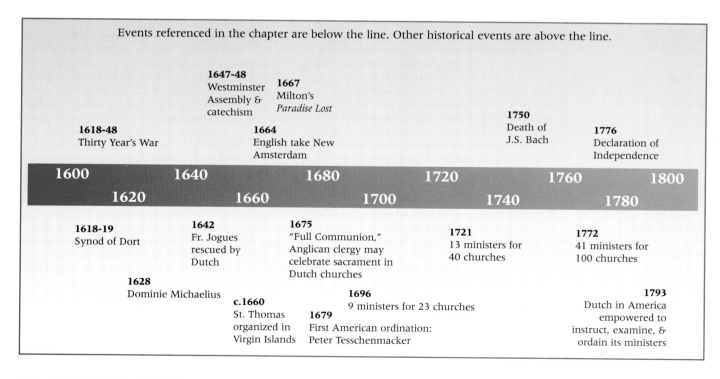

Events referenced in the chapter are below the line. Other historical events are above the line.

Above the line:

1647-48 Westminster Assembly & catechism

1667 Milton's *Paradise Lost*

1618-48 Thirty Year's War

1664 English take New Amsterdam

1750 Death of J.S. Bach

1776 Declaration of Independence

Timeline: 1600 1620 1640 1660 1680 1700 1720 1740 1760 1780 1800

Below the line:

1618-19 Synod of Dort

1642 Fr. Jogues rescued by Dutch

1675 "Full Communion," Anglican clergy may celebrate sacrament in Dutch churches

1721 13 ministers for 40 churches

1772 41 ministers for 100 churches

1628 Dominie Michaelius

c.1660 St. Thomas organized in Virgin Islands

1679 First American ordination: Peter Tesschenmacker

1696 9 ministers for 23 churches

1793 Dutch in America empowered to instruct, examine, & ordain its ministers

Early Ecumenism

"The first Jesuit missionary who entered within the borders of the State of New York [and, by the way, one of the first to carry the cross into Michigan] was Father Isaac Jogues. . . . He was captured by the Mohawks in 1642 and treated with great cruelty. He was beaten with clubs and stones; all his fingernails were pulled out, and the fore-finger of each hand gnawed by the savages...

Father Jogues was at length permitted a little more freedom, and he instructed some Indians in the faith and baptized some dying children. He afterward escaped to the Dutch at Fort Orange, who protected him against the wrath of the Indians, and finally paid them one hundred pieces of gold for his ransom. This was subsequently remitted to them from France. Domine Megapolensis secreted him until he went to New Amsterdam. Gov. Kieft kindly received him, and gave him clothes and lodged him in the Fort. . . . He sailed for France and was received with great honor. He returned to Canada in 1646, and returned to central New York and was killed by the Mohawks."

Ecclesiastical Records of the State of New York, vol. 1 (Albany: J. B. Lyon, 1905), 106.

because of his past criticism of Governor Minuet and other officials. Megapolensis, the first minister to Albany, learned the language of the Mohawk Indians, converted several, and was instrumental in their becoming members of the First Church of Albany. Nonetheless, he intended to return to the Netherlands because the company had never forced van Rensselaer, for whom he worked, to pay his salary in full. The wonder is that any good pastors could be found who were willing to accept the risks of the new world.

Later, under English rule, the company no longer was obligated to recruit or to finance ministers for New Netherland. Instead, the Dutch church members of the English colonies were responsible for finding and paying their own dominies—but always in relationship to the Classis of Amsterdam. Sometimes ministerial salaries continued to be paid in part by taxation, although there were frequent complaints that the English authorities did little to enforce the collection of taxes for the Dutch church. In other instances, portions of revenue-yielding acreage, called "glebe lands," were set apart to provide a part of the minister's compensation.

Financial problems were only a part—and perhaps the least part—of the difficulties involved in securing a minister. Few congregations knew whom they were calling. They addressed one of

Polity: The way in which the church is governed. In the Reformed Church in America, the polity is described in its *Book of Church Order*. The Liturgy and the Doctrinal Standards are also a part of its Constitution.

the classes in the Netherlands, or a minister, or an individual known to be in sympathy with their needs. The party contacted would try to find a minister willing to venture across the ocean on a three-to-twelve-week voyage to a land and church he had never seen.

To bring this previously unseen and unheard dominie to their settlement, the congregation had to risk a considerable amount of money. When congregations at Poughkeepsie and Fishkill cooperated and called Dominie Cornelius van Schie to their double pastorate in 1731, the expenses to bring him and his family amounted to more than his salary for an entire year. On some occasions, churches sent candidates for the ministry to the Netherlands to complete their educations and obtain ordination with the

We Need Floorboards

Peter Stuyvesant

In 1654 the colonists on Long Island had promised Domine Johannes Polhemus a salary of one thousand florins plus a parsonage. After two years, the fifty-six-year-old Polhemus and his family were still sleeping in unfinished rooms on bare ground, and the congregations of Midwout, Amesfoort, and Breuckelen had to be compelled to contribute their share of his salary.

Polhemus brought the matter to the attention of Director Stuyvesant in a letter dated December 14, 1656:

Noble Sir, Honorable General in New Netherland.

I am compelled to respectfully complain to your honor, that I must see the planks, given by your honor out of compassion and presented to the community here to finish my house against this cold winter, being taken and lost this way or that; for instance two were lost on the way here by having been left on the beach in nobody's care: after having been brought into the village without my knowledge, twenty-four were delivered to Jan Eversen Meyer; six were put down at the Church for benches; of the balance sixty-nine were taken away with the consent of Jan Snedicker and Jan Strycker; seventeen carried to Thomas Swartwout and his brother Albert Swartwout to dry malt; so that my house remains open as it was and I with my wife and children must live and sleep on the bare ground and in the cold…. In order not to make my situation worse by keeping silence, I write this to your Honor.

In haste,
Your Honor's obedient servant,
Joh. Th. Polheym.

Stuyvesant, in turn, wrote the magistrates of Midwout:

Honorable, Dear, Faithful.

When last with you in Breuckelen at the house of Albert Cornelissen it was agreed in parting, by expectation of long pastorates after they returned.

The congregation at New Paltz, together with two neighboring churches, had with that expectation paid the expenses of Barent Vrooman. When, within two years of his return, Vrooman accepted a call to the larger Schenectady congregation, that church had to compensate New Paltz more than a hundred pounds (equivalent to about a year's salary at that time) for its previous expenses. Further expenses accruing to the Schenectady church eventually raised its total outlay for obtaining Vrooman to 255 pounds—before the congregation even began to pay his salary.

Evidently, the Schenectady church found it worthwhile to invest in a minister who had at least a two-year reputation in New

mutual consent and approbation of yourselves and the other delegates from the villages of Breuckenlen and Amersfoort, that you should together make an estimate of the funds, out of which the preacher, Domine Polheym, was to be paid and placed above want and report it to us and the Council within eight days. As this time has passed and we are not yet informed of the result, we have deemed it necessary to remind you of it through the Schout and this open letter, that you fulfill your promise; else we shall be compelled by our official position and duties to take steps and give such orders and provide for such means, that the Minister be duly paid and placed above want. The said Domine Polheym, who was then present, complained further of the uninhabitable state and inconvenience of his dwelling house, which has as yet neither ceiling or wainscoting....The winter being imminent, this is unbearable and improper, and in order to remedy it we sent you...one hundred hemlock planks....I am however credibly informed now, that the said boards have not been used for the purpose intended by us, but that the Commissaries dispose of them privately according to their pleasure...while nothing whatever is done to finish the Minister's house, which is most urgent to do, the winter being so near at hand. We command therefore herewith, that the boards be brought together again upon receipt hereof, and put to their proper use and to no other as we have ordered.

P. Stuyvesant.

Archives of the Reformed Church in America

First Church Brooklyn

To pay their share of the minister's salary, the magistrates of Midwout levied an annual real estate tax ranging from six to twenty florins, since "every one of the inhabitants and neighbors has not the same amount of property, one having less, the other more." Those in Breukelen, however, tried to get out of paying altogether, claiming that they had never called the pastor to begin with and that "during the two weeks he comes here only for a quarter of an hour on Sunday afternoon, [he] gives us only a prayer instead of a sermon, from which we learn and understand little and when we think, that the prayer or sermon, whatever it be called, is beginning, it is already over, so that he gives small edification to the congregation." Only after another threat from Stuyvesant did the congregation agree to pay for one year, but for one year only.

Ecclesiastical Records, vol.1, 362-69.

1656 Pulpit

The 350-year-old pulpit is the focal point of the sanctuary of the First Church in Albany, New York—a congregation that dates back to 1642. The Van Rensselaer patroon was having arguments with the Trading Company and insisted that the church be organized on the east side of the river. Two years later, after Van Rensselaer's death, the congregation moved to the west side of the river near the fort, worshiping in a converted storehouse. The need for a better place of worship was recognized in 1654 and a pulpit was ordered from the Netherlands. The church was completed in 1656 and doubled as a blockhouse.

The structure was built of heavy wooden timbers in a square configuration with canons mounted behind loopholes in the overhanging balconies. It was erected squarely in the middle of the intersection so as to command excellent views of anyone approaching the town from the north, the west, or the south, the river forming a natural barrier towards the east. During church services, the women were assigned the pews on the ground floor while the men sat in the balcony where they would be available to man the canons should the need arise.[1]

The price for the pulpit was twenty-five beaver pelts. Unfortunately, when the pelts arrived they were wet and worthless, but the church in Amsterdam shipped the pulpit anyway.

The pulpit is finely carved and made of oak. On one side is mounted a delicately fashioned hourglass to time the length of sermons.

Among other items from the church's early history is the original brass weathercock (also dating to 1656) and a silver beaker fashioned in 1678 by New York's first silversmith.

---

[1] Robert S. Alexander, *Albany's First Church: And Its Role in the Growth of the City, 1642-1942*, (Albany: First Church, 1988), 38.

Photos: First Church in Albany

Paltz rather than risk an unheard and unknown person from the Netherlands, for such ministers were not always satisfactory. There were a few complaints that sermons were too short, and others that their dominies were too stringently against worldly amusements. At other times ministers themselves became too involved in worldly amusements, as in the case of one clergyman who was deposed because of bigamy and six others deposed because of repeated drunkenness. Others were dishonest, two having forged their credentials, while others were churlish, two being deposed because they were unable to get along with their colleagues. Eleven ministers were deposed, which would seem like a small number except that there were only forty ministers in active service at the end of the colonial period. Even the stringent Church Order of Dort standards for ministry could not always guarantee high-quality results.

From time to time the Dutch churches in America found other ways to fill their pulpits. The Dutch

St. Thomas Reformed Church

Christopher Columbus discovered the Virgin Islands on his second voyage in 1493. Dutch settlers began to arrive as early as the 1640s, and soon St. Thomas became a commercial center in the slave trade and commodities market.

St. Thomas Reformed Church was organized about 1660—early church records no longer exist. The congregation, which originally was a member of the Classis of Amsterdam in the Netherlands, transferred to the Reformed Church in America in 1827.

Donald J. Bruggink photos

The congregation erected its first building around 1718. It was destroyed in the 1730s by storm or one of the many fires that plagued St. Thomas over the years. Its second building, constructed in 1744, was burned in 1804, rebuilt, and finally destroyed in 1806. The present church building, a classical revival structure dating to 1844, suffered massive damage by hurricane Marilyn and was rebuilt in 1996, largely by Reformed Church in America volunteers.

in the colony of New Jersey were without any ministerial service prior to 1709. That year they sent a self-taught, gifted lay preacher, Guilliam Bertholf, to the Netherlands, where he was licensed to preach by the Classis of Middleburg. Gradually, as the number of pastors in America grew, the church began to avail itself of the possibilities in the Church Order of Dort for ordaining men on these shores. Between 1714 and 1776, seventy-five ministers were added to the church. Twenty were educated and ordained by classis-authorized committees in America, and ten other American-born pastors were educated and ordained in the Netherlands, while the majority—forty-five—came directly from Europe.

Although the situation improved as the church grew, the impact of church polity upon the size of the Reformed Church must not be minimized. In 1676 there were only two Dutch ministers preaching in the colonies, and by 1690 there was only one Dutch minister in all of the Dutch Reformed churches in North America. By 1696, the number had increased to nine, but with twenty-three churches to serve, the ratio was still unsatisfactory—more than two to one. In 1721 thirteen ministers served forty churches, and as late as 1772, just before the church received its independence from the Classis of Amsterdam, there were forty-one ministers for one hundred churches.

In contrast, from 1702 to 1776 the Society for the Propagation of the Gospel of the Church of England sent sixty missionaries to the New York colony. In 1710 the Reverend Thomas Barclay of the society reported to London that at Schenectady about a hundred Dutch families were his "constant hearers." There had been no Dutch pastor for five years (nor was there one in Albany at the time), and as a result Barclay had performed baptisms and marriages for the Dutch as well as preaching. Dutch

More Early Ecumenism

To the Noble, High, Honorable Sir, Major Edmund Andros, Governor-General of all his Royal Highnesses Territories in America.

Noble, High and Honorable Sir:

A minister according to the order of the Church of England, lawfully called, is sufficiently qualified to be admitted to the serving and administering of the sacraments in a Dutch Church belonging under his Majesty's dominion, when he has promised to conduct himself in his service according to the Constitution of the Reformed Church of Holland.

Noble, High, Honorable Sir,
Your excellency's Servants and Subjects,
The Consistory of the City of New York,
In the name of all.
        Wilhelmus Van Nieuwenhuysen, Pastor

New York
October 1, 1675

Ecclesiastical Records, vol. 1, 681.

ministers warned the Classis of Amsterdam that with many vacant churches the Dutchmen assuredly would go over to the Episcopalians as "some have already done."

Strict adherence to Reformed Church order, which ordinarily required ministerial training and ordination in the Netherlands, had only served to keep the Dutch church in America woefully short of ministers, with never more than

Peter Tesschenmacker:
First American Ordination

To the Right Honorable Sr. Edmund Andros Kt. Signor, of Saucamares; Lieutenant and Governor General under his Royal Highness James Duke of Yorke and Albany and Dependants.

The humble Pettison of Severall of the Inhabitants of Esopus humbly sheweth unto your Honor,

Whereas this place is destitute of a Minister for the Instruction of the people, it is our earnest desire and humble request, with all submission, that your Honor will be pleased to be siding and assisting; in the procuring one for us; that can preach both English and Dutch, which will be most fitting for this place, it being in its Minority; and having great charges is not very able to maintain two Ministers; neither to be at the Charge of Sending for one out of England or Holland, and we are informed, Mr. Peetar Taschenmaker is at liberty, who is a person, well known to your Honor and officiated in this place, for some time, And if it be procured, is very well approved of and much desired by most, he being a man of a sober life and conversation having Deported himself to satisfaction of ye Inhabitants, Wherefore we

Archives of the Reformed Church in America

The first Dutch church in Esopus (later Kingston), erected 1679.

humbly pray that your Honor will be pleased to be Instrumental in the same and your Honor's humble petitioners shall every pray, etc.

[Then follow the signatures or marks of the sixty-nine petitioners.]
Ecclesiastical Records, vol. 1, 683-84.

According the *Historical Directory of the Reformed Church in America, 1628-2000*, Peter Tesschenmaeker was in Dutch Guiana, South America, sometime between 1676 to 1678, after which on October 9, 1679, the secretary recorded a call from "the congregation of the South River" to Petrus Tesschenmaacker. It was also noted that this "was without precedent" but "the Dutch ministers here, at the request of his Excellency, Governor Edmond Andros, and upon production of the testimonials of the preparatory examination of said Domine Petrust Tesschenmaacker, written by the Dutch and English Consistories at the Hague, have been satisfied, in view of said congregation's distress, to confirm this candidate as minister to that place, and to ordain him."

Ecclesiastical Records, vol. 1, 726-27.

one pastor for every 2.4 churches. Nonetheless the church survived: Albany, without a pastor in 1710, and which lost its first pastor, Megapolensis, because van Rensselaer wouldn't pay his full salary, is today the prestigious First Church in Albany. Schenectady, which in 1710 had been without pastoral ministration for five years except for the Anglican, the Reverend Thomas Barclay, grew into a thriving family of ten Reformed churches.

But what of all those Dutch who lived on the fringes of the Dutch settlements? Eventually, they became English-speakers, like the majority of their neighbors. And the polity that made it impossible to obtain suitable Dutch ministers meant that their spiritual nurture was provided by others.

Incredibly, by 1790 only thirty-nine ministers served an estimated 97,500 Dutch in New York, New Jersey, and Pennsylvania. In addition, an estimated 9,250 Dutch had settled in Delaware, Connecticut, Massachusetts, Vermont, Rhode Island, Maine, New Hampshire, Maryland, Virginia, North Carolina, South Carolina, Georgia, Kentucky, and Tennessee, with but one church, one mission station, and one pastor.

The careful polity of the Reformed Church had two results: On one hand, it shackled the ability of the church to meet the need of thousands of Dutch settlers for a minister. And the more widely scattered the Dutch were, the less likely they were to receive ministerial service. On the other hand, larger communities that were willing to work and to take risks in order to obtain the services of ministers (who also had to be willing to work and to take risks) sometimes received pastors who were able to provide Christian nurture equivalent to the best that the church of the Netherlands could offer. Many of those churches remain to this day as testimonies to God's grace.

Resources for Further Study

Albany's First Church: And Its Role in the Growth of the City, 1642-1942, by Robert S. Alexander. Albany: First Church in Albany, 1988.

Clarity, Conscience, and Church Order: Reflections on the Book of Church Order, ed. Russell L. Gasero, http://www.rca.org/images/aboutus/archives/bcoreflections.pdf.

Constitutional Theology: Notes on the Book of Church Order of the Reformed Church in America, by Allan J. Janssen. The Historical Series of the Reformed Church in America. Grand Rapids: Eerdmans, 2000.

From Dordt to the GPC: The Changing Role of the Particular Synod, by Russell L. Gasero, http://www.rca.org/images/aboutus/archives/hh35.pdf.

Gathered at Albany, by Alan J. Janssen. The Historical Series of the Reformed Church in America. Grand Rapids: Eerdmans, 1995.

Meeting Each Other: In Doctrine, Liturgy, and Government, by Daniel Meeter. The Historical Series of the Reformed Church in America. Grand Rapids: Eerdmans, 1993.

4

Big Conflicts for a Little Church

The image above, printed and sold by Paul Revere, depicts Custom House Guards firing on unarmed citizens in Boston, March 5, 1770. Such broadsides contributed to the conflicts between Rebels and Tories.

The ordination of women, membership in the World and National Councils of Churches, abortion, and homosexuality have all caused dissension within the Reformed Church in America. However, these disagreements have been mild compared to three areas of strife that racked the Dutch Reformed Church before 1771: pietism versus orthodoxy, Coetus versus Conferentie, and Rebels versus Tories.

Pietism versus Orthodoxy

Theodorus Jacobus Frelinghuysen had been nurtured in the piety of the Netherlands through his family, teachers, and friends. Pietism emphasized experiential religion, and pietists' sermons were marked by extensive inquiry into the experiences and the motivations of the hearers. The only true Christian was one who felt his or her sinfulness, felt contrition and remorse, felt this not out of fear but out of love for God, and experienced a conversion that could be recounted with sufficient clarity to convince one's hearers—the ministers and elders with whom one sought membership within the church. This pietism also included stringent ethical demands and belief in freedom in prayer, which translated into a disregard for much of the required liturgy of the church. When Frelinghuysen accepted a call to "Rarethans" (Raritan), thinking it was in

Flanders or Brabant, his devotion to God was such that he maintained his acceptance even when he found the location to be across the Atlantic in New Jersey.

The churches in New York were orthodox. They followed the doctrine, church order, and liturgy of Dort. Their order of worship and prayers were fixed. The sermons tended to be long, with their biblical content highly structured into theological form followed by application for holy living.

The poles of pietism and orthodoxy met in 1720 when the New York pastors, Boel and DuBois, extended a friendly greeting to the newly arrived Frelinghuysen, inviting him to preach from their pulpit. As orthodox ministers, Boel and DuBois read the prayers as stipulated in the liturgy. As a pietist, Frelinghuysen thought these written prayers lacked sincerity. True to his principles, Frelinghuysen omitted even the Lord's Prayer and substituted a

Events referenced in the chapter are below the line. Other historical events are above the line.

1758
William Wilberforce begins his antislavery campaign

1702
William III dies, states-general resume control of affairs

1738
Handel's Israel in Egypt

1776
Declaration of Independence

1703
Birth of John Wesley

1740
Great Awakening in America

1760
George III, King of England

1789
French Revolution

1700 **1720** **1740** **1760** **1780** **1800**

1706
Request to form a Coetus

1720
Dominie Theodorus Jacobus Frelinghuysen arrives in New York

1747
Death of Dominie Frelinghuysen

1771
Livingston's Plan of Union

1709
Classis Amsterdam refuses

1738
First meeting to organize a Coetus

1755
Five members of Conferentie

1776
Beginning of War of Independence, Rebels versus Tories

"howling" free prayer. As a gracious host, DuBois nonetheless invited Frelinghuysen to his home for dinner. Frelinghuysen, more concerned with his principles than with being a gracious guest, asked why DuBois had such a large wall mirror, suggesting that such ostentation was unjustified.

Until then, the Raritan Valley had known only one Dutch minister, Guiliam Bartholf, a mild man of pietistic sympathies. Frelinghuysen was not mild. He had the temerity to bar from the Lord's Table the wife of a prominent church member, Jan Teunissen, although no one seemed to know what the charges were. Yet, when the teenage boy whom Frelinghuysen had brought with him as a helper was accused of serious breaches of morality, the boy was nevertheless admitted to the Table. Tensions from differences escalated as Frelinghuysen suggested that many church officers were among the unregenerate. The names of the elders who ranged themselves against Frelinghuysen can be recognized even at the distance of more than two and one-half centuries: Dumont, Wyckoff, Vroom, Van Sebering. Frelinghuysen soon found himself confronted by the hostility of Bartholf's successor, Dominie

Coens. Frelinghuysen suffered a psychosis and was described as "robbed of his senses." Coens then stirred up the disaffected, baptized children in Frelinghuysen's parish, and even organized an opposing consistory. For fifteen years the battle raged. Before it ended not only were the ministers of New York and New Jersey drawn into its turmoil, but also the civil courts, the Classis of Amsterdam, and the religious press of the Netherlands and Germany.

While Frelinghuysen was certainly not possessed of great tact, he was committed completely to the Calvinist cause—as interpreted by those of the pietistic persuasion. And whether his prayers were howling or not, he preached with emotional power. Frelinghuysen's primary goal was the conviction and conversion of sinners. Matters of liturgical and social tradition were swept aside. In fact, the revivals begun by Frelinghuysen were gradually spread by others until New Jersey, New York, and New England were all caught up in the Great Awakening.

One would not wish to question the great benefits to Christ's church that resulted

Gualtherus Du Bois

Coetus: From the Latin, meaning an assembly. It was more than a consistory, because it was composed of ministers of the Dutch churches, but neither was it a classis, for that would infringe upon the prerogatives of the Classis of Amsterdam that had oversight of the churches in America.

Conferentie: The assembly of ministers who wished to maintain tight ties to the Classis of Amsterdam (and thus in opposition to the Coetus), out of theological conservatism and to protect the rights given by the English in the charter of 1696.

Great Awakening: Begun by Frelinghuysen in New Jersey. His emphasis upon a transforming, regenerative change—a conversion—was soon adopted by the four Presbyterian Tennets. The awakening, or revival, spread to New England, with Jonathan Edwards as its most famous exponent. It spread to the South, and north to Nova Scotia as late as the 1770s. It reshaped the way many viewed entry into the Christian life.

Pietism: The emphasis upon a heartfelt experience of sin and grace.

Orthodoxy: In the context of this period, faithfulness to the theology of Dort together with its liturgy of fixed prayer for public worship.

Rebels: Those in America who rebelled against the British government and fought for self rule as exemplified by the Declaration of Independence.

Tories: In America, the title given to those who wished to remain as a part of Great Britain, obedient to the established rulers.

Theodorus Jacobus Frelinghuysen— Forerunner of the Great Awakening

Theodorus Jacobus Frelinghuysen, a Dutch Reformed Church minister, played a key role in what became known as the Great Awakening, a spiritual revival that spread through the colonies in the eighteenth century. Frelinghuysen's sermons focused on the conversion of sinners rather than on the nurture of believers and were aimed at his own parishioners, most of whom he viewed as spiritually lacking and bound for hell:

Come here, you careless ones at ease in sin; you carnal and earthly-minded ones; you unchaste whoremongers and adulterers; you proud, haughty men and women; you seekers after pleasure; you drunkards, gamblers, disobedient and wicked rejectors of the gospel; you hypocrites and dissemblers. How do you think the Lord will deal with you?...Be filled with terror, you impure swine, adulterers, and whoremongers. Without true repentance, you will live with the impure devils. All who burn in their vile lusts will be cast into a fire that is hotter than that of Sodom and Gomorrah.[1]

More often than not Frelinghuysen's sermons ended with a clear call to repentance.

Cursing, lying, adultery, licentiousness, stealing, and similar sins must no longer be found among us. Each of us must search his ways, mourn over, and depart from these sins. Each has done his part toward inflaming the wrath of God, so each must work to extinguish it. A holy reformation and change must take place among us, for this is the only way to sustain a sinking land....I beseech you beloved, by the mercy of God, by the blood of Jesus Christ, by your spiritual and temporal welfare, by the love you bear wife and children, by all that you hold dear, turn to the Lord. Fall at his feet.[2]

And,

Jesus stands before us with extended arms, inviting sinners and the ungodly to repentance. Oh let him who senses his sins and his state of condemnation before God surrender himself to the Lord Jesus! Let him who senses his helplessness and unwillingness and is convinced of Jesus' all-sufficiency and willingness turn to God. Let him who desires to be reconciled to God through the merits of Christ and to be sanctified by his Spirit go to the Lord Jesus. He that cometh to him, he will in no wise cast out.[3]

---

[1] Joel R. Beeke, ed., *Forerunner of the Great Awakening: Sermons by Theodorus Jacobus Frelinghuysen (1691-1747)*, The Historical Series of the Reformed Church in America. Grand Rapids: Eerdmans, 2000, xv.
[2] Ibid., 164.
[3] Ibid., 104.

from the Great Awakening to which Frelinghuysen so largely contributed. At the same time, the Dutch church was ravaged by the dissension occasioned by Frelinghuysen and other pietists.

Coetus versus Conferentie

The second great struggle in the eighteenth century was about local versus overseas control. It pitted against each other the parties of the Coetus (pronounced *see-tus*) and Conferentie (*con-fur-en-tee*).

All European churches assumed responsibility and control of their congregations in other lands. Thus it was not unusual that the Reformed Church in the Netherlands should, through its Classis of Amsterdam, assume responsibility for and control of the churches in New Netherland. That control of the Dutch churches continued when the colony became New York.

Not only were examinations and ordination for ministry in the hands of the Classis of Amsterdam, but every problem arising in the colonies had to be adjudicated by the classis. In 1662 Dominie Polhemus of Flatbush suggested forming an association of ministers in New Netherland for better communication with one another. In 1706, the Reverends DuBois, Anthonides, and Beys requested of the Classis of Amsterdam permission to hold a fraternal gathering once a year for the Dutch ministers in the province. This association of ministers came to be

To the *Honourable*
RIP VAN DAM, Esq
PRESIDENT of His Majestys Council for the PROVINCE of NEW YORK
This View of the New Dutch Church is most humbly
Dedicated by your Honours most Obedient Sert Wm Burgis

Garden Street Collegiate Church, Org. 1663

known as the Coetus. It had no jurisdictional authority, membership was voluntary, and affairs were settled by mutual consent. In 1709 the Classis of Amsterdam replied that "the formation of a classis among you, to correspond to ours at home, is yet far in the future and we hardly dare to think of it."

However, after fifteen years of correspondence over the Frelinghuysen disputes, in 1735 the Classis of Amsterdam itself suggested some sort of yearly meeting to promote church order—

provided it didn't infringe upon the prerogatives of the classis. One would have expected the American clergy to welcome such a suggestion, but the plan encountered opposition from those who favored control by the Classis of Amsterdam as a bulwark to keep the church "in the Dutch way."

The advantages of maintaining close ties with Amsterdam seemed obvious to the four ministers who formed the Conferentie. Their English charter of 1696 would ensure their ecclesiastical liberty as long they continued the extant relationship to the Netherlands. These four, all ministers in New York and close to the seat of English power, feared that a change in relationship might also mean the erosion of their liberties to worship as a Dutch church. Continuance with the Classis of Amsterdam also meant continued high standards for the ministry in education and orthodoxy.

On the other hand, the men who favored a strong Coetus wished to be able to ordain and educate men in America. Generally they leaned toward pietism rather than rigid orthodoxy and were not nearly so zealous of their Dutch connections as were the Conferentie's ministers. By 1754 these ministers voted for a strengthened Coetus. Sharper division resulted, and both clergy and congregations took sides.

One must not, however, lose sight of the size of the church when it was torn by this conflict. At the first meeting in 1738 there were fourteen Dutch ministers in all of the colonies of New York and New Jersey, of whom ten were for the Coetus. By the division of 1755, there were five ministers in the Conferentie, although it rose to its peak strength of ten in 1765.

New York's Liberty Bell

It rang for George Washington's Wall Street inauguration. It tolled for the funerals of presidents Washington, Lincoln, Grant, and Kennedy. It's older than the Liberty Bell of Philadelphia (which dates to 1753), and today it stands atop the Middle Collegiate Church in New York City.

Cast in Amsterdam in 1731 out of silver coins, the bell measures three feet tall and weighs eight hundred pounds. On July 9, 1776, the bell announced the signing of the Declaration of Independence in Philadelphia five days earlier.

Archives of the Reformed Church in America

The Old Dutch Church of Sleepy Hollow

Old Dutch Church is the oldest building of the Reformed Church in America still in existence. The church attained considerable publicity in the nineteenth century with Washington Irving's *The Legend of Sleepy Hollow*. In his legendary story of the headless horseman, Irving describes the setting of the church:

Donald J. Bruggink photos

It stands on a knoll surrounded by locust trees and lofty elms, from which its decent, whitewashed walls shine modestly forth, like Christian purity beaming through the shades of retirement. A gentle slope descends from it to a silver sheet of water bordered by high trees, between which peeps may be caught at the blue hills of the Hudson. To look upon its grass-grown yard, where the sunbeams seem to sleep so quietly, one would think that there at least the dead might rest in peace.

Vredryck Flypse built the church in the 1690s for his family and the tenants of his manor. He imported the pulpit from the Netherlands— indicating the importance placed on the proclamation of God's Word. The walls, which are two feet thick, were built of stone from the area, but the yellow bricks around the doors and windows came from the Netherlands. There was

no heat in the church except for the foot warmers brought from home—live coals in a metal pan, inserted in the wooden container. The special pews in the front of the church were for the elders and the minister's family.

Today the congregation worships in the Reformed Church of Tarrytown, New York, just down the street, but once a year worship services are held in the historic building. Old Dutch Church remains a popular site for those interested in colonial history and is used frequently for weddings. Among those buried on the church grounds are black slaves and soldiers of the Revolutionary and Civil Wars.

Feelings about these two parties ran high among congregations as well as ministers. Dominie Theodorus Frelinghuysen of Albany (son of the Raritan Frelinghuysen) was a leader of the Coetus. He knew firsthand the difficulties resulting from control by the Classis of Amsterdam. He had been captured at sea and held for six months while returning from a Dutch ordination, and two of his brothers had died at sea returning from their education and ordinations. Nonetheless, even though he was a leader in the Coetus, he did not attend meetings for several years because of opposition to the Coetus within his congregation. One can only imagine the emotional trauma experienced by this man as a result of his own imprisonment as well as the loss of his two brothers, and all to support a church order for which he personally saw no compelling need.

Dina van Bergh—Saved by a Swordfish

The life of Dina van Bergh, born in the Netherlands in Amsterdam in 1725 to a wealthy merchant family, illustrates pietism at its best. Dina died at age eighty-one in New Brunswick, New Jersey, the widow successively of the Reverend John Frelinghuysen (son of Theodorus Jacobus) and the Reverend Jacob Rutsen Hardenbergh.

At age seventeen, Dina had an experience she was later to describe in her diary as "my soul set free." We don't know how many diaries Dina kept, when she began, or when she ended. What we do have is her diary from February 1746 through 1747, written when she was a young woman in the Netherlands.

Nieuwe Kerk, Amsterdam. Begun in 1408, twice destroyed by fire, its present structure dates to 1645.

Spanning less than two years, the diary contains over 62,000 words, all of them in a vein similar to the brief samplings that will be used to illustrate her story.

It was five years since my soul was set free. I was blessed with an occupied mind, and enjoyed close communion with the Lord that day. I was greatly assisted as I reflected upon the Lord's merciful faithfulness granted to me so far. I was constrained to acknowledge that the God of Israel is God who indeed had helped me till now. His grace was the only reason that I am who I am. But my soul felt greatly ashamed of my abject state as I so lacked in conformity to God and my unreadiness in self-denial in all things concerning the service of the Lord. This grieved my heart all the more, since I had a lively sense of the benefits of God towards me.[1]

While Dina had a circle of female friends with whom she often gathered to pray, the gathering in no way meant neglecting the services of the church, which Dina attended morning, afternoon, and evening: "In the evening I was in the house of God, under the service of my much-beloved pastor and teacher, the Reverend Temmink." Not only did Dina go to church but she remembered the text, the psalms sung, the nature of the sermon, and her personal appropriation of it.

In the afternoon I went to church by Reverend Phijzers. His Reverence had chosen to preach about the twenty-ninth Lord's Day of the Heidelberg

Bitterness, rancor, and confusion destroyed much of the effectiveness of the Dutch churches. As early as 1748, Dominie DuBois of New York had observed that internal strife contributed to the languishing of the congregations and transfers to other churches. That strife went on until the Reverend John Henry Livingston, a native-born American and a graduate of Yale, went to the Netherlands for his theological education and had the foresight to meet with the Classis of Amsterdam and the Synod of North Holland. Livingston gave them a firsthand interpretation of the situation and found a solution that would be satisfactory to everyone. It affirmed allegiance to the Classis of Amsterdam and the Church Order of Dort and maintained high standards of ministry with a theological professor from the Netherlands to be chosen by the Classis of Amsterdam. These

Catechism. We are fed and nourished in all regards from the Lord, even in mind and other powers of the soul. I was happy to be able to see it and I desired to continue in this state of utter dependence. And after psalms in the morning, I sang my favorite Psalm, Psalm 31:15-18, 23-24, and Psalm 38:9-10, 17-22.

Neither was Dina a stranger to the sacraments:

The following Lord's Day was time for the Lord's Supper, and my soul panted after the blessed sacrament. There were many things that had disquieted me this week. Wherefore it occurred to me whether I should not forego this time. But experience has sometimes taught me that this may be a snare of the adversary, and that by waiting and heeding such a suggestion we may find the way shut up altogether. I even said to my soul, "O soul, this is not the place of your rest. You will not be quieted here, this is a field of conflict." But the Lord Jesus rose up before my imagination, calling, as on the great day of the feast, "Whoever is thirsty, let him come to me and drink." I was so much aware of my soul's desire and the need of the strengthening of my faith, knowing that all I could bring was an empty soul, that I could not withdraw myself from the presence of my King.

Dina's reflection on this occasion goes on for another thousand words in a similar vein.

Dina's faith and her trust in God involved not only herself and her family but also her nation. She prayed about flood victims who had "been brought into distress on account of the water. I became aware of what it means to bear one another's burdens. Yet, at the same time, my heart remained convinced of the Lord's fatherly love and compassion." On another occasion she writes,

I also was occupied with my country during this time as I earnestly made supplication and called on the spirit of judgment and might as often as I had the impression of God's hand smiting us, especially in the recognition of disease among the cattle.... Concerning the enemy of our country [France] I continued to believe that the Lord would not give us over into her hand but at this same time the water froze so severely, that it could serve the enemy as a bridge to attack us.... On a certain Sunday the cold became so severe that I was compelled to acknowledge that, unless the Lord would be merciful, who would be able to stand?... And praised be his goodness, on Tuesday morning, there was as strong and delightful a thaw as was ever seen. O how humble and grateful this made me before my merciful God who had not rejected my prayers, but who taught me anew to entrust myself to the Lord. Especially as our enemies had boasted that they would undertake something that would resound through all of Europe. Yet now I could say, "The daughter of Zion laughs thee to scorn, O enemy, and shakes her head over thee, for the Lord has made strong the bars of our gates."

However, news came that

Sluys in Flanders had been taken by the French. My friend and I were greatly startled, but the Lord kept me from unbelief and discouragement, and my thoughts were drawn to the words, "There is no searching for his understanding; therefore, wait provisions satisfied the Conferentie. The church in America would have the right to educate and ordain its own ministers, satisfying the concerns of the Coetus. Finally, the Classis of Amsterdam and the Synod of North Holland were satisfied by retaining the right to review all decisions made in America as well as the right to appoint the professor of theology, thus insuring the new ministers' orthodoxy.

This solution was accomplished after thirty-five years of strife and eighteen of division. When Livingston in 1771 gathered the ministers of the colonies to effect

upon the Lord and be strong."

With the selection of the Prince of Orange as stadtholder, admiral, and captain general, Dina has prayers of thanksgiving that extend over five thousand words.

There were moments even in good times when Dina, at age twenty-two, wished to be with the Lord:

It was good for me to draw near to God. Then I heard what was a special blessing to me from my beloved spiritual father, Rev. Mr. Temmink. It was a discourse on the 22nd Lord's Day of the Catechism, 57, 58, the resurrection of the body and eternal life. The Lord was present, and I would fail, should I attempt to give any description of this precious discourse. It was permitted to the preacher to ascend to Pisgah's top, and take a view of the goodly land, and so I was blessed with such a view of heaven, and what was laid up for me there, that I was scarcely able to endure the sight. I felt powerfully drawn towards the heavenly state, while at the same time I joyfully desired to serve the purposes of God here below.

Dina did not seem to be in the best of health. She makes frequent references to her faintness and to her lack of strength. On June 12, 1747, Dina suffered a violent sickness attended by fainting spells and fever. The next Sunday, however, found her again in church. In August, Dina contemplated a trip by barge through the canals to Utrecht, a distance of approximately thirty-five kilometers. After considerable vacillation, she believed she was led by the Lord to go, and in September she made the journey. But by the eighteenth of the month, she again fell ill with a high fever.

I was in great distress with exceedingly high fever.

Professor Osterdijk was called and prescribed for me. As soon as I had taken the medicine, my disease took a change and I became much worse, so that the professor was called again. He was astonished and said he had never had so feeble a patient. I committed myself into the hands of the Lord. That day the professor came by three times. He and everyone else thought that I should die. He also expressed much concern that my parents were not with me and proposed that they should be written to immediately. I said, "My dear sir, there could be no more joyful news to me than that I should die, for I am reconciled to God; I step with Jesus into eternity."

Although she did not so note in her diary, it was during this visit to Utrecht that she first met Johannes Frelinghuysen. Johannes was a theological student awaiting examination and ordination and a return to America. Some two years after that meeting Dina wrote,

Some few notes on how my heart through hidden instructions, was prepared and afterwards bent by the Lord towards marital relations with the Reverend Mr. Johannes Frielinghuysen, minister at Raritan in New Netherland: The way of my God with me in these matters is an elevated one because it involves my being torn away from my parents, sister and dear friends with whom the greatest possible bond of tender affection connects me. Concerning the person in question, it all came to me quite unexpectedly. In my relation with him I never had expected anything of that nature. About two years ago I learned to know his Reverence in Utrecht through a providential direction of the Lord.

Dina's notes of over eight thousand words recount her resistance to this proposal. Throughout, reconciliation and plan for the future, there were but twenty-two in attendance.

Rebel versus Tory

The third dispute to rack the church was between Rebel and Tory, and this time civil commitment was added to ecclesiastical commitment. While we might like to think that all of our forefathers were "Rebels" or "Patriots" fighting for the cause of independence from England, out of a total of forty-one clergy of the Dutch church, four openly declared themselves on the side of the

---

she refers to "his Reverence" and never to "Johannes." She struggles against the idea. She hopes that her parents' refusal to let her go will put an end to the matter, but she succumbs eventually to what she sees as the Lord's leading, all the while hoping that it is but a test as God tested Abraham in the sacrifice of Isaac. She insists that Frelinghuysen return to America and come back after several years to wed her, again hoping that something will intervene to save her from this marriage, but in the end, contrary winds prevent Johannes from sailing and she ultimately agrees to be wed.

Once married, Dina embarked on a voyage across the North Atlantic. During the voyage a terrible storm arose, battering the boat. Its wooden hull sprang a leak. The pumps were unable to keep up with the flow, and the captain despaired of saving the vessel. However, Dina calmly sat in a chair tied to one of the masts and prayed for their safety. As she prayed, the water stopped rushing into the hold. The pumps were able to empty the ship of the water that had come in. The ship was saved. Later it was found that a swordfish was wedged in the open seam of the hull, effectively stopping the leak. The chair Dina used was called the "Ebenezer chair," and she used it throughout her life.

The obligations in Dina's life in New Netherland evidently precluded the continuation of her diary. On their arrival, Johannes and Dina began building a home with the bricks and money sent by her family to house the furniture also sent by them. During his pastorate in the Reformed Church in Somerville, Johannes was also involved in the training of students for ministry in America. Two children were born to Dina and Johannes, Frederick in April 1753 and Eva in September 1754. Tragedy struck ten days after the birth of Eva, when Johannes contracted pneumonia and died on his way to a Coetus meeting on Long Island.

Dina prepared to return to her family in the Netherlands. However, before she completed her arrangements she was confronted by a young man of eighteen years, Jacob Rutsen Hardenbergh, a theological student of her late husband. Jacob proposed! And Dina responded, "My child, what are you thinking about?" and went ahead with her preparations to leave. But once again a storm intervened, and Dina saw the hand of Providence at work. She married Jacob despite eleven years' difference in their ages. After Jacob was ordained to the ministry, he was called to the church formerly served by Johannes and Dina, and later to congregations at Raritan, Bedminister, North Branch, Neshanic, and Millstone.

Ten children were born to Jacob and Dina, of whom eight survived infancy. Dina continued to be a support to her husband in godly life and conversation among the women of the congregation. In 1789, Jacob was called to be pastor of the First Reformed Church in New Brunswick as well as president of Queens College. Both prospered under his leadership. Jacob died of consumption (probably tuberculosis) in 1790, while Dina, subject to faintings and fevers in her twenties, survived him, dying in 1807 at the age of eighty-one.

To trust in the Lord, to seek his will, to ponder Scripture, to attend church and be nurtured in catechism and song, to be fed by the sacraments, to be obedient to the Lord's commands, to be faithful in prayer, to be ready for death, but to be active in God's service throughout one's life—that was the life of Dina van Bergh Freylinghuysen Hardenbergh.

---

[1]All quotations are from the unpublished manuscript of Dina van Bergh's diary, translated by Gerard Van Dyke and held by the Joint Archives of Holland (Michigan). The authors are deeply indebted to Dr. Van Dyke for his translation of the diary and his research into the life of Dina van Bergh.

Tories, and four more were clearly sympathetic to that cause. A total of eight ministers does not sound very large, until we consider that it represented one-fifth of the clergy.

It has been estimated that even more of the Dutch church as a whole, about one-third of its members, favored the side of the Tories. Some congregations were in favor of revolution, while others were in favor of the British crown, but most congregations contained supporters of both parties. With the nationhood of the United States a long-established fact, we tend to forget that the third of our church members and the fifth of its ministers who supported the British crown had good reasons for doing so. Largely, their political decisions followed their ecclesiastical decisions. If one felt comfortable with the constituted authority of Dort, the Classis of Amsterdam, and the charters of the British crown to the Dutch church, then it was very natural to take seriously the injunctions of Romans 13 and the Belgic Confession, which enjoined obedience to those in rule—in this instance, George III.

Research has shown that the very ministers and congregations that favored the orthodox party of the Conferentie also favored the conservative Tory party and British rule. Conversely, those who favored greater freedom in worship and greater freedom and independence in church government also favored greater political freedom. Those who remember America's involvement in the Vietnamese conflict will remember the marked differences of opinion among the citizenry and within the churches—and Vietnam was a conflict that took place on the other side of the globe. Remembering this discord will give some inkling as to the degree of conflict that must have torn the Dutch church when the war involved the land in which they lived, their homes, and their churches—some of which were burned and others of which were used as stables. The church was divided about a war in its midst, with Dutch Tories serving with the British armies while Dutch Patriots fought against them. Is it not a wonder that out of such discord God by grace could build a church?

One final note: The depth of the colonial dissension may be judged by the memory carried for more than two centuries by members of the church. In the early 1980s both of the denomination's theological seminaries, New Brunswick and Western, received million-dollar gifts from the estate of Miss Florence Charavay. No one at either seminary was familiar with this benefactress, so they inquired among people in her New Jersey congregation. Finally an elderly person was found who remembered the deceased, and her comment was, "Oh, her family were Tories."

Resources for Further Study

The Diary of Dina van Bergh, trans. Gerard Van Dyke with an introduction and notes by J. David Muyskens, http://www.rca.org/images/aboutus/archives/vanberg.pdf.

Forerunner of the Great Awakening: Sermons by Theodorus Jacobus Frelinghuysen (1691-1747), ed. Joel R. Beeke. The Historical Series of the Reformed Church in America. Grand Rapids: Eerdmans, 2000.

Piety and Patriotism, ed. James W. Van Hoeven. The Historical Series of the Reformed Church in America. Grand Rapids: Eerdmans, 1976.

5

Indian and Dutch

NOVÆ SVECIÆ Seu PENNSYLVANIÆ IN AMERICA DESCRIPTIO.

The story of the relationship between the Dutch and Native Americans is a tale—perhaps familiar even today—concerning a people's relationship with a little-understood culture.

The Dutch, like the other nations of Europe, touted the prospect of converting the "heathen" to Christianity as one of their goals in settling the New World. The record of accomplishment, while containing a few bright spots, is by and large dismal.

The Europeans, little accustomed to dealing with people of other cultures, assumed their own was superior. Their inability to understand Indian behavior often resulted in their attributing stupidity to Indians. This attitude appeared in the first minister to New Netherland, Domine Jonas Michaelius, who in 1628 wrote:

As to the natives of this country, I find them entirely savage and wild, strangers to all decency, yea, uncivil and stupid as garden poles, proficient in all wickedness and godlessness.... How these people can best be led to the true knowledge of God and of the Mediator Christ is hard to say.

Their language, which is the first thing to be employed with them, methinks is entirely peculiar....It also seems to us that they rather design to conceal their language from us than to properly communicate it....

It would be well then to leave the parents as they are, and begin with the children who are still young....But they ought in youth to be separated from their parents; yea, from their whole nation....I hope to keep a watchful eye over these people, and to learn as much of their language as will be practicable, and to seek better opportunities for their instruction than hitherto it has been possible.[1]

Michaelius stayed only four years. His successor, the Reverend Everardus Bogardus, was embroiled in disputes with the governor, Willem Kieft. During this time "no efforts were made to convert the heathen, between whom and the settlers an unlicensed intercourse generally prevailed."[2] Others were more successful than Michaelus and Bogardus.

Events referenced in the chapter are below the line. Other historical events are above the line.

1763
Treaty of Paris. France cedes Canada to Great Britain

1664
English take New Amsterdam

1775
Battle of Lexington, beginning of Revolutionary War

1704
French and Indians attack in Connecticut

1618-48
Thirty Years' War

1755-63
French and Indian War

1812-14
War of 1812

1861-65
Civil War

| 1600 | 1650 | 1700 | 1750 | 1800 | 1850 | 1900 | 1950 |

1629
Dominie Michaelius

1690
Dominie Dellius & Indian conversions

1881
Women's Board for Domestic Missions

1903
Geronimo is baptized

1643
Governor Kieft massacres Indians

1911
Mildred Cleghorn born

1731
Dominie Drissius reports tribe Christianized

1895
Frank Hall Wright commissioned

1644
Dominie Megapolensis

1898
Cheyenne church in Colony, OK

1911
Apache church in Mescalero, NM

The Reverend Dr. Jonas Megapolensis, called to the patroonship of Rensselaerwyck with the responsibility "for the edifying improvement of the inhabitants and the Indians," was both a more perceptive observer of Indians and their culture and more adept in learning their language. Still, in 1644 he too complained, "This nation (the Mohawks) has a very difficult language, and it costs me great pains to learn it, so as to be able to speak and preach in it fluently."

Sketch by Champlain, published in 1613

Megapolensis goes on to write:

Though they are so cruel to their enemies, they are very friendly to us, and we have no dread of them. We go with them into the woods, we meet with each other, sometimes at an hour or two's walk from any houses, and think no more about it than if we met with a Christian. . . .

When we deliver a sermon, sometimes ten or twelve of them . . . will attend . . . and will stand awhile and look, and afterwards ask me what I am doing and what I want, that I stand there alone and make so many words, while none of the rest may speak. I tell them that I am admonishing the Christians that they must not steal, nor commit lewdness, nor get drunk, nor commit murder, and that they too ought not to do these things; and that I intend in process of time to preach the same to them

in their own country . . . when I am acquainted with their language. Then they say I do well to teach the Christians; but immediately add . . . "Why do so many Christians do these things?"[3]

It is interesting to note that the directors of the East India Company did not seem to share the same concern for the Indian's conversion. In a remonstrance to the directors in 1650, the ministers complained, "The Directors have made no effort to convert to Christianity either the Indians, or the Blacks or Slaves, owned by the Company there." The directors replied, "Every one conversant with the Indians in, and around New Netherland, will be able to say, that it is morally impossible to convert the adults to the Christian faith. Besides, 'tis a Minister's business to apply himself to that, and the Director's duty to assist him therein."[4]

The Classis of Amsterdam evidently desired that the conversion of Indians take place and obviously wanted to believe the best. However, in a letter dated July 15, 1654, Megapolensis and Drisius wrote to the classis:

> You make mention in your letter, that you have gathered from our letters, that the knowledge of the Gospel is making great progress among the Indians here. Speaking with all deference, we do not know or think that we have furnished any such intelligence in our letters. We greatly wish indeed, that such were the state of things among the Indians, but as yet, there is little appearance of it.[5]

The concern for the conversion of Indians seems to have been real—at least for many of the clergy. But even those who made noble attempts frequently despaired of the results. In 1657, writing from New Amsterdam, Megapolensis and Samuel Drisius put their names to the following:

> We can say but little of the conversion of the heathens or Indians here, and see no way to accomplish it, until they are subdued by the numbers and power of our people, and reduced to some sort of civilization; and also unless our people set them a better example, than they have done heretofore.[6]

Yet the Dutch ministers' concern for the salvation of Indians was also mixed with hatred of Roman Catholicism and fear of a French invasion from the north. In 1658 one of the reasons for requesting two more ministers for New Netherland was that "the Jesuits in Canada or Nova Francia are seeking to force an entrance among us, and introduce their idolatries and superstitions."[7]

Cultural clashes were apparent, too, in the Dutch Reformed Church's expectations for people becoming Christians. The high standards of the Reformation were upheld for Indians and blacks—they were not treated as inferiors when it came to expectations for the faith—but these expectations were unrealistic culturally and even linguistically. When the ministers in New Netherland sought advice concerning the baptism of Indians and blacks, the Classis of Amsterdam replied that it should not be done without previous instruction and confession of faith, nor should their children be baptized unless the parents were confessing Christians.[8]

Success in the conversion of Indians was not recorded until 1690, when it took place at Albany under the ministry of Domine Dellius. The domine had left Albany with the intention of returning to the Netherlands, and the consistory wrote to the Classis of Amsterdam requesting his return:

> Dellius' departure grieves also the very heathen; for during the past year his Reverence made it his duty to instruct them and bring them over to the Christian faith. He was so far successful in this work, that he has already incorporated quite a number, after public confession and baptism, in the church, much to the astonishment of everybody. He then also received them into the communion of the Holy and

Willem Kieft

Relations between the Indians and Dutch were relatively good, considering the vast cultural differences. The Indians, in fact, did much to befriend and supply the Dutch with food to sustain them in the early years of the colony, and carried on an active trade with them.

The Indian tribes were often at war with one another, as was the case in 1643 when the Mohawks, with whom the Dutch at Albany maintained a good relationship, came south in a war against the Algonquins, who had been friendly to the Dutch of New Amsterdam.

In the diary of David Pieterszoon de Vries, artillery-master and then patroon in New Netherland, is the record of Willem Kieft's actions toward the Indians. Willem Kieft was appointed director general of New Netherland in September 1637 and served in that capacity until July 1646.

DeVries was present on February 24, 1643, when Kieft told him of his plan to "wipe the mouths" of the savages [Algonquins]. De Vries argued against the proposed massacre, recalling the friendship of the Indians and indicating reprisals would surely lead to the spilling of "Christian blood." Twice de Vries interceded with Kieft against the action, quoting himself in the second appeal: " 'Let this work alone; you wish to break the mouths of the Indians, but you will also murder our own nation, for there are none of the settlers in the open country who are aware of it.'"[1]

When it was day the soldiers returned to the fort, having massacred or murdered eighty Indians, and considering they had done a deed of Roman valor, in murdering so many in their sleep, where infants were torn from their mother's breasts, and hacked to pieces in the presence of the parents. . . . After this exploit the soldiers were rewarded for their services, and Director Kieft thanked them by taking them by the hand and congratulating them. At another place, on the same night . . . forty Indians were in the same manner attacked in their sleep and massacred. . . . Did the Duke of Alva in the Netherlands ever do anything more cruel? . . . As soon as the savages understood that the [Dutch] had so treated them, all the men whom they could surprise on the farm-lands, they killed; but we have never heard that they have ever permitted women or children to be killed. . . . So there was an open destructive war begun.[2]

Subsequently, the Indian chiefs demanded reparations, which were minimally given by Kieft, but they did not satisfy the Indians. While the chiefs tried to maintain peace, young braves engaged in reprisals. No one but de Vries dared to be alone with the Indians, and when he left on October 8, his final words to Kieft were "that this murder which he had committed on so much innocent blood would yet be avenged upon him. . . ."[3]

---

[1] Jameson, *Narratives*, 227.
[2] Ibid., 228-29.
[3] Ibid., 234.

Most Precious Supper of the Lord. The respect and affection which these new converts had for him greatly favored his Godly undertaking; and the number coming to the public instructions arranged by his Reverence for every day, increased so greatly, that we firmly believe that God has a great following among them. We are much obliged to his Reverence because he is the first who has taken upon himself at his own expense, and of his own motion and out of pure love, the troublesome labor of converting the heathen.[9]

Once Dellius reached Boston, a consistory member there persuaded him to return to Albany because of this success in converting Indians.

What began solely as a spiritual endeavor did change with time. In the following year, the correspondence and exchange of gifts between the "praying Indians" and the new governor, Sloughter, makes it clear that the civil authorities and Indians understood that this also involved a military alliance against the French and their Indian allies.

The success of Domine Dellius, coupled with civil desires for Indian allies, sparked emulation not only among the Dutch but the British as well—New Netherland had become New York in 1664. The New England Society for the Propagation of the Faith was urged in 1696 to undertake missionary work. The Onondaga Indians requested Protestant missionaries in 1697. Domines Freeman of Schenectady and Lydius of Albany were

appointed in 1700 to teach Indians. Even the bishop of London commended Dellius's work among the Indians. In 1701, the Anglican Society for Propagation of the Gospel in Foreign Parts was formed, and missionary work among Indians was included in its mandate.

With the increased numbers of missionaries and converts, more cross-cultural tension arose. In 1716 the Indians complained that they felt poorly dressed in their bearskins while the Dutch were so well dressed in church. In 1722 a separate church was built for the Mohawks.

Nonetheless, the work of the pastors at Albany continued. Following Dellius, the Reverend Johannes Lydius continued the work of catechizing, even though his salary was often in arrears. By the time the Reverend Peter Van Driessen wrote to the Classis of Amsterdam in 1731, he could testify that the Indian tribe around Albany had "now been altogether Christianized" and that two-thirds of an adjacent tribe had "enlisted under the banner of Christianity . . . ."[10]

Unfortunately, international conflicts impinged upon these promising beginnings. The French and Indian War raged from 1755 to 1763, from New England across New York and into Ohio, and north to Quebec. The French enlisted Indian tribes to fight on their side, while the British enlisted tribes in their fight against the French. With mutual massacre and treachery, churches, missions, and Christian witness suffered. All the while further immigration from Europe

Geronimo and the Apache Mission

Reformed Church missionary Walter C. Roe described Geronimo as "short, thickset but spare, and of great endurance."[1] U.S. General Miles said, "He was one of the brightest, most resolute, determined-looking men that I have ever encountered. He had the clearest, sharpest, darkest eyes I think I have ever seen, unless it was that of General Sherman when he was at the prime of life and just at the close of the great war. Every movement indicated power, energy and determination."[2]

From hidden camps in the Sierra Madre Mountains, Geronimo, a Chiricahua Apache medicine chief, led hit-and-run raids on settlers over a ten-year period. About to be overcome by the U.S. military, Geronimo surrendered in 1886. His entire band was transported to Florida—the men were imprisoned in the dungeons of old Fort Pickens, the women and children kept at nearby Fort Marion. When the damp climate of the eastern seaboard proved fatal to many, the Indians were moved to Mount Vernon, Alabama, but they continued to die from tuberculosis and dysentery. After seven years the remaining Indians were moved again, this time to Fort Sill just south of Colony, Oklahoma. They were held captive there from 1894 to 1913 on a reservation six miles square.

Shortly after Walter and Mabel Roe met with the Women's Executive Committee of the Board of Domestic Missions in late 1898, more than one thousand dollars was raised to begin work among the Apaches of Fort Sill. Within months, a school was built and an appeal went out to Reformed churches for needed supplies:

In response to the earnest efforts of Rev. and Mrs. Roe last fall, we received from auxiliaries and individuals, churches and Endeavor Societies, the sum of $1,462.17 for the Apache Mission.

With this sum the necessary building has been erected, a modest little structure, answering the purpose of schoolhouse and residence for the workers as well. This amount provides also for the first expenses for our workers. But now an appeal is made for some immediate needs for this mission. Will you not present them to your societies.

A central point in the reservation has been chosen for the school building, but as the Indians are scattered over several miles, a horse and wagon will be needed.

Inside the building will be needed maps and pictures for the walls of the schoolroom, seats and desks for the scholars, and also the teacher's desk. Books and stationery, slates and pencils, are essential for the work, and lamps must be provided for the church service, which will also be held in this room.

One of the workers on the field writes: "I do wish, on account of freight, that most of the dear friends would send their gifts in money, so as to avoid duplicates, and let many of the bulky things be purchased at the nearest market town."

So we ask you to take this list of "needs" to your fall meetings, and send to the treasurer the money, which will be immediately invested in these very necessary articles for the Apache schoolhouse.[3]

In the summer of 1903, Geronimo was baptized and joined the Fort Sill congregation. It is reported, however, that he was later expelled from the church for incessant gambling. The descendents of the imprisoned Apache tribe became the nucleus of two other Reformed churches, both in New Mexico: Mescalero and Jicarilla Apache (in Dulce).

---

[1] Women's Executive Committee, Board of Domestic Missions, *Mission Field*, September, 1899, 176.
[2] Ibid.
[3] Ibid., 178.

continued to pressure Indian lands and ways of life. While the British won the French and Indian War, by 1774 they were confronted by a revolution among the thirteen colonies. The Boston Tea Party was followed by the Battle of Lexington in 1775, and the War for Independence continued until 1783. The Dutch Reformed Church, located in the Middle Colonies, bore much of the brunt of the fighting, with churches burned, pillaged, and used to house troops or horses. Less than two decades later the young nation was again at war with Britain, from 1812 to 1814. Is it any wonder that in view of the devastation and distractions of war, Indian missions continued to diminish?

Nonetheless, until wars intruded, the record of the ministry of the Dutch to the Indians is not without merit when one considers the resources available. The opinions of Domine Michaelius were uttered in 1628, when he was the only minister in New Netherland. Megapolensis first wrote in 1644, when he was one of only two ministers in the colony that stretched from Albany to the Delaware. When Dellius began to have some success at Indian conversion in 1690, he was one of seven Reformed ministers, of whom three were French, ministering to French congregations. Notwithstanding those meager resources, Dellius could in 1693 count two hundred Christian Indians in Albany, and by 1731 Van Driessen could report the entire tribe Christianized, with two-thirds of an adjacent tribe accepting the gospel.

A year after the War for Independence ended, the General Synod of the Dutch church was presented with a draft report for "the extension of the borders of the church." The question of extension became a regular issue. Such

Apache Indians near Dulce, New Mexico, circa 1930.

recommendations and efforts that came to modest fruition were concerned primarily with providing new churches for the Dutch on America's expanding frontier.

However, as early as 1784, the New York Missionary Society, a voluntary society including Reformed, Presbyterian, and Baptist churches, with John H. Livingston serving as vice president, was established with the purpose of evangelizing Indians. However, it was 1799 before its first missionary, the Reverend Joseph Bullen, was sent to the Chickasaw Indians of Georgia. In 1797, the Northern Missionary Society, with the Reverend Dirck Romeyn of First Schenectady as president, sent missionaries to the Indians of central and western New York.[11] In 1817 the Reformed Dutch Church joined Presbyterians and Associate Reformed in forming the Society for Foreign Missions, and by 1820 the society had sent eight males and nine females to the Osage Indian tribe in Missouri. A year later, that voluntary society was joined by the New York Missionary Society, becoming the United Foreign Missionary Society, which established missions among the Tuscaora, Seneca, Cataraugus, Chippewa, and Machinaw tribes.[12]

The responsibility for ministry to Indians had moved from parish ministers to missionaries sent by voluntary societies of churches. In 1831, the Dutch Reformed Church began to move away from those

The Radio at the Comanche Mission

From the *Christian Intelligencer and Mission Field*, April 3, 1929:

Through the Collegiate Church of St. Nicholas, Fifth Avenue and Forty-eighth Street, New York, a very fine Radiola set, of the semi-portable type, was presented by Mrs. L. W. Coleman, 77 Park Avenue, New York, to the Comanche Mission at Lawton, Oklahoma. This was something we had been wishing for for several years and it was offered to us without our even asking. You should have seen the group gathered around it the first Friday evening after it came, at the regular weekly social. There were Fred and David, both practically blind, and so unable to even watch the carrom games which the Indians like so well. All Indians like music, both these men are good singers of Indian songs and they seemed to appreciate it so much. Robert Chaat had charge of the radio for the evening and interpreted to the older people where this or that was coming from and also some of the words of the songs.

On the day President Hoover was inaugurated the Women's Missionary Society was having their weekly meeting. The radio was turned on and we soon picked up Washington and it looked for a while as though there would not be much sewing done. But the most interested gathered up close with their work, the children were sent out-doors to play and now and then all would stop to listen, then someone would interpret to the older ones. One interested listener was Mrs. Padahpony, who does not understand a word of English, but when the patter of the horses' hoofs of the cavalry in the parade came in perfectly clear and she was told what it was, you should have seen the look on her face! It was better to her than all the wonderful music to which we had listened.

The mission workers, so largely isolated from much that is going on in the outside world, appreciate this splendid addition to the mission equipment....All appreciate the thoughtful generosity of the friends who sent it.

—J. Leighton Read, Lawton, Oklahoma

Mary Thunderbull and her two grandchildren, Albert Bringingood and Clifford Whiteman, in Colony, Oklahoma.

voluntary societies, and in 1832 it established the Board of Foreign Missions, making missions the institutional business of the denomination.[13] Seventy years later, the domestic board reported that it had aided 230 churches and missions and was aiding 164 missionary pastors.[14] It would appear, however, that these were churches of the denomination, rather than missions to Indians.

However, "a visit by Mrs. John Bussing, president of the [Women's Board of Domestic Missions], and Mrs. Charles A. Runk, chairwoman of the Committee on Indian Mission,

to the Rev. Frank Hall Wright, a Choctaw Indian minister recovering from tuberculosis in New York City, led to his appointment to begin specific work among the Indian tribes."[15] Commissioned in 1895, Wright organized churches in Oklahoma among the Cheyenne near Colony in 1898, and among the Comanches near Lawton, with services beginning in 1901 and formal organization in 1907. Services were also held among the Apaches imprisoned at Fort Sill, Oklahoma. In 1907 services were begun among the Apaches in Mescalero, New Mexico, and in 1911 a church was organized. In 1908 services were begun among the Omahas at Winnebago, Nebraska, and established as a church in 1911. The Walter C. Roe Memorial Mission in Dulce, New Mexico, was established in 1921,

The Rev. Robert Paul Chaat (greeting a church elder) was born in Fort Sill, Oklahoma, and was the first ordained native American pastor in the Reformed Church in America (1934). He served as pastor of the Commanche Memorial church in Lawton, Oklahoma, from 1931-69.

and, in 1934, the Reformed Church in America assumed responsibility for the church in Macy, Nebraska, organized by the Presbyterians in 1857. Five remain as Reformed churches, with a combined membership of more than eight hundred.

The challenge confronted by pastors, societies, and boards in their mission to the Indians is one the church continues to face: being faithful to the gospel in the context of another culture while being sensitive to that culture.

Mildred Cleghorn—An American Apache

At age seventy-five, Mildred Cleghorn, then chairperson of the tribal council for the Chiricahua Apaches, was one of eighty people awarded the Ellis Island Medal of Honor during the one-hundred-year anniversary celebration of the Statue of Liberty in 1986. She, along with Walter Cronkite, Jacqueline Kennedy Onassis, Jo DiMaggio, Coretta Scott King, and others, "exemplified the ideal of living a life dedicated to the American way while preserving the values of a particular heritage group."

Archives of the Reformed Church in America

Born a prisoner of war at Fort Sill in Oklahoma, Cleghorn was the first woman elected to the office of elder at the Jicarilla Apache Reformed Church, a congregation her parents helped start. She was a charter member of the Reformed Church's American Indian Council and served on the denomination's General Program Council for six years. A graduate of Oklahoma State University, Cleghorn worked for the Bureau of Indian Affairs and for the university extension service.

When she worked in Kansas, she joined a church guild made up of white women. It taught her how little white people knew about Indians. "Indians are as different from each other as Germans are from Italians," she said. "They have different languages, different customs, different dress. You can't just view them as one type of people."[1]

As head of the tribal council and as one of the last surviving prisoners of war, Cleghorn spoke in 1986 at a ceremony, held at Geronimo's grave, marking the one-hundredth anniversary of his surrender. Geronimo, she said, should be remembered as a man who tried to save his homeland. "We lost our land and most of our heritage," she said. "What we have now, we are trying to retain."[2]

Cleghorn was one of the Chiricahua Apaches featured in the award-winning 1988 PBS documentary, *Geronimo and the Apache Resistance*, of the American Experience series. In 1996 Cleghorn became one of the lead plaintiffs in a class action suit filed on behalf of more than 300,000 Indians who were seeking reliable accounting of hundreds of millions of dollars in Indian trust funds managed by the Bureau of Indian Affairs. That same year, on the anniversary of the Oklahoma City Bombing, Cleghorn helped read the 168 names of the bombing victims.

Mildred Cleghorn died April 15, 1997, at the age of eight-six. She was driving her great-grandson to school when her car was hit broadside by another vehicle. She was killed instantly.

---

[1] "Mildred Cleghorn: An American Indian," by John Stapert. *Church Herald*, Dec. 5, 1986, 10.
[2] Jack Elliot, Associated Press writer, "Ceremony Marks Surrender of Geronimo Apaches," *Saturday Oklahoman and Times*, Sept. 27, 1986.

[1] Hugh Hastings, *Ecclesiastical Records of the State of New York*, vol. I, 56-61.

[2] Ibid., 216.

[3] J. Franklin Jameson, *Narratives of New Netherland* (New York: Barnes & Noble, 1909), 172-78.

[4] *Ecclesiastical Records*, vol. I, 266-67.

[5] Ibid., 326.

[6] Jameson, *Narratives*, 399.

[7] Ibid., 434.

[8] *Ecclesiastical Records*, vol. I, 508.

[9] *Ecclesiastical Records*, vol. II, 1003.

[10] *Ecclesiastical Records*, vol. IV, 2548-49.

[11] Marvin D. Hoff, *Structures for Mission*, The Historical Series of the Reformed Church in America (Grand Rapids: Eerdmans, 1985), 26-27.

[12] Ibid., 29.

[13] Ibid., 31.

[14] Ibid., 34.

[15] Ibid., 48.

Resources for Further Study

The Dutch Reformed Church in the American Colonies, by Gerald F. De Jong. The Historical Series of the Reformed Church in America. Grand Rapids: Eerdmans, 1978.

Ecclesiastical Records of the State of New York, vols. I-VII, published under the supervision of Hugh Hastings, 1901-1916.

Geronimo and the Apache Resistance, WGBH/Boston, WNET/New York, KCET/Los Angeles, video 1988.

Historical Directory of the Reformed Church in America, 1628-2000, by Russell L. Gasero. The Historical Series of the Reformed Church in America. Grand Rapids: Eerdmans, 2001.

Structures for Mission, by Marvin D. Hoff, The Historical Series of the Reformed Church in America. Grand Rapids: Eerdmans, 1985.

Jicarilla Apache, Dulce, New Mexico
(originally Walter C. Roe Memorial Mission)

Commanche Reformed Church, Lawton, Oklahoma

Winnebago Reformed Church, Winnebago, Nebraska

6

Slave and Free

New Amsterdam ca. 1642

In the 1750s, shortly after the death of her husband, Johannes, the pious Dina van Bergh Frelinghuysen wrote a long letter to her brother-in-law. One paragraph begins with the disposition of her husband's books and ends, "As to the blacks, they are submissive to me, but I should like to be rid of them." The Frelinghuysens, first family among the Dutch pietists of America and leaders in the Coetus, like their opponents in the Conferente, seemingly saw nothing wrong with the keeping of slaves.

The story of slavery in New Netherland begins even before that of the Dutch church. In 1625 the black company slaves of the Dutch West Indies Company arrived in New Amsterdam.[1] In the keeping of slaves the Dutch were no different from the Anglicans in Virginia or the Puritans in New England or, for that matter, the Quakers in Pennsylvania, where the founder of the "Holy Experiment," William Penn, held slaves until his death in 1718. A century and a half after the first African Americans came to New Amsterdam, the Roman Catholics of Maryland held approximately three thousand black slaves. One of the slaveholders was Father John Carroll, subsequently the first bishop in the United States.

Any attempt to understand the lack of moral outrage against the slave trade must take two points into account: context and time. Prior to the sixteenth century, slavery was not an issue for the Protestant countries of northern Europe, for there had been very little trading contact with sources of the slave trade. Northern Europe was already overpopulated with a ready source of inexpensive labor in debtors' prisons and among the peasant classes. Those who fell into debt could be indentured as servants for a specified length of time, depending upon the size of debt. Their debts were then paid by the persons to whom they committed themselves for labor.

In the colonies of the seventeenth century, however, the situation was very different. In New Netherland, in particular, the Dutch simply were unable to attract enough people to take advantage of the available resources. The Indians proved difficult to enslave because they outnumbered the early settlers and were in their native habitat. Africa, however, proved a ready source of labor. It also had a preexistent slave trade as a result of

Events referenced in the chapter are below the line. Other historical events are above the line.

Above the line:

- **1609** Henry Hudson's voyage of discovery
- **1664** British seize New Amsterdam
- **1725-1807** John Newton, captain of a slave ship. Converted, 1779 wrote "Amazing Grace"
- **1787** Wilberforce begins battle against slavery
- **1759-1833** William Wilberforce
- **1807** Abolition of slave trade by British
- **1833** Abolition of slavery in British dominions

Timeline: 1600 — 1650 — 1700 — 1750 — 1800 — 1850

Below the line:

- **1628** Slaves arrive in New Amsterdam
- **1639-55** Dominie Bogardus baptizes Negroes
- **1644** Blacks in New Amsterdam freed and given land to till
- **1649** Nicholas Manuel Angola baptized in St. Nicholas
- **1750s** Dina van Bergh would be rid of her slaves
- **1746-60** Quaker John Woolman speaks against slavery
- **1774** Pennsylvania Quakers disown slaveholding members
- **1816** General Synod affirms blacks as part of our congregations
- **1832** Colored woman praised in *Christian Intelligencer*
- **1855** How, "Slave Holding Not a Sin"
- **1856** Van Dyke, "A Reply"

African Baptisms

New Amsterdam was a seaport trading post inhabited by Dutch fur traders, merchants, sailors, and enslaved Africans. Many of the Africans—who comprised nearly 20 percent of the colony's population—were skilled workers. They were carpenters, farmers, blacksmiths, weavers, and ship builders.

Early church documents record the baptisms of African children with surnames of Angola and Congo. Christopher Moore, a historian and member of West End Collegiate Church in New York City, is an eleventh-generation descendent of Emanuel and Christina Angola, whose child Nicholas Manuel was baptized in St. Nicholas Church in 1649 (third record down).

intertribal warfare in which the victors sold unneeded captives to the slave merchants. The new market in the Americas greatly increased the demand for slaves and the resultant suffering and degradation.

Northern Europeans (except for those who went on voyages of discovery to Africa, the Indies, or the Americas) commonly knew only persons of varying shades of pink. The Dutch in the Province of Holland had never really assimilated the Friesians and looked down on the Gelderlanders. It was no wonder that they had difficulty relating to people of different colors and cultures from different continents. So, what would Dina van Bergh Frelinghuysen Hardenbergh's reaction have been to her black slaves in America in the 1750s?

From her Bible, with which she was very familiar, she would have known of slavery in both the Old and New Testaments. She would have known no biblical condemnations of slavery. In fact she would have found the apostle Paul sending Onesimus back to his master, and she would have known the exhortations to slaves to respect their masters and of masters to treat their slaves with kindness. By the 1750s, slavery would have been an accepted institution for over a century in the Dutch-dominated colony. Her slaves were perhaps the first black persons she had encountered in her life and they were obviously different; they were there to serve.

Quakers: A Christian religious group, followers of George Fox (1624-91) in England, who believed in the direct inspiration of the Holy Spirit available to whomever God would choose. He rejected a professional ministry, sacraments, oaths, and military service. Quakers were regarded as disturbers of the peace, and a threat both to right belief and the social order. They were persecuted both in England and the English colonies.

Rebaptized: To be baptized a second time. Baptists insisted upon rebaptism, claiming the baptism of infants to be invalid. Non-Baptist churches regard rebaptism as a sin insofar as it is a denial that the efficacy of baptism belongs to God through the work of Jesus Christ, and that it is a gift, not a work effected either by the person, the minister, or the church.

The Dutch were not alone in seeking economic advantage from slavery and the slave trade. In the mid-seventeenth century, not even the Quakers were against the slave trade. It might also be well to recall that the enslavement of fellow northern Europeans was not unknown and that prisoners of war were pressed into service frequently as galley slaves—John Knox had served as a galley slave of the French. The practice of indenturing whites was in some respects even more arduous than slavery. A slave owner had an investment to protect for the future and therefore was under the constraint of self-interest to provide adequate nourishment and rest for his slaves. The person who held an indentured servant had no such long-term self-interest.

At the beginning of the colony of New Netherland, an inducement for the Dutch to come to America was not only the offer of patroons (estates), but there was this further inducement: "The Incorporated West India Company shall allot to each Patroon twelve black men and women out of the prizes [i.e., ships captured by the Dutch] in which Negroes shall be found, for the advancement of the Colonies in New Netherland."[2] In 1648, correspondence from Peter Stuyvesant, governor of the colony, to its directors in Holland requested the right to send ships directly to Angola in Africa to bring "Negroes to be employed in farming" back to New Netherland.[3] In contrast, in the Netherlands, as early as 1679, the Reverend Jacobus Hondius published *Swart Register van Duysent Sonden*, in which he "declared the slave trade to be one of the major sins of his time and warned his fellow Christians not to get involved in it."[4]

Moving toward the middle of the eighteenth century, one finds an interesting work that was pro-slavery but that, perhaps by its circumstances of writing and promotion, betrayed an excessive eagerness to justify the institution. The work, in Latin, was *Dissertatio Politico-Theologica de Servitute, Libertati Christianae non Contraria* (i.e., *A Dissertation on the Politics and Theology of Slavery, which is not Contrary to Christian Liberty*). The author was a student of theology at one of the Netherlands' most prestigious schools, the University of Leiden. The principal theme of the work was that slavery was not contrary to Christian freedom. What is so interesting about the work is that its author was himself black. Subsequently ordained in the Dutch Reformed Church, the Reverend Jacobus Elisa Johannes Capitein (1717-1747) was the first African Negro ordained into the

Enslaved Africans as skilled laborers

Protestant ministry.

Capitein's dissertation quoted from Aristotle, Seneca, and Calvin as well as extensively from Holy Scripture. He had prepared his treatise under Professor Jan van den Honert, one of the country's most reputable theologians. The dissertation was soon translated into Dutch, published, and went through four editions within a year.

Jacobus Capitein

Before returning to Africa as a missionary, Dominie Capitein preached to overflowing crowds in some of the churches in the major cities of the Netherlands. The fact that a black was willing to condone slavery indicates merely that as a scholar he was reflecting the ethos of his own time and country and of millennia of Judaic and Christian tradition. The fact that the Dutch accepted him and his message so readily may be indicative of the fact that they wished for affirmation of an institution that was beginning to be questioned.

It was between 1746 and 1760 that Quaker John Woolman toured congregations from North Carolina to New England, pleading with his coreligionists to liberate their slaves. By 1774 his message had sufficient impact that the Quakers of Pennsylvania voted to disown members who bought or sold black people. It should be noted, however, that this took place a century and a half after the Dutch came to New Netherland. During the same time that Quaker Woolman was itinerating on behalf of the freedom of slaves, the great evangelist George Whitefield, while urging the evangelization of slaves, nonetheless owned eight and after 1750 purchased many more to cultivate his plantation.

When Whitefield urged the conversion of the slaves in the late eighteenth century, he was only doing what had been urged upon Christians since the beginning of the seventeenth century. Even the Reverend Jonas Michaelius, two years before coming to New Netherland in 1628, had suggested two young mulattos be sent from Guinea in Africa to the Netherlands for Christian training that they might become missionaries. It must be recognized that from the very first the conversion of Negroes (as well as Indians) was one of the objectives of the Classis of Amsterdam as contained in a letter to the brethren in New Netherland. In 1640, the Classis of Brazil "stated that the primary purpose for obtaining Negro slaves ought not to be for profit but 'to bring them to the knowledge of God and salvation.'"[5]

The same year in New Netherland, Dominie Evardus Bogardus in New Amsterdam requested of the classis and

company that a schoolmaster be sent to the colony in order "to teach and train the youth of both Dutch and blacks in the knowledge of Jesus Christ."[6] It was this same Dominie Bogardus who not only baptized blacks but performed their marriages and included them in the records of the church. In 1650, when complaints were made about the conduct of the West India Company, one of those complaints was that "the Directors have made no effort to convert to Christianity either the Indians or the blacks, or slaves, owned by the Company."[7]

In the early 1660s, when the Reverend Adrian van Beaumont inquired of the Classis of Amsterdam concerning the baptism of Negroes and Indians, he was told

> The Classis deems it necessary that you observe the good rule of the church here in this land, where no one, who is an adult, is admitted to baptism without previous confession of his faith. Accordingly, the adult Negroes and Indians must also be previously instructed and make

confession of their faith before Holy Baptism may be administered to them. As to their children, the Classis answers, that as long as the parents are actually heathen, although they were baptized in the gross (by wholesale, by the Papists), the children may not be baptized, unless the parents pass over to Christianity, and abandon heathenism.[8]

In the same year, however, the Reverend Samuel Drisius of New Netherland inquired concerning "a certain person thirty years of age, baptized by the Mennonites, but now manifesting an inclination toward the true and Scriptural Reformed Religion," as to whether or not he should be rebaptized. The classis replied, "Since he has been baptized once, he need not be baptized." While this paragraph is between two that deal with the relationship of New Netherland to the West Indies churches, there is no indication whether the "certain person" was white or black, slave or free.[9]

Blacks, however, faced a "glass ceiling" in terms of Dutch expectation when it came to baptism, as is indicated by a letter of the Reverend Henry Selyns to the Classis of Amsterdam, dated 1664, June 9:

> As to baptisms, the Negroes occasionally request, that we should baptize their children, but we have refused to do so, partly on account of their lack of knowledge and of faith, and partly because of the worldly and perverse aims on the part of said Negroes. They wanted nothing

else than to deliver their children from bodily slavery without striving for piety and Christian virtues. Nevertheless when it was seemly to do so, we have, to the best of our ability, taken much trouble in private and public catechizing. This has borne but little fruit among the elder people who have no faculty of comprehension; but there is some hope for the youth who have improved reasonably well. Not to administer baptism among them for the reasons given is also the custom among our colleagues.[10]

Selyns alludes to one of the perceived financial problems in baptizing slaves, i.e., whether when a slave was baptized and became a Christian he or she should not be set free. Dominie Udemans, in 1638 (in the Netherlands), published a book in which he argued precisely this point. When New Netherland became an English colony in 1664, English courts "generally followed the rule that Negroes could be held as slaves until they became Christian, at which time they were to be freed."[11] These laws were not binding upon the colonies, and "between 1664 and 1706 six of the colonial legislatures, including those of New York and New Jersey . . . passed acts which declared it was legal for a Christian to be held as a slave."[12] "In 1747 the Classis of Amsterdam declared that 'the acceptance of Christianity . . . does not make servants, male and female slaves, free persons.'"[13] Yet, in spite of that uncertainty, Bogardus, a century earlier, between 1639 and 1655, baptized one to three Negro children annually into the Dutch Reformed Church of New Amsterdam, and that in turn indicated that there were adult Negroes who had also become full communicant members.

However, in total numbers, the evangelistic efforts to convert black slaves could hardly be seen as a triumph. Undoubtedly the greatest impediment to bringing slaves to Christianity was their experience at the hands of their masters. The institution itself frequently separated husband from wife and parents from children. Brutality visited upon slaves was all too frequent. The discrepancy between

By Grace Alone

Harlem, New York, 1832

For nearly a week past there have been no cases of cholera or deaths. The colored woman who nursed the lamented Dr. Arnold and Mr. and Mrs. Hinton in their sickness is a most faithful domestic in the family of William Randell, Esq., of Harlem. She is not dead as was announced in the papers. She is still living and has recovered from the illness into which her unwearied watchings with the sick and dying had brought her, and long may she live to reap the reward of her works and labors of love and mercy.

—*Christian Intelligencer*, August 4, 1832

Punishment for slave uprisings of 1741

Christian teaching and Christian practice was all too apparent to those who lived in slavery.

It is true that in New Amsterdam in 1644, eleven slaves were freed and given free land to till to their own advantage. However, even these bounteous gifts were not free of Dutch self-interest. Governor Willem Kieft had embarked upon a series of murderous raids against Indian encampments (the raids were opposed vigorously by Dominie Bogardus), and the Indians, not surprisingly, began to conduct their own raids against the Dutch. New Amsterdam at that time stretched only about a mile north of the fort at the tip of Manhattan, and farms on the edge of the village bore the brunt of Indian attack. It was to these vacated farmsteads with their inhabitants slaughtered that the newly freed blacks were moved, not only to provide food for the village, but also to constitute the first line of defense against Indian attack.

The English, after the conquest of 1664, questioned the legitimacy of free black ownership, and the former Dutch governor, Peter Stuyvesant, sent a letter to the English authorities explaining that this was land the blacks have cleared and cultivated . . . and they have owned and possessed unmolested. All of these parcels of land were given to the aforesaid Negroes in true and free ownership with such privileges as all tracts of land are bestowed on the inhabitants (of this) province. . . .In acknowledgment of the truth I have signed this with my own hand. Done at the island of Manhattan on this 20 April 1665.[14]

However, it should also be noted that by 1712 the New York Assembly had passed a law restricting black land ownership. There is a certain amount of fiscal irony in the fact that the last parcel blacks were forced to sell is the land upon which the Empire State Building now stands.

While the status of slavery seesawed back and forth, those Christians who articulated its moral offense gradually grew in numbers. It is interesting that in 1816 the General Synod could declare

in the church there is no difference between bond and free, but all are one in Christ. Hence blacks are to enjoy the same privileges, etc. (see Constitution of 1792, Article 59). Resolved that hereafter, the blacks within the bounds of our congregations be enumerated as a part of them. [15]

The article of the constitution to which it refers says simply, "Adults, by baptism, are initiated into the Christian church, and received as members thereof in full communion; and therefore are bound to partake of the Lord's Supper, which they shall promise at their baptism." Just eleven years after synod acted, the New York legislature freed all remaining slaves in that state on July 4.

All of this is not to say, however, that the hearts of all Christian people had been changed. In 1855, the North Carolina classis of the German Reformed Church, because of a theological disagreement within its denomination, requested transfer to the Dutch Reformed Church. Dr. Wyckoff of Albany and Dr. Bethune of Brooklyn objected that the peace of the church would be endangered and that the church would be distracted by the question of slavery. The Reverend Isaac G. Duryee of Schenectady objected to receiving the classis of North Carolina because "slave holding was a sin and the Dutch Reformed Church should not hold fellowship with slave holders."[16] The Reverend Samuel B. How, pastor of the First Reformed Church of New Brunswick, addressed the synod on behalf of the German classis. He began by stating the obvious, that slavery had existed within the Reformed Dutch church for generations. For biblical justification, he cited 1 Timothy 6:1-5, claiming that Paul was communicating in this passage that slavery was not temporary as it had been for Jews enslaved to Jews, but was a permanent condition from which slaves could not escape. Quoting the Old Testament, he pointed to

Genesis in which God makes a covenant with a slaveholder, Abraham. Through a slaveholder God promised to bless all the nations of the earth. The Reverend How found Jesus in favor of slavery by citing Matthew 8:5-13, where Jesus healed the slave of the centurion. Interestingly, it was an elder, John Van Dyke, who responded to the Reverend How. Van Dyke began by pointing out that How was addressing the situations of Abraham and Paul, rather than those of the horrors of American slavery, especially in the South. The Reverend How, said Van Dyke, had "coolly transferred the scene of the conflict from cotton fields and rice swamps, the slave pens, the auction blocks and whipping posts of the South [to the time of Abraham and Paul]." Van Dyke further asked,

> . . . is it sinful or is it not, to forever separate a husband and a wife? You know it is perfectly lawful to do so in the slave states; and you know, also, that it is the daily practice, whenever it is the will of the master to do so, but is it sinful or right in the sight either of God or man?[17]

Returning to How's argument concerning Abraham, Van Dyke took the argument to its logical conclusion:

> [Abraham] not only had men servants . . . but he had a female

Samuel B. How

slave also Hagar, by whom in the lifetime of his wife, he had an illegitimate child, without ever having been censured or reproved for it by the Almighty; but will you undertake to reason from this that the patriarchs of the present day, the great heads of the church, may now do the same thing and be innocent, on the ground that Abraham was allowed to do so without disapprobation?[18]

The upshot of this last great public argument concerning slavery before General Synod was that the classis of North Carolina was not received into the Dutch Reformed church. However, it's worth noting that a spirited defense of slavery was mounted by one of the leading ministers of the denomination, a former college president and minister of the prestigious First Reformed Church of New Brunswick, and that it was rebutted by an elder.

When one considers the level of self-interest in the keeping of slaves, and the societal pressures to preserve the institution for the benefit of whites, one must be grateful for those persons who acted on behalf of blacks: Dutch pastor Jacobus Hondius, Quaker John Woolman, Dominie Evardus Bogardus, even Peter Stuyvesant, Drs. Wyckoff and Bethune, the Reverend Duryee, and elder Van Dyke. They too acted by God's grace.

---

[1] Howard, Dodson, Christopher Moore, and Roberta Yancy, *The Black New Yorkers: 400 Years of African American History*, The Schomburg Illustrated Chronology (New York; John Wiley & Sons, 2000).
[2] *Ecclesiastical Records of the State of New York*, vol. I, 79.
[3] Ibid., 228-29.
[4] Gerald F. De Jong, "The Dutch Reformed Church and Negro Slavery in Colonial America," *Church History*, vol. 40, December 1971, 424.
[5] Ibid., 428.
[6] Ibid., 429.
[7] *Ecclesiastical Records*, vol. I, 266.
[8] Ibid., 508.
[9] Ibid., 513.
[10] Ibid., 548.
[11] Gerald F. De Jong, "The Dutch Reformed Church and Negro Slavery in Colonial America," *Church History*, vol. 1, March 1971, 431.
[12] Ibid., 431.
[13] Ibid., 432.
[14] Christopher Moore, "Land of the Blacks," *Seaport, New York's History Magazine*, fall-winter 1995, 11.
[15] *Minutes of the General Synod of the Reformed Church in America*, 1816, 18.
[16] Noel L. Erskine, *Black People and the Reformed Church in America* (New York: Reformed Church Press, 1978), 46-47.
[17] Ibid., 51.
[18] Ibid., 52.

Resources for Further Study

Black People and The Reformed Church in America, by Noel Leo Erskine. New York: Reformed Church Press, 1978.

The Dutch Reformed Church in the American Colonies, by Gerald F. De Jong. The Historical Series of the Reformed Church in America. Grand Rapids: Eerdmans, 1978.

Santa and Pete: A Novel of Christmas Present and Past, Christopher Moore and Pamela Johnson. New York: Simon & Schuster, 1998. A film version of *Santa and Pete*, with James Earl Jones and Hume Cronyn, is available on DVD at Amazon.com.

7

Freed to Grow

Archives of the Reformed Church in America

The Reformed Church in America owes more to the Reverend John Henry Livingston than to any other one person. Through him the Coetus-Conferentie dispute was resolved and a plan of union effected. To him the Reformed Church owes the Explanatory Articles for its constitution, as well as a hymnal that served the church for over a century. Livingston's Plan of Union provided an effective decision-making synod on American soil, and it included a way to provide for the education, examination, and ordination of ministers. Article XX of the Plan of Union (October 15-18, 1771) states:

we, with the approbation of the Reverend Synod of North Holland and the Reverend Classis of Amsterdam, assume the long desired privilege of holding the Preparatory and Final Examinations, and of further qualifying those who are lawfully called agreeably to the usage of the Netherlands.

Articles XXVII and XXIX provided that the professorate would be appointed according to the advice of the Classis of Amsterdam and would be from the Netherlands. Before the classis could respond, however, the Revolutionary War began, making it difficult if not impossible for the Classis of Amsterdam to provide a professor. In 1784, after the cessation of revolutionary hostilities, Livingston again brought the issue before the church. The same year, Livingston was nominated as theological professor. The trustees of Queens College (now Rutgers) elected him to the Chair of Theology but provided no money for salary. (Students provided a fee of five pounds, given when a certificate of licensure was granted, but that was totally inadequate compensation.) As a result, for a decade Livingston maintained his full pastoral duties in New York while lecturing in theology to students in his home. However, due to the high cost of living in New York City, the synod of 1794 requested that Livingston move to Flatbush. He acceded to the request, giving up many of his pastoral duties and half his salary. The synod provided no recompense for the move. In 1795 Queens College closed its doors for lack of funds. In 1807 the trustees of Queens acted to combine the college with the theological professorate, with all of the monies from the New York churches going

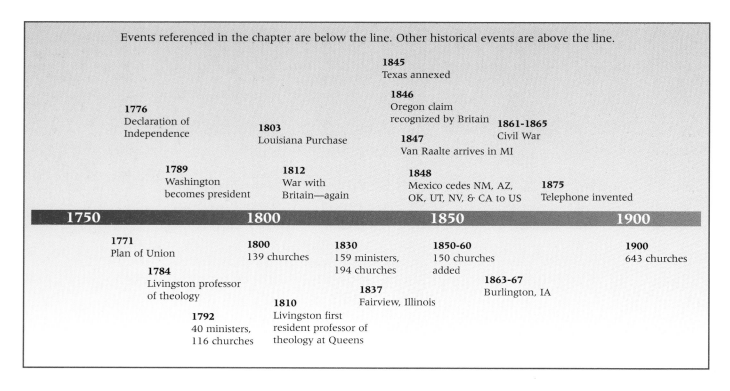

Events referenced in the chapter are below the line. Other historical events are above the line.

1845
Texas annexed

1846
Oregon claim recognized by Britain

1847
Van Raalte arrives in MI

1776
Declaration of Independence

1803
Louisiana Purchase

1861-1865
Civil War

1789
Washington becomes president

1812
War with Britain—again

1848
Mexico cedes NM, AZ, OK, UT, NV, & CA to US

1875
Telephone invented

1750   1800   1850   1900

1771
Plan of Union

1800
139 churches

1830
159 ministers, 194 churches

1850-60
150 churches added

1900
643 churches

1784
Livingston professor of theology

1863-67
Burlington, IA

1792
40 ministers, 116 churches

1810
Livingston first resident professor of theology at Queens

1837
Fairview, Illinois

to the latter. Livingston was again called to the post, but he refused to move until monies were in hand to support him. Finally, in 1810, Queens, which was to become New Brunswick Theological Seminary, gained its first resident theological professor, John Henry Livingston.

It is hardly possible to overemphasize the importance of New Brunswick Theological Seminary to the life of the Reformed Church. In 1792, seven years after Livingston had begun to teach students in his home, there were 116 Reformed churches, but only 40 ministers. Twenty years after Livingston took up residence at New Brunswick, the number of ministers had leaped from 40 to 159. True, there were now 194 churches to be served by those 159 ministers, but the ministerial ranks had multiplied nearly four-fold in just thirty-nine years.

Without the leadership of John Henry Livingston and resident theological education at New Brunswick, the remarkable growth of the Reformed Church in the nineteenth century would not have been possible. With the right to examine and ordain ministers in this country and a school at which to train them, the outpouring of men for the ministry resulted in outstanding growth for the church. At the beginning of the nineteenth century, the Reformed Church had 139 churches. Within the first decade, 38 churches were added; in the second, 37 more; in the third, an unprecedented 107 churches. The next two decades fell behind that pace with 84 and 85 churches, respectively. Then, in the ten-year

"Old Queen's," which at one time housed all of Queen's College plus the theological school. The cornerstone was laid in 1809, but the structure was not completed until 1825, the same year the school's name was changed to Rutgers.

period from 1850 to 1860, 150 churches were added. In a single decade, more congregations were added to the Reformed Church in America than had been formed in the previous 172 years from 1628 to 1800.

The Reformed Church has never again equaled that decade of 1850-1860 for church growth. But throughout the nineteenth century, growth continued. From 1860 to 1870, 103 churches were added. In the next decade, 91, 90 in the following, and in the final decade of this marvelous century, 138 churches were added. Altogether, 923 new churches were formed during the nineteenth century, representing church growth of 764 percent.

The magnitude of this achievement becomes apparent when compared to the "good old days" of church growth after World War II. In the Reformed Church in America's greatest twentieth-

Explanatory Articles: When the Reformed Dutch Church organized itself in the United States apart from the Classis of Amsterdam, it adopted the church order of the mother church in the Netherlands. However, that was a church where the Doctrinal Standards described the state as responsible for the maintenance of the church, even as the church was to be a guide to the state (Cf. Article 32 of the Belgic Confession). In America, the relation of church and state was one of separation, requiring "explanatory articles" to adapt the old church order to a new political situation.

century decade of growth, from 1950 to 1960, 110 new churches were formed. Certainly that is something to celebrate, but, considering the 150 churches that had sprung up a century earlier from a much smaller base of churches, the celebration should contain a degree of humility.

What caused the church to grow so phenomenally during the nineteenth century? Many factors played a part. It was a time when America surged from the Atlantic to the Pacific, expanding its national boundaries to their present limits. Population growth was unprecedented. Larger numbers of Dutch immigrants arrived than had come to New Netherlands originally. Some stopped in New Jersey, and others went on to Michigan, Wisconsin, Illinois, Indiana, and Iowa.

Nonetheless, the key to the success of the church in the

The Old Mud Meeting House

The congregation faced each other eye-to-eye across a long Communion table—women on one side, men on the other, segregated at the entrance of their church by a unique double door.

The congregation of Dutch settlers had left Pennsylvania in 1789 seeking fertile farmland west of the Allegheny Mountains. They traveled by flatboats down the Ohio River and then by wagon along the Cumberland Mountains to what is now Mercer County, Kentucky. The Reverend Peter Labagh, a Reformed Church missionary, organized the congregation in 1796, and the Classis of New Brunswick helped fund the construction of the meeting house.

The Mud Meeting House, which is on the National Registry of Historic Buildings, measures thirty-four by forty-six feet. Its fourteen-feet-high walls were filled with wattle (split saplings) and daub—a mixture of clay silt from the nearby creek combined with twigs and straw.

The church's first and only Reformed Church pastor, the Reverend Thomas Kyle, served the congregation from 1804 to 1816, when he resigned to become a Methodist. The congregation applied to the classis for a successor. The classis replied that the distance between the Kentucky congregation and the Reformed churches in the east was too great to assure viability and recommended that the church become Presbyterian. In 1826 the Cumberland Presbyterian Church took over the meeting house and used it until 1847, when a majority of the congregation moved to a newly constructed facility. Since then the meeting house has been used by a variety of denominations, and in 1928 it became the property of the Harrodsburg Historical Society.

James L. Ballard photos

Unlike many churches today built of the finest materials, but with little concern for Word or Sacrament, Old Mud's walls were common, but pulpit and table were prominent and finely crafted.

Elias Van Bunschooten

In 1810 the Reverend Dr. John Henry Livingston, who had served the Collegiate Church in New York City for almost forty years, resigned to spend his remaining years training theological students at Queen's College (now Rutgers University) in New Brunswick, New Jersey. Since 1784 he had been a professor of theology, but only on a part-time basis.

When he arrived in New Brunswick, Livingston discovered that most of the students preparing for theological study at Queens needed financial help and that the college had little money available for scholarships. For help Livingston turned to a childhood friend, Elias Van Bunschooten.

In a letter dated July 31, 1810, Livingston appealed to Van Bunschooten, then a minister serving in Clove, New York, who was known for his frugality and eccentricities (One story has Van Bunschooten, unable to cross the rain-swollen Delaware River, shouting marriage vows to the bride and groom standing on the opposite bank):

What, my dear old friend and brother—what if God should put it into your heart to dispose in your last will and testament of a respectable part of your property for the benefit of the Theological Institution? It will be no injury to any [since he was a bachelor] if you should make the Reformed Dutch Church your principal heir. The very idea must be pleasing to your mind and will warm your heart. It will prove how much you loved the church which has so long loved and respected you. I have suggested this with freedom and without reserve.

Four years later, Van Bunschooten appeared on the floor of General Synod, which was meeting in New York City. He marched down the aisle and placed a package on the presiding officer's table. It contained ten bonds worth $13,800 and $800 in cash, a substantial amount in those days. The money was to be invested and the interest paid to Van Bunschooten during his life. Upon his death, the income was to be used to educate the future leaders of the church.

The Reformed Church's first planned gift, however, came with one stipulation: The terms of the gift must be read at future meetings of the classis and synod, not to memorialize the donor but to encourage similar gifts.

---

nineteenth century is the Reverend John Henry Livingston, architect of the Plan of Union, compiler of the Reformed Church hymn book, first professor of theology, first to hold the chair of theology at New Brunswick, and mentor to hundreds of seminarians. He brought concord out of dissension. He provided the ecclesiastical structure to examine and ordain for the ministry, and, preeminently, he trained men for ministry. Those were the men who, despite the huge growth in the number of churches, left fewer pulpits vacant at the end of the expansion than when it began. When people who understand the minuscule colonial origins of the Reformed Church ask, "How did you ever get as big as you are?" the answer must include John Henry Livingston.

Two questions about the nineteenth century remain to be answered: To what extent was the wave of Dutch immigrants in the nineteenth century responsible for church growth? and, Why did so many Reformed churches disappear by the end of the century?

First, it should be noted that of the 923 new churches of the nineteenth century, only 237 appear to have been started as a result of the new waves of Dutch immigration to the Midwest and Far West, while 686 were started by the

RCA Constitution: The constitution of the Reformed Church in America is composed of three elements: the *Book of Church Order*, the Liturgy, and the Doctrinal Standards. In short, how we govern ourselves, how we worship, and what we believe.

eastern churches. Clearly the older churches of the East formed the base for the bulk of church expansion in the nineteenth century. New immigration accounted for only about one-quarter of the expansion.

"But what happened to this expansion?" Obviously 139 plus 923 totals 1,062, but the Reformed Church in America ended the nineteenth century with only 643 churches. What happened? Let's look at the 150 churches of the great decade, 1851-1860. Sixty-eight are still in existence as

Reformed churches. Seven are affiliated with other denominations. Eleven merged with other Reformed Church congregations, while 43, or 29 percent, were dissolved or dropped from the denominational records. In almost every instance, the demise of these churches came because of a lack of members or a lack of funds.

It is interesting to note that the fate of the churches in the Midwest was remarkably similar. Of the 150 churches established between 1851 and 1860, 34 were immigrant

The Oldest Reformed Church in the Midwest

Having received reports that America's western region was "ripe for the harvest of souls," the 1836 General Synod encouraged the Board of Domestic Missions to "go forward in the enterprise with energy, and plant churches as extensively as can be done where desirable fields offer, and suitable men can be obtained."[1] The board made the first successful step toward its goal of establishing a classis for Illinois, Indiana, Michigan, and Wisconsin in Fairview, a small enclave in central Illinois with three log cabins, a log schoolhouse, and one frame building. On October 16, 1837, the Reverend A. D. Wilson of the Classis of New Brunswick organized the Fairview Reformed Church, a congregation of eight individuals.

The erection of the Fairview Reformed Church building was a monumental achievement. These dedicated pioneers gathered the wood, nearly all black walnut, from native forests, floating the large timbers, and putting them in place. They hewed the finishing wood by hand, made the framing for more than a thousand window lights, and built the high pulpit and the pews. Financial problems followed, however, and there were delays. Once an appeal was made to the East, and $468 came to assist. But the church was built and still stands today as it stood in 1841 when it was finally dedicated.[2]

Photo: Clarence Liang

Fairview Reformed Church

---

[1] *Acts and Proceedings of the General Synod of the Reformed Protestant Dutch Church in North America*, June 1836, 521.
[2] Willis J. Vander Kooi, "The Oldest Reformed Church in the Midwest," *Church Herald*, April 19, 1968, 16.

churches of which 8 (24 percent) were dissolved or dropped—again for lack of members or lack of funds.

The Reformed Church in America forebears in the nineteenth century might be faulted for overestimating the possibilities of extension in a given place, but they can never be faulted for lack of zeal, courage, or daring. The numbers speak for themselves.

Letters from Iowa

Letters from D. A. Budde in Burlington, Iowa, to J. A. Wormser in Amsterdam:

December 23, 1852

We Hollanders, plus a few German families, have affiliated with De Hollandsche Gereformeerde Kerk [The Reformed Church in America] of New York, and we have a small congregation in Burlington under the name of De Hollandsche Gereformeerde. Our Rev. [J. B.] Madoulet is from Nijmegen and preaches each Sunday, once in High German and once in the Dutch language. The financial costs are borne largely by the synod [of the RCA]. The church has the same [creedal and liturgical] forms in their church books as they do in Holland, and that includes the Canons of Dort, but it is all in English. Last October…I attended a classis meeting at Ferview [Fairview], Illinois, sixty miles from here. Everything was in English, but most everyone was of Dutch ancestry, and some could still speak some Dutch. We were all like one big family.…We now are hoping to build a church next summer, but we do not know whether we will be able to collect sufficient funds. We have already sold at least ten acres of our land for 450 dollars to help the good cause along.

May 29, 1854

Our congregation here is not growing much. We have to put up with a lot of grief. It is small, consisting of seventeen families, all by our selves, over against all the other denominations. We are under very strict scrutiny, and as I wrote you before, the family of our minister does not conduct itself in a Christian manner, and as a result he lost his influence both inside and outside the congregation. So we had no choice but to dismiss him.

—From Johan Stellingwerff, *Iowa Letters: Dutch Immigrants on the American Frontier*, ed. Robert P. Swierenga, trans. Walter Lagerwey, Historical Series of the Reformed Church in America, Grand Rapids: Eerdmans, 2004.

Nonetheless, 29 percent of the churches founded in one decade disappeared within a century. It appears that sometimes it was a case of misplaced judgment—the establishment of a church where people failed to gather. It is also possible, however, that sometimes the churches were intended to appeal to people who were Dutch, or of Dutch ancestry, and when not enough such people gathered in a given spot, the church collapsed. It's an interesting possibility to consider, especially in light of the fact that the Reformed Church, with its emphasis upon an educated ministry, showed that in the nineteenth century a well-trained ministry that proclaimed the Word of God could be successful.

The Fulton Street Prayer Meeting

A prayer meeting that began in Old North Dutch Church in New York City in 1857 ignited a spiritual revival that spread across the continent. Faced with immigrants from every part of Europe and a declining membership, Old North employed Calvin Lanphier—a businessman with a talent for singing and a gift for praying—as a neighborhood missionary. He began a program of visitation to area families to bring them into the church and to recruit children for the Sabbath school.

With permission from a dubious consistory to hold a noontime prayer meeting, Lanphier began praying alone September 23. Within a half-hour a second person joined him, then five others—a total of six men from four denominations. At the next prayer meeting September 30, twenty men attended. When forty showed up a week later, it was voted to hold the meetings daily. Within four months, the three lecture rooms at Old North were filled.

Soon the movement spread throughout the city—in January twenty meetings were held simultaneously in churches of several denominations. At John Street Methodist Church, two thousand people gathered daily in the sanctuary and basement. The rules were simple: no prayers more than five minutes long, no sermons, no controversies, no meetings more than an hour long, and no one excluded.

Soon the prayer meetings spread elsewhere—to Philadelphia, Albany, Detroit, Chicago, Portland, and overseas to France, England, and Ireland. Although intended for Christians, thousands of unbelievers were converted.

Although Old North Dutch Church was disbanded in the late 1800s, the Fulton Street daily prayer meetings continued until 1961.

—To read more of this story, see Marvin Hoff, "The Fulton Street Prayer Meeting," *Reformed Review*, September 1963.

Resources for Further Study

The Dutch-American Experience: Essays in Honor of Robert P. Swierenga, ed. Hans Krabbendam and Larry J. Wagenaar. Amsterdam: VU Univ. Press, 2000.

Dutch Chicago: A History of the Hollanders in the Windy City, by Robert P. Swierenga. The Historical Series of the Reformed Church in America. Grand Rapids: Eerdmans, 2002.

Equipping the Saints: The Synod of New York, 1800-2000, ed. James Hart Brumm. The Historical Series of the Reformed Church in America. Grand Rapids: Eerdmans, 2000.

Iowa Letters: Dutch Immigrants on the American Frontier, ed. Johan Stellingwerff, trans. Walter Lagerwey. The Historical Series of the Reformed Church in America. Grand Rapids: Eerdmans, 2004.

"Makers of the Modern Reformed Church: John Henry Livingston and the Rise of the American Mission Movement," by John W. Beardslee III, in *Historical Highlights* (Issue No. 30, Vol. 8, No. 2, October 1989), http://www.rca.org/images/aboutus/archives/hh30.pdf.

Two Centuries Plus, by Howard G. Hageman. The Historical Series of the Reformed Church in America. Grand Rapids: Eerdmans, 1984.

Vision from the Hill, ed. John W. Beardslee III. The Historical Series of the Reformed Church in America. Grand Rapids: Eerdmans, 1984.

Zion on the Hudson: Dutch New York and New Jersey in the Age of Revivals, by Firth Haring Fabend. New Brunswick: Rutgers Univ. Press, 2000.

8

Tai-Hoey for Amoy

Hope and Wilhelmina Hospitals at Amoy at the beginning of the twentieth century.

Archives of the Reformed Church in America

John Henry Livingston was not only the father of the
Reformed Church but also the father of its missionary
movement. As the denomination's only seminary professor, for
forty-one years Livingston had a direct influence on almost every
person entering the ministry of the Dutch Reformed Church. For
four decades his was the dominant voice in theology and on behalf
of missions.

In 1804 Livingston preached "The Everlasting Gospel," a sermon
destined to become famous in its pamphlet form. Based on
Revelation 14:6-7, it partook of themes common to the American
Protestant missionary movement: the expectation that Jesus' return
was to be preceded by the conversion of the nations; the optimism of
a young United States, whose people saw a God-given destiny to
play a role in that conversion; and the clarion call to go out and
preach the everlasting gospel.

The Reverend David Abeel responded to that call. A son of the

Reformed Church and a graduate of New Brunswick Theological Seminary, he spent time in Java, Siam, and China before being assigned to the mission in Borneo in 1841. By the next year he was convinced that China was a field with far greater potential for the spread of the gospel. The Reformed Church began its work in China in 1842 in the city of Amoy (now Xiamen) on the island of Amoy, a few miles off the coast from Kulangsu (and three hundred miles north of Hong Kong). The mission in Borneo soon closed, while that in China began to flourish.

For those whose concept of foreign mission has been colored by such descriptions as are found in James Michner's *Hawaii*, or other far worse media presentations, the story of the Reformed Church mission to China is instructive.

Michner's fictional missionaries tried to make New Englanders out of Hawaiians and were unwilling to trust church leadership to native Hawaiians. The missionaries of the Reformed Church have quite a different record.

The first Protestant church in China to be erected for a Chinese congregation was dedicated in 1849. Sensitive to the Chinese culture, the missionaries respected the Chinese custom of separating men and women in public meetings by building a ten-foot-high screen down the middle of the church. By 1856 the congregation was formally organized, with a consistory of Chinese elders and deacons. Three years later, a second church was built, and it soon was led by the first Chinese pastor, the Reverend Yap Han-chiong, who was ordained in 1863.

The missionaries did not make the Chinese church subservient to its American mother. They were remarkably ecumenical for their

Events referenced in the chapter are below the line. Other historical events are above the line.

Above the line			
1823 Monroe Doctrine	1846-48 War with Mexico	1898 Spanish-American War	
1824 Erie Canal	1844 Morse's telegraph		1941 War with Japan and Germany
1831 Beginning of abolitionist movement	1863 Emancipation Proclamation	1917 U.S. declares war on Germany	1950 War in Korea
1804-06 Lewis & Clark expedition	1861-65 Civil War		

1800	1850	1900	1950

Below the line			
1804 Livingston preaches "The Everlasting Gospel"	1849 Building of first Chinese Protestant church	1866 Wakasa Murata baptized	1908 John Van Ess assists British in oil exploration	1948 African mission begun
1836 Elihu Doty arrives in Batavia	1862 Lap-Han-Chiong ordained		1920 Mission poultry farm
1842 David Abeel settles in Amoy	1890 Cantine & Zwemer begin Arabian Mission	1925 Chiapas mission begun

The House of Happiness

On October 16, 1889, James Cantine left New York City to begin the Arabian mission. Nine months later, Samuel Zwemer set sailed to join him in Beirut. Both were responding to their seminary professor's dream of preaching the gospel to the people of Islam.

Cantine and Zwemer explored the region extensively. Their initial voyages took them to Cairo, south through the Red Sea, and around the Arabian Peninsula. They stopped in Aden, Belhaaf, Makallah, Muscat, Bahrain, Bandar Abbas, and Bushire—finally settling in Iraq, where they opened a Bible shop in Basrah and performed simple medical and dental procedures in villages along the Tigris River. Over time, Reformed Church in America missionaries would help establish hospitals, dispensaries, schools, orphanages, Christian bookstores, and churches in Kuwait, Oman, and Bahrain.

One of those orphanages was the House of

Archives of the Reformed Church in America

Um Miriam leading prayers in women's clinic.

Happiness in Bahrain. The story is told that one of the sweepers at the mission hospital found a newborn baby in the hospital garbage. Reformed Church missionary Josephine Van Peursem asked Um Miriam, a Persian woman, if she would care for the baby boy as one of her own. As other children were abandoned at the hospital, a home was constructed on the hospital compound for Um Miriam, her three children, a niece, and nine orphans.

Um Miriam had first come to the mission hospital seeking help for her six-year-old son, Aboud, who had been blinded permanently when the wrong medicine had been applied to his eyes on an earlier occasion. Through the care and witness she received, Um Mariam became a Christian, followed by Aboud, who married a Jordanian Christian. Aboud became a leader in the Bahrain congregation, his sister served as principal of the mission school, and four grandchildren attended Reformed Church colleges.

day—far more so than the parent church in America.

The Amoy region was served by three communions that arrived in rapid succession: the Reformed Church in America (1836), the London Mission Society (1844), and the English Presbyterian Church (1850). They divided the area agreeably to avoid competitive duplication. The Reformed missionaries got along so well with their English Presbyterian counterparts, who had a similar polity and doctrine, that they participated jointly in translation, the production of tracts and books, medical and educational work, and in ordaining the first Chinese pastors. Their cooperation was based on a common commitment to Christ and to establish an indigenous Chinese church. Accordingly, they acted together to organize the first Chinese consistory/ session in 1856.

Four years earlier, back in the United States, the General Synod had directed the Reformed missionaries at Amoy to apply to the Particular Synod of Albany when they were ready to form a classis in China. With the formation of the first consistory in 1856, the General Synod again directed the missionaries to form a classis of the Reformed Church in relation to and under the control of the Particular Synod of Albany. The synod understood polity as exercised in the United States, and the polity as previously exercised by the Classis of Amsterdam—one in which

Elihu Doty

The Reverend Elihu Doty began his missionary career in Batavia (now Jakarta, Indonesia) in 1836. He served next on the island of Borneo from 1839 to 1844, then in Amoy, China, from 1844 to 1864. He died at sea in 1864, four days before reaching the United States. Doty's journal, which covers most of his career, indicates the hardships, sacrifices, and challenges often faced by nineteenth-century missionaries.

June 7, 1836. After being detained for nearly a week by contrary winds and rain, this afternoon we received directions to repair to the ship, which is to carry us from our native land to the field of our future labors....On board we found all the missionary company composed of Brethern Ennis, Nevius, Youngblood, with their wives, and Miss Condit, and had the happiness for the first time to sit down in our cabin and take a cup of tea together.

August 23. Gales and squally weather almost constantly for the past week. On Saturday evening we experienced a most tremendous tempest. The gloominess of the midnight storm at sea is indescribable....Lightning in livid glare flashed in quick succession followed by the awful thunder clap. The winds drove through the ship's tackling with frightful roar. All sails were furled and the helm lashed, and our rocking, trembling, groaning ship, with naked spars, was committed to the mercy of the waves. The billows ran high....About 2 o'clock a heavy sea came over the poop and quarter deck, deluged the cabin of the officers and leaking down into one state room soon expelled us from our berths and left us to seek shelter in some other place. Sabbath morning clear but strong winds. No preaching in consequence of the weariness of seamen from preceding nights labors and rough weather.

September 15. This morning at 10 o'clock the anchor was cast about 3 miles from Batavia. Brother Ennis and myself accompanied the Captain ashore, to make arrangements for the disembarkation of the missionary family. Thus after being prisoners of the ocean for near 100 days, we once more stept upon "terra firma."

September 18. Our first Sabbath in this land of spiritual darkness and death. Passed the day with the mission family at Parapatan. A day long to be remembered, when with the people of God though few in number, we had the privilege of entering his courts. O how refreshing to the weary pilgrim is a rest place, so to me have the place of worship and privileges of the sanctuary proved today.

October 9. The apartment of Brother Nevins was entered last Thursday night and robbed of watch and clothing, etc. This circumstance has made us all feel that we have no security and need not look for abiding peace and serenity short of the heavenly source. O that I could without any reserve and with a perfect confidence cast all my cares upon Him who careth for us.

November 29. This morning went into the market near us with a number of Chinese tracts for distribution. Before I had fairly entered the place and as soon as it was known that I had Chinese books they flocked around me in numbers so that I was unable to proceed until entirely released from my load. The avidity of the Chinese to obtain a printed tract or book is truly astonishing. The majority can read and with eagerness grasp at any thing to read. It is not because they are Christian books that they desire them, but because they are books which they can read, and would doubtless with as much eagerness, grasp at a work on any other subject as that of the religion of Jesus Christ. They will read and it is to be hoped that the truth thus brought in contact with their minds may find its way to the heart and with some, produce the peaceable and peaceful fruits of righteousness. This was my first attempt at distribution and oh that it may prove the beginning of much usefulness and good. So precious, the ignorant and perishing immortal souls.

ecclesiastical polity transcended both geography and culture. It was not that synod was against the formation of a Chinese classis (it had learned that much from its history with Amsterdam), but it was to be answerable to the General Synod through the Particular Synod of Albany.

However, the missionaries were single minded in their determination to create a united, indigenous Chinese church. It should perhaps be recognized that indigenous meant, in reality, free from foreign control. Accordingly, in 1862 action was taken founding the Classis/Presbytery of Amoy. Since there was no Chinese word for either classis or presbytery, it was called the Tai-hoey, meaning "Great Meeting of the Elders." The Tai-hoey (tai-hoy) was initiated with the attendance of all of the Reformed and English Presbyterian missionaries and one elder from each of the five organized churches. Minutes were kept in Chinese.

At the very next meeting of the Tai-hoey, members decided that they had the right to examine and ordain Chinese candidates for ministry. They also authorized the organization of a sixth church. It had taken the Dutch Reformed in America over a century and a half to gain these privileges from the Classis of Amsterdam. Now the missionaries had given an amalgamated classis/presbytery that power unilaterally only twenty years after the first missionary of the Reformed Church had set foot in Amoy.

The General Synod was outraged. Its directives to make the classis subservient to the Particular Synod of Albany had been ignored. The missionaries had granted privileges to that indigenous (independent) classis that had taken the mother church 145 years to achieve, and it had united with two denominations to achieve a single church—something the mother church had never achieved. Even the presence of missionary John Van Nest Talmage at the General Synod of 1863 could not sway the synod. It again ordered its missionaries to organize a classis of the Dutch Reformed Church through the Particular Synod of Albany.

The missionaries remained polite but unswayed, and, in a letter to the Board of Foreign Missions, they suggested that "Synod must have mistaken our position on this question." They went on to state that if synod insisted on its position, "We can see no other way than to recall us."[1] With this threat of resignation by all five Reformed Church missionaries in the field,

Ecumenical: The recognition that Christ, as the head of the church, desires that Christians live in oneness in him (cf. John 17). Ecumenical Christians are those who at minimum refrain from slandering other Christians. More often the term refers to those who work for mutual understanding and toward the goal of full communion: recognition of the validity of the ministry and sacraments of other faith communions. To achieve this goal, churches have been engaged in far-reaching discussions, seeking understanding and agreement in doctrine. Notable recent achievements have been the Formula of Agreement between the Reformed Church in America, the Evangelical Lutheran Church in America, the Presbyterian Church USA, and the United Church of Christ; and the Joint Declaration on Justification by Faith between the Lutheran World Federation and the Roman Catholic Church.

Archives of the Reformed Church in America

Pastor Lap

"The Rev. Lap-Han-Chiong, the present pastor of the church at Sio-Ke, is the oldest ordained minister connected with the Amoy Mission. It is believed that he is also one of the oldest ordained ministers in China, if not the very oldest. The thirtieth anniversary of his ordination was celebrated about two years ago, when the good pastor received many tokens of the high estimations in which he is held by missionaries, Chinese Christians and non-Christians alike. His high character, spotless reputation, good judgment and kindly feeling and manner, have justly won for him a place in the affections and esteem of all who know him, and even exceptional influence with Chinese officials. He is one of the noblest fruits of the gospel in China. His wife is likeminded. Their lives and work have been of signal service to the cause of Christ."

—*Mission Field*, 1894-95, 274

Indigenous church:
The church native to
the country. For
example, the Church
of South India.

the synod of 1864 affirmed its policy but allowed the brethren "to defer the formation of the Classis of Amoy."[2] The matter was not brought before synod again.

The missionaries' support for an indigenous, self-ruled, Chinese church did not mean anyone who wished to join could do so. Those Chinese who wished baptism were invited to small weekly meetings where, virtually one-on-one with the missionaries, they were, through conversation, instructed in the faith and examined as

to their experiential knowledge of the Holy Spirit's work in their hearts. . . .This brings us into the closest personal contact with their minds, and enables us to give instruction, to correct misconcep-

tions of truth, guide the inquiry, encourage, warn and exhort. . . .[3]

When the Rev. John S. Joralmon arrived as a new missionary in 1856, he observed,

I have no hesitation in saying that the brethren here are far more careful in the reception of members than are the churches at home. . . .I have far less doubt of the genuineness of their conversion than I have of the majority of those in church fellowship at home.[4]

Furthermore, excommunication could result for persistence in breaking the Sabbath or dealing in drugs, intoxication, sexual

The Baptism of Wakasa Murata

When commercial treaties with Japan opened the doors of that country to foreigners in 1859, two Episcopal, one Presbyterian, and three Reformed Church missionaries—the Reverends Guido Verbeck and Samuel Brown, along with medical doctor D. B. Simmons—were the first Protestant missionaries to arrive. Brown and Simmons went to Yokohama in the north; Verbeck settled in Nagasaki to the south.

Perhaps most prominent among these early missionaries to Japan was Guido Verbeck, whose ministry there spanned nearly forty years. He taught in government schools, helped organize the University of Tokyo, served on committees that revised the Old and New Testaments for the Japanese, and became a trusted adviser to high government officials. Verbeck is also remembered for baptizing Wakasa Murata,

Archives of the Reformed Church in America

WAKASKI. THE FIRST BAPTIZED BELIEVER IN JAPAN.

the First Councillor under the district of Saga's feudal lord Naomasa Nabeshima.

In 1855, Murata was in Nagasaki leading a group of *samurai* who had been patrolling the harbor since the arrival of English and Dutch ships. A small package was found floating in the water. Inside was a book that Murata took home with him to Saga.

Murata's curiosity led him to send one of his men back to Nagasaki to learn what he could about the book. He discovered that it was a Dutch New Testament. When Murata heard that a Chinese version was available, he sent an emissary to Shanghai secretly to obtain a copy, and Murata, along with his younger brother Ayabe and a few close friends, began studying the Scriptures privately.

In 1862 Murata's brother, seeking someone who could help them understand the Bible more fully, made contact with Verbeck. For the next few years, Murata and Verbeck communicated by messenger between

immorality, or gambling. The Chinese church was anything but consumer-oriented, but the church did grow—against virtually insurmountable odds.

However, the above should not be taken to suggest that the missionaries were interested only in doctrine and personal morality. As early as 1842, Dr. William H. Cumming arrived as a medical missionary. Physical healing went hand in hand with spiritual healing. Larger issues also occupied the missionaries' view. John Van Nest Talmage was scathing in his indictment of the opium trade forced on China by the English:

> The money which Christian nations have received from China for this one article [opium] far exceeds all the money which has been expended by all Protestant churches on all Protestant missions in all parts of the heathen world since the days of the Reformation.[5]

Nor did the illiteracy of most of the population go unchallenged. The exceedingly complicated, classical Chinese writing system of thousands of intricate characters limited literacy to the upper classes, people with the leisure for such study. The missionaries recognized almost immediately that if the classical system alone was available they would never conquer illiteracy to the extent that the common people could read the Scriptures. Accordingly, by 1851 (less than ten

Presbytery: The same as a classis in the Reformed Church in America, with the former name used commonly in Scotland, the latter in the Netherlands. In establishing the church in Amoy, China, the Presbyterian and Reformed missionaries refused to use either term, or to separate their converts, but insisted upon establishing an indigenous church with a tai-hoey ("great meeting of the elders").

Saga and Nagasaki, a two-day's journey south. On May 14, 1866, the two met for the first time:

> His eyes beamed love and pleasure as I met him. He said he had long known me in his mind, had long desired to see and converse with me, and that he was very happy that now in God's providence he was permitted to do so.
>
> At this time there was admitted to our parlour Wakasa, Ayabe, Wakasa's two sons, young men of twenty and twenty-two respectively, and the servant, Motono, who had acted the part of messenger between us for four years.
>
> They showed great familiarity with their Bibles, made several pertinent quotations, and when during the conversation I referred them to sacred passages they readily identified them and always accepted them as conclusive proof. They were prepared to believe all that Jesus said and to do all that he required.
>
> We spent a delightful afternoon in conversing on the saving love and power of Christ, and just as I thought my friends were about to leave me, Wakasa took me by surprise by inquiring if I would object to baptizing him and his brother Ayabe before they left town. I was surprised because so many Japanese had at different times talked to me of the great peril of becoming Christians in the full sense of the word.
>
> The following Lord's Day, the Day of Pentecost, was chosen, the hour selected being seven o'clock p.m. At last when the Sabbath evening came, the two candidates presented themselves, attended into the room by none but Motono....The shutters were closed, the lamps lit, a white cloth spread on the center table, a large cut-glass fruit-dish, for want of anything better, was prepared to serve as a font. Besides Motono, my wife was the only witness present, so that there were but five persons in the room. I began by reading Matthew twenty-eight....I exhorted them not to be discouraged in their peculiarly difficult situation, but rather by a life of faith, of love, and of holiness, to disarm all the criticism of their neighbors and even persecution itself.[1]

Murata, who was fifty-one at the time, informed Lord Nabeshima of his baptism and was allowed to live out his life in Saga without punishment. He died in 1874.

---

[1] Gordon D Laman, "Guido F. Verbeck: Pioneer Missionary to Japan," in *Historical Highlights: Newsletter of the Historical Society of the Reformed Church in America*. vol. I, no. 4, Fall 1980.

years after Abeel's arrival from Borneo) Talmage was explaining how the use of an adapted Roman alphabet could communicate Chinese speech and make it possible for the masses to read.

The Reverends Elihu Doty and John Van Nest Talmage of the Reformed Church, along with the Reverend Carstairs Douglas of the English Presbyterian Mission, were tireless in effectuating this new system with translations, publications, grammars, and lexicons.

The missionaries also were concerned with the elevation of the

In the Pursuit of Oil

Henry Bilkert

Archives of the Reformed Church in America

Although Reformed Church missionaries John Van Ess, Paul Harrison, and Henry Bilkert believed the petroleum industry in Arabia would likely introduce destabilizing factors like materialism and nationalism into the region,[1] they did offer some assistance in the pursuit of oil.

In 1908 Van Ess helped the first British group in its explorations.

An Englishman, named [George] Reynolds, came to my house in Basrah and asked me to hire forty mules for him. He said he was going across the border into Persia to prospect for oil. I got him the mules and the upshot of the expedition was that oil was discovered, and the net result was the Anglo-Iranian Oil Company.[2]

In 1929 Henry Bilkert agreed to accompany Charles Crane in Kuwait. Crane was an American industrialist who, along with Henry King, led the King-Crane Commission that reported the desire of the people of "Greater Syria" for self-rule to President Wilson following World War I.

On Monday, January 21, the two-car cavalcade was ambushed in the desert by a small party of Ikhwan marksmen, and Bilkert was mortally wounded. He received a bullet through the shoulder which passed through to sever his spine, paralyzing him. The cars raced back over the excruciatingly rough desert track to Basrah, but Bilkert died before they arrived.[3]

At the time, the American consul in Bagdad wanted to hold the Iraqi government accountable for the incident, since officials failed to warn Bilkert and Crane of the danger of such a trip. But John Van Ess persuaded him otherwise, believing that such an act would risk the good relations they had built up over time and desiring rather to show true Christian forgiveness.

Lewis Scudder, in *The Arabian Mission's Story*, tells the rest of the story. Some years after the shooting, one of the gunmen came to the mission hospital in Bahrain for treatment. The Bedouin, who had been part of a group who attacked travelers and carried out raids on the Iraq/Kuwait border, admitted the killing to Dr. Paul Harrison. To the man's astonishment, Harrison was able to show the same love and care he had for all his patients.

Postscript: Henry Bilkert had developed the desire to be a foreign missionary in his early years. While he was at New Brunswick seminary about to make formal application for an appointment as a missionary, his father died. Since he was an only son, he questioned his call and asked his mother's guidance. She responded by telling him that from his childhood they "had consecrated him to the Lord's service in whatever way He saw fit to use him, and that she would be happy in his carrying out his missionary purpose as they had looked upon such a decision as an answer to their prayers."[3]

[1] Dorothy F. Van Ess, *Pioneers in the Arab World*, The Historical Series of the Reformed Church in America (Grand Rapids: Eerdmans), 121.
[2] Lewis R. Scudder III, *The Arabian Mission's Story: In Search of Abraham's Other Son*, The Historical Series of the Reformed Church in America (Grand Rapids: Eerdmans, 1998), 72.
[3] *Christian Intelligencer and Mission Field*, February 6, 1929, 82.

status of Chinese women. Contrary to encouraging patriarchy, the missionaries did much to improve the lives of women. Not only did the missionaries give medical attention to women, but they also sought to bring education. "Bible women" were hired to visit in homes when public meetings for women proved impractical. Ultimately, sufficient educational inroads were made so that a few parents allowed their daughters to go to school.

The impact of Christ's teaching was such that shortly after the turn of the century the screens separating men and women in church began to come down. As early as the 1890s, the London Missionary Society was using deaconesses, and in 1916 the South Fukian Synod upheld the right of churches to appoint women as deacons. By 1936, at the district conferences held for consistory members, a third of those attending were women, and they included not

The Mission Poultry Farm

Reformed Church missionaries John and Henriette De Valois arrived in Katpadi, India, in 1920 to establish an agricultural institute to foster rural reconstruction and development. John was a graduate of Iowa State College, with expertise in poultry husbandry and agricultural cooperative societies.

In 1929 the institute enrolled twenty-six boys. After morning prayers, they engaged in practical work on the farm, such as digging a pit silo and preparing synthetic farmyard manure from waste straw. Several of the boys had never been in school before. On the last Sunday, Communion was celebrated.[1]

Archives of the Reformed Church in America

MISSION
POULTRY FARM

Katpadi, South India.
Catalog 1930-'31.

The parents of the boys and several special visitors were present. We were all very happy indeed when 15 of the boys publicly confessed Jesus Christ as their Saviour and joined the Church in full communion. Several of the boys were already members of the Church. Four of the Hindu boys begged us to baptize them, which, however, we thought unwise without their parent's consent.[2]

Perhaps most noteworthy was the institute's effort to improve India's poultry stock through its

Mission Poultry Farm. While local chickens were hardy, they only produced small eggs in limited quantity. So the institute imported high quality White Leghorns and Rhode Island Reds from Iowa State College.

The poultry flock of 400 to 1,000 birds are all pedigreed, trap-nested stock either imported or from newly imported birds. Importations are made yearly to maintain stamina and breed characteristics. Utility is our first consideration but the many cups and medals which our birds have been winning at leading Indian Poultry Shows prove that our birds are up to show standards as well.[3]

The goal was to encourage villagers to keep improved fowls as a cottage industry. The institute would buy the eggs on a cooperative basis every Wednesday and Saturday, carefully candle them, test and grade them, and sell them on standing orders of two dozen or more.

[1] J.J. De Valois, "A Farmer's Short Course in India," Mysore, India: Wesleyan Mission Press, 1929, 3.
[2] Ibid., 13.
[3] "Mission Poultry Farm Catalog 1930-31" (Vellore, India: Victoria Press), 3.

Up, Up, and Away

Through the 1950s, Reformed Church missionaries traveled to and from their overseas assignments by passenger ship. When Henry Bovenkerk, mission secretary for Asia, realized that the ship on which Glenn and Phylllis Bruggers were scheduled to travel home from Japan in 1958 would arrive too late for Glenn to attend an important workshop, he asked them to fly. It had always been assumed that flying cost more, but when total costs were compared, air travel became standard fare for most Reformed Church missionaries.

Resources for Further Study

The Arabian Mission's Story: In Search of Abraham's Other Son, by Lewis R. Scudder III. The Historical Series of the Reformed Church in America. Grand Rapids: Eerdmans, 1998.

The Call of Africa, by Morrell F. Swart. The Historical Series of the Reformed Church in America. Grand Rapids: Eerdmans, 1998.

Doctor Mary in Arabia, by Mary Bruins Allison. University of Texas Press, 1994.

Doctors for the Kingdom, Paul L. Armerding. The Historical Series of the Reformed Church in America. Grand Rapids: Eerdmans, 2003.

From Mission to Church: The Reformed Church in America Mission to India, by Eugene P. Heideman. The Historical Series of the Reformed Church in America. Grand Rapids: Eerdmans, 2001.

Grace in the Gulf, by Jeanette Boersma. The Historical Series of the Reformed Church in America. Grand Rapids: Eerdmans, 1991.

"In Celebration of the 150th Anniversary of the Amoy Mission: Letters from David Abeel," *Historical Highlights*, Issue No. 34, February 1992, http://www.rca.org/images/aboutus/archives/hh34.pdf

"India Mission Records: Jacob Chamberlain Letters," *Historical Highlights*, Issue No. 33, September 1991, http://www.rca.org/images/aboutus/archives/hh33.pdf

Mission to Borneo, by Gerald De Jong. http://www.rca.org/images/aboutus/archives/borneo.pdf

Pioneers in the Arab World, by Dorothy F. Van Ess. The Historical Series of the Reformed Church in America. Grand Rapids: Eerdmans, 1974.

The Reformed Church in China, 1842-1951, by Gerald F. De Jong. The Historical Series of the Reformed Church in America. Grand Rapids: Eerdmans, 1992.

Through the Changing Scenes of Life: The American Mission Hospital Bahrain, 1893-1993, by Angela Clarke. American Mission Hospital Society, Bahrain, 1993. Available from RCA Distribution Center, Grand Rapids, Mich.

only women deacons but also women elders.[6] The South Fukian Synod was fifty-six years in advance of the Reformed Church in America in ordaining women as deacons.

For the story of the war years, readers will have to review the book to which this chapter owes so much, *The Reformed Church in China, 1842-1951*, by Gerald F. De Jong. Suffice it to say that the 150 Reformed Church missionaries who served in Amoy laid a good foundation. The church survived the persecutions of the Chinese governments of the twenties and thirties, the Japanese occupying forces of the thirties and forties, and a half-century of communism. The church of China not only survived; it expanded like seed sown in good soil.

Nor has the involvement of the Reformed Church ceased. The Reverend Dr. Marvin D. Hoff, president of Western Theological Seminary from 1985 to 1994, has from 1969 served as secretary and trustee of the Foundation for Theological Education in Southeast Asia, and from 1994 as its executive director. As such, he has been instrumental in bringing international aid to the seventeen seminaries in a newly opened China. Through the United Bible Society, a Reformed Church mission partner, the Amity Press (formed in 1988) printed more than eighteen million Chinese Bibles in its first decade.

---

[1] John W. Beardslee III, ed., *Vision from the Hill* (Grand Rapids: Eerdmans, 1984), 75-76.
[2] Ibid, 76.
[3] Ibid, 41.
[4] Ibid, 43.
[5] Ibid, 57.
[6] Ibid, 206-207. Cf. Henry Poppen, "Amoy Again Pioneers," *Intelligencer Leader*, Dec. 2, 1936, p. 12.

Chiapas, Mexico

Chiapas, Mexico, was once the center of Mayan culture. It is a place where animistic beliefs continue to grip people strongly. It's a place where, in spite of persecution and poverty, Reformed Church missionaries working with the National Presbyterian Church in Mexico has helped grow a church that now numbers over 180,000 members in fourteen hundred places of worship.

Western Seminary Collection of the Joint Archives of Holland

The story of the Reformed Church in Chiapas begins in 1925, when the Southern Presbyterian Church invited the Women's Board of Domestic Missions to join in evangelizing the Indians. The Reverend Jose Coffin, a Presbyterian missionary, had been working out of Tapachula and needed help. There in the rugged hills of southern Chiapas, Coffin had located over eighty scattered groups of believers who had been evangelized originally by Guatemalan coffee pickers who crossed the border into Mexico each year. In greetings to the Reformed Church, Coffin notes, "We feel that our work has one end only, namely, to bring men and women to a saving knowledge of Christ."[1]

The first Reformed Church missionaries to answer the call were newlyweds John and Mabel Kempers. They arrived by train in 1926.

We are in Chiapas at last....A frantic whistling of our engine, a stop, much moving and flurry tells us we are arriving in Tapachula. And here we see friends! A tall, stately man with a large dark mustache and laughing eyes and all the courtesy in the world, meets us—Senor Coffin! Here is a short, smiling woman who speaks to us in English and jokes with us—Dona Luz, Senora de Coffin. Oh, we have heard and read of them often.[2]

In 1926 it literally took months to visit the various groups of believers. The trips could only be taken in winter and spring due to the heat, and even then torrential rains often made the roads and trails impassable. John Kempers recounts one such trip:

The first incident of the trip took place at the very outset. While saddling the horses in the darkness a large scorpion, which hid in the saddle bags, stung my thumb. Though we have killed dozens of them, this was the first time I have been stung...the pain continued until noon.... Rain had made the roads exceedingly slippery and fording streams was difficult, but we finally reached Nazaret where we had an evening service. After the service, several more families arrived so we found another text and started over again. We slept in the chapel that night.

Next day we crossed the Huixtla River, my horse being almost swept away in the swift current, and went on to Santa Rita, to reach which we had to climb a steep mountain for five hours....We had a religious service at night.[3]

The next Reformed Church missionaries to arrive were Garold and Ruth Van Engen. Others followed, like Paul and Dorothy Meyerink and Sam and Helen Hofman. They came with the same goal: to reach as many people as possible with the gospel and to train indigenous Christian leaders to reach others for Christ.

Western Seminary Collection of the Joint Archives of Holland

[1] *Christian Intelligencer and Mission Field*, September 16, 1925, 584.
[2] Ibid., March 13, 1929, 172.
[3] Ibid., October 15, 1930, 674.

Into Africa

On September 11, 1946, the Board of Foreign Missions of the United Presbyterian Church invited the Reformed Church in America to join in mission work among the Anuak tribes in southern Sudan. Although a merger of the two denominations never took place, the mission partnership in Africa yielded results.

The first Reformed Church missionary appointed to go to Sudan was Wilma Kats, a graduate of Central College who was teaching in Denver, Colorado. Next were Bob and Morrell Swart, followed by Harvey and Lavina Hoekstra.

Harvey Hoekstra's early impressions are recorded in a letter home dated May 9, 1949:

Geleb house and grainstore

> The key to the heart of Africa lies in her villages. It is in the African village with its mud houses and grass roofs with lounging men, playful children and hard-working women that the real victory for Christ will be won.
>
> If I could take you with me to one of our villages, you would find, perhaps ten to twenty of these small huts. The walls are made of mud and sticks and are about as tall as a short man. You cannot see these walls from the outside because long grass from the roof comes down to the ground protecting them from the rains. On one side we noticed a small opening. We enter but see nothing until our eyes become accustomed to the darkness.
>
> Inside the hut we see a small baby lying on an animal skin on the floor. The mother sits nearby. Flies are crawling all over the little baby. If we look more closely, we will likely find the baby's eyes are sore and infected....
>
> From the roof of the hut we notice a wing or two of a bird, possibly the shriveled up head of a chicken, several horns from cattle and some tobacco hanging to dry. Each of theses items has some special relation to the spirits of whom the Anuak lives in constant fear.

Walking through the village, we notice that here and there are mounds of dirt with several tall sticks on the top of which are the horns of some former cow. Tied to the sticks are ears of corn. Buried beneath the mound of dirt are the fetish bones and charms and even, possibly, the body of some relative who has died and is buried there.

> Often, as I preach in the villages, I see on either side of me these pagan shrines and know that only as Jesus comes into their hearts and transforms them will the fear and superstition that haunts our people's hearts be taken away....[1]

Sudan gained its independence in 1956, after spending most of its modern history under the control of either Egypt or Great Britain. Since then, however, civil war has raged almost continuously between the fundamentalist Islamic government in the north and rebel groups in the south (where much of the country's wealth is generated by its oil reserves). The government has been responsible for countless human rights violations, many of which have been directed against Christians. Despite persecution, the church in Sudan continues to grow at an estimated annual rate of 30 percent.[2]

In 2001, Dr. Haruun Ruun, executive secretary of the New Sudan Council of Churches, appealed to the General Synod to advocate for the cause of peace and justice in Sudan. In response, the Reformed Church in America voted to communicate with government officials in the United States and Canada, suggesting policies that would assist the peace process.[3]

---

[1] Harvey T. Hoekstra, *Honey, We're Going to Africa!*, Mukilteo, Washington: WinePress Publishing, 1995, 63.
[2] Reformed Church in America, *Minutes of the General Synod, 2001*, 232.
[3] Ibid., 233.

9

Black and White

First Reformed Church, New Brunswick, New Jersey

In 1855, just six years before the Civil War, the Reverend How, minister of the First Reformed Church in New Brunswick, was still arguing on behalf of slavery as a biblical and permanent institution. When it comes to race relations, the Reformed Church has a history that sometimes represents the gospel and at other times reveals a prejudiced racism. On the gospel side, as early as 1816, the General Synod could declare:

"in the church there is no difference between bond and free, but all are one in Christ." Hence blacks are to enjoy [the] same privileges. . . . Resolved, that hereafter, the blacks within the bounds of our congregations be enumerated as a part of them.[1]

Again, on the gospel side of race relations was the fact that

There have not infrequently been [African-American students] in the New Brunswick Seminary during the last quarter of a century. They are not perhaps always specifically alluded to, as such, in the reports. The pastors of the colored churches in New Brunswick (Methodist and Baptist) have sometimes become special members of the seminary. References are given to five, the earliest one, Mark Jordan, was licensed by the Classis of New

York as early as 1822.[2]

The Reformed Church was also a supporter of the American Colonization Society, which was first organized in 1817 and in 1820 brought to the attention of the synod. Year after year, synod commended the society to its churches for their offerings. The American Colonization Society helped escaped slaves and other freed blacks who so wished to return to Africa as colonizers and as bearers of the gospel. While it has been popular in the late twentieth century to deride the American Colonization Society as a way to get rid of blacks, within its historical context it was seen as an opportunity to enable blacks who wished to do so to return to Africa (specifically Liberia), to ensure their freedom, and to have the opportunity to act as missionaries of the

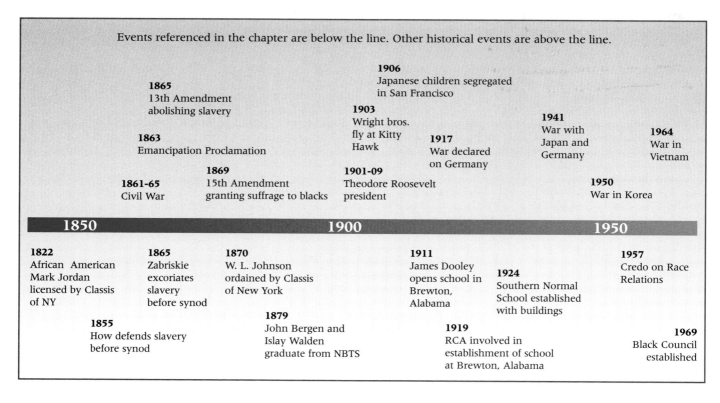

Events referenced in the chapter are below the line. Other historical events are above the line.

1865
13th Amendment abolishing slavery

1863
Emancipation Proclamation

1861-65
Civil War

1869
15th Amendment granting suffrage to blacks

1906
Japanese children segregated in San Francisco

1903
Wright bros. fly at Kitty Hawk

1901-09
Theodore Roosevelt president

1917
War declared on Germany

1941
War with Japan and Germany

1950
War in Korea

1964
War in Vietnam

1850 | **1900** | **1950**

1822
African American Mark Jordan licensed by Classis of NY

1865
Zabriskie excoriates slavery before synod

1855
How defends slavery before synod

1870
W. L. Johnson ordained by Classis of New York

1879
John Bergen and Islay Walden graduate from NBTS

1911
James Dooley opens school in Brewton, Alabama

1919
RCA involved in establishment of school at Brewton, Alabama

1924
Southern Normal School established with buildings

1957
Credo on Race Relations

1969
Black Council established

John Bergen and Islay Walden

In 1879 John Bergen and Islay Walden became the first African-American graduates of New Brunswick Theological Seminary. Bergen was ordained by the Classis of New Brunswick and went on to serve as a missionary and peddler of religious books in Columbus, Georgia.

Born a slave in North Carolina, Walden was sold from the auction block several times and moved from plantation to plantation as a youth. When slavery was abolished following the Civil War, he set off on foot heading north to obtain an education and to fulfill his mother's wish that he become a minister.

Along the way Walden supported himself in creative ways. On the streets of Washington he sold copies of original poems he composed, and

John Bergen

in towns in Pennsylvania and New Jersey he gave lectures on anatomy, having memorized several chapters from a textbook.

When his travels took him to New Brunswick, Walden met a Rutgers College professor who helped him obtain financial aid for his education from the Second Reformed Church there. Walden left immediately for Washington to enroll in Howard University. He came back to New Brunswick for his theological training.

Upon ordination, Walden returned home to North Carolina and worked as an evangelist for the Presbyterian Church at Lassater Mills until his death in 1884.

Archives of the Reformed Church in America

gospel to Africa. Synodical resolutions to support the society and its work continued through 1868.

Based on the records of the General Synod, however, the Reformed Church failed to stand in the vanguard of the movement for the emancipation of the slaves. At the beginning of the Civil War, C. Van Santvoord, chairman of the Committee on National Affairs, while sponsoring a resolution in support of the government and regretting the conflict, said nothing about the issue of slavery. In the following year, the report under J. Romeyn Berry alluded to slavery in the prayer that God "will in infinite wisdom guide us in a way by which in the best manner every yoke may in his own time be broken and the oppressed go free."[3] In the following year, the resolutions

presented by Charles Wiley pledged full support to the president and the nation, but regarding slavery they only sought

a peace founded on the full ascendancy of law and rightful authority, and guaranteed in its permanency by the removal or the sufficient coercion and restraint of whatever causes tend necessarily to imperil the existence of the nation.[4]

Finally, in 1864, under the chairmanship of R. D. Van Kleek, slavery was openly addressed:

In time past, the General Synod has not deemed it necessary to give forth a judgment in regard to the system of American slavery, inasmuch as it existed in the regions beyond the bounds of our Church; if, as in the overruling Providence of that

God, who knows how to make the wrath of man to praise Him, there is a prospect opened for the ultimate and entire removal of that system which embodies so much of moral and social evil.[5]

The synod was even more outspoken in 1865 when, under the chairmanship of F. N. Zabriskie, it spoke of "the destruction of the system of oppression, and the prospects of returning harmony and prosperity." At the same time, the synod under Zabriskie's leadership resolved to

> pledge ourselves to use our utmost exertions for the harmonizing and evangelizing of the population, the amelioration of the condition of the freed men, and the restoring of the waste places of Zion by our domestic missionary operations.[6]

The Reformed Church, regrettably, did not live up to its own resolutions. In the post-war years, the Presbyterian Church in the United States (Southern Presbyterian Church) repeatedly approached the Reformed Church in America for assistance in the amelioration of the freedmen. Appeals came before the Reformed Church from 1877 through 1896, but while these were recommended to boards and committees to study, the ultimate result was that the Reformed Church declined "on account of pressure of work in other fields."[7]

It was not until 1902 that the Reformed Church became involved officially with a ministry to African-Americans. It took place through the persistent efforts, begun in 1896, by a black pastor, the Reverend Dr. W. L. Johnson. Johnson was born in New York City in 1844, graduated from Lincoln University in 1869, and was ordained by the Classis of the Dutch Reformed Church in New York in 1870. During that intervening year, or perhaps before, Johnson must have studied at New Brunswick, for while there is no record of him in the list of graduates, the Board of Domestic Missions, in its report to the General Synod of 1898, refers specifically to the Reverend Dr. W. L. Johnson as a graduate of New Brunswick Theological Seminary and it does so again in its report to the General Synod of 1902.

Johnson began his career as an evangelist in North Carolina from 1869-74, served briefly as a pastor of Somerville, New Jersey, in 1874-75, and moved to Orangeburg, South Carolina, where he served from 1876 until his death in 1913. Dr. Johnson's pleas for Reformed Church aid began in 1896. Despite a lack of response, he continued to solicit the synod of 1897 for assistance, at which time synod appointed a committee to study the matter. The committee recommended that funds be solicited from the churches to assist Johnson through the Executive Committee of Colored Evangelization of the Southern Presbyterian Church.

The committee's resolution was put before the Board of Domestic Missions, which rejected the idea insofar as it could not undertake a mission through another church's agency. Even this, however, did not put an end to Johnson's efforts. In 1899 he sent a progress report to the synod, stating that he had established two new mission churches and eighty-five Sunday schools, which ministered to three thousand black children—all without the denominational connection that he sought.

Johnson also applied to the Classis of New York, asking it to receive his churches (New Hope Reformed Mission Church and Criston Reformed Mission Church) under its care. The Board of Domestic Mission and the General Synod both insisted that the Classis of New York had the prerogative under Reformed Church polity to take Johnson's churches under its care, but the classis, of which Johnson was a member, did not accept his churches. However, the importunate Johnson finally obtained his goal when the Classis of Philadelphia accepted his transfer from the Classis of New York and also accepted Grace Church in

James Dooley

James Dooley dreamed of starting a school for black children where industrial training and academic work would go side by side—all in a Christian environment. In 1911 he saw his opportunity when he happened upon an abandoned reformatory in Brewton, Alabama. The photograph below shows Dooley with two students on the school's farm soon after the school opened.

The early years were tough. There was no problem finding willing students. The challenge was funding, and for that Dooley would venture north accompanied by a few students.

It was on one of those visits that he first came into contact with the Reformed Church. He afterward recalled that the first time he entered a church of our denomination was in 1914, when he visited Detroit. There the First Church gave him and his helpers an opportunity to speak and to sing their Negro songs. Some other western churches visited in those early days were in the Classes of Germania and Pleasant Prairie; and in later years, when the school was firmly on its feet, those churches raised funds and erected a dormitory building, which was named "German Hall."

It was in response to the desire of those Western churches that the Board of Domestic Missions, in 1919, took the responsibility for the Negro School at Brewton. Mr. Dooley continued as the honored Principal, and the growth and development of the institution have been steady. No phase of our Domestic Mission work makes a stronger appeal to our Churches.[1]

James Dooley with some of his boys on the farm of the school he started in Brewton, Alabama.

Archives of the Reformed Church in America

---
[1] "James Dooley," *Christian Intelligencer*, June 11, 1930.

Typing class at Southern Normal School, 1965.

church was suitable for blacks and as to whether or not the Southern Presbyterian Church might not like to take over the work. Johnson died January 27, 1913. The *Christian Intelligencer* (predecessor to the *Church Herald*) paid "tribute to William Johnson as a representative of the American Sunday School Union. He had a plan for every Sunday School to become a church." The *Intelligencer* acknowledged candidly that "although Johnson was disappointed regarding his expectation from the Dutch Reformed Church for black people, yet he never gave up hope in the ultimate outcome."[9] The black churches of South Carolina continued to be members of the Philadelphia Classis until 1926, when they were transferred to the North and South Carolina Presbytery of the Presbyterian Church in the United States.

That did not, however, mean the end of Reformed Church association with African-Americans. In 1919 a school for black children had been founded in Brewton, Alabama, by James A. Dooley, a graduate of Tuskegee Institute. In the same year, the Reformed Church assumed responsibility for the institution, and by 1924 building had begun on five classrooms and an auditorium seating three hundred, with contributions by the church and funds from the legacy of Julia Van Vorst. That construction, begun in 1924, was to become the Southern Normal School of Brewton, Alabama. Students and professors at Western Theological Seminary

Orangeburg, along with his several Sunday schools. Johnson, whose testimonials were of the highest character and his reputation at Orangeburg unblemished, had at last obtained for his churches a denominational connection with the Reformed Church.

Johnson was a man with a vision. In 1904 he solicited help from the Classis of Philadelphia to found a "classical and industrial academy for black people at Orangeburg."[8] Classis demurred. One wonders at the forces involved in the second thoughts that immediately began to be expressed in the synod about ministry to African-Americans. Assertions were made that the Baptists and Methodists were already there. Questions were raised as to whether or not the polity of our contributed scholarships for students at Brewton.

The Reverend Andrew Branch, a graduate of Alabama State Teachers College, taught English and music at Southern Normal School. In 1939 he entered New Brunswick Theological Seminary, graduating in 1943 and becoming pastor/director of the school at Brewton. By 1945 Branch could report that in the twenty-six-year history of the school, "eight thousand Negro boys and girls have been brought in direct contact with the Christian gospel and have been given concrete experiences in Christian living."[10] Among the many notable graduates of Southern Normal School are the Reverend Samuel Williams, who graduated from Central College and Western Theological Seminary and served his entire ministry in the Reformed Church in America, and Dr. Manford Byrd, another honored graduate, who became superintendent of the public schools of the city of Chicago.

A side benefit of Brewton, which is easily overlooked in the twenty-first century, is that during the 1940s and '50s, Branch, often accompanied by his choir, was the first personal contact many midwestern Reformed Church folk had ever had with blacks. Brewton educated whites in the North concerning the common humanity they shared with African-Americans.

The civil rights movement of the 1960s and '70s brought new

Graduation at Southern Normal School, 1965.

Archives of the Reformed Church in America

educational opportunities for blacks and radical changes in the purpose of Brewton. As opportunities in public education became more equal in the nation, Brewton's educational function grew less necessary. In 1996 the Reformed Church responded to a local request and turned over the school to a board that was both local and African-American.

The civil rights movement of the '60s and '70s accelerated a change in race relations within the Reformed Church. This era saw the development of an integrated ministry, something envisioned by the General Synod as early as 1816. The church was challenged not to abandon its churches as neighborhoods changed, and, in New Lots in Brooklyn, Mott Haven in the South Bronx, and Elmendorf and DeWitt in Manhattan, integration began to take place.

In 1958 the synod asked the

Credo on Race Relations

The Credo on Race Relations, adopted by the General Synod in 1957 and distributed widely the following year, called upon the church to support the U.S. Supreme Court decision on the ordered, gradual desegregation of the public schools, to respect interracial marriages, and to actively support groups and agencies that are striving to achieve social justice. The credo began by stating these beliefs:

I.   We believe that the problem of race is a problem of human relations. We believe that the Scriptures of the Old and New Testaments provide the final authority for all matters of human relations. We believe that all problems of human existence are resolved in the love of God....

II. We believe that in the light of the Biblical revelation, we have fallen short in the demonstration of that love. We hereby make an act of confession and repentance for:

1—our insensitivity to the needs of others.
2—our acquiescence through silence in a sub-christian social pattern which denies the full rights of human dignity to some minority groups within our national borders.
3—our failure to realize the mission of the Church in our own communities, while advancing the Church's mission at a distance.
4—our persistence in pursuing the historical pattern of ethnic exclusivism in the face of the mounting pressures of social heterogeneity.
5—our emotional prejudices which often sap our spiritual vitality and snap our moral nerve.
For these and other acts and attitudes, Gracious Lord, forgive us.

III. We believe that sincere repentance manifests itself in acts of obedient love. We, therefore, believe that our sincerity will be demonstrated through concrete local acts, such as:

1—identification with minority groups victimized through unjust discrimination.
2—conscientious efforts to open the doors of all churches to all people.
3—the support of those laws and agencies designed to uphold and guarantee the rights and health of all.
4—the promotion of inter-group discussions, where in atmospheres of understanding and good-will, the forces for reconciliation may operate creatively.
5—the education of our youth in the privileges and responsibilities of life in a free, mixed society.[1]

---

[1] Reformed Church in America, *Minutes of the General Synod , 1957*, 181.

Manford Byrd, Jr.

A graduate of Southern Normal School, Central College, B.A., Atlanta University, M.A., Northwestern University, Evanston, Ph.D., Professor of Graduate Studies, Illinois State University, General Superintendent of Schools, Chicago Public Schools. A member of seventy-six service groups, including seven in the United Church of Christ, as well as the Board of Trustees of Southern Normal School and Central College, and the recipient of one hundred eighteen awards, including honorary doctorates from Central College, Hope College, and the National College of Education. The father of three and husband of Cheribelle Warfield for forty-eight years.

Black Power: The phrase was coined by Stokley Carmichael. Radicalized by the brutal treatment he received as a follower of the Reverend Dr. Martin Luther King's nonviolent efforts at racial integration, Carmichael urged Black Power. In his 1967 book, he defined Black Power as "a call for black people in this country to unite, to recognize their history, to build a sense of community. It is a call for black people to define their own goals, to lead their own organizations." However, in his speeches Carmichael became increasingly radical, perhaps contributing to the racial riots of the late 1960s. He retired to Africa in 1969. Black Power became a rallying slogan for a whole political direction. While an important contribution to a sense of black empowerment, it was the nonviolent methods of King that proved the most effective and lasting.

entire denomination to subscribe to a "Credo on Race Relations" (see box), which stressed racial inclusiveness and open housing. In 1964 the Christian Action Commission recommended racial inclusiveness as one of the criteria for the use of denominational funds for church extension.

Impatient with the slowness of change and emboldened by the success of the Reverend Dr. Martin Luther King Jr., a more radical vision, Black Power, came to the fore in American society. In 1969 Black Power met the General Synod in the person of Charles Foreman and his "Black Manifesto." Out of that educative confrontation, with its demands for substantial reparations, came the development of the Black

Council—an agency funded by General Synod, with an initial offer of $100,000 per year to be distributed by the Black Council as it saw fit.

Wise leadership within the council rejected the $100,000, refusing to become a funding group, and instead opted for full participation in the decision-making life of the church, with representatives on every body from the General Synod Executive Committee on down. The Black Council also called together the Black Caucus, to which blacks from throughout the church were invited to share their identity, concerns, and programs.

Among the most influential leaders of the Black Council (now the African-American Council) was

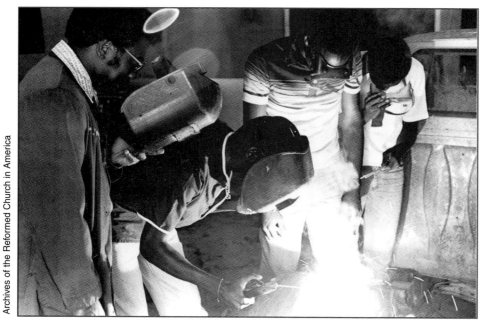

Instruction in welding, Southern Normal School.

opportunity to provide theological training to gifted minority pastors. Hageman began to meet this need through the establishment of off-campus, metropolitan-based training. That Hageman had assessed the need correctly became manifest in the growing number of pastors who became seminarians. Through the continued efforts of the oldest theological seminary in America, under the leadership of President Norman J. Kansfield, the need for advanced biblical and theological training of minority ministers throughout the area of metropolitan New York continues to be met. At the turn of the century enrollment stood at 240 students.

It is one of the strange ironies of the early twenty-first century that as African-American and other minorities are flocking to New Brunswick Theological Seminary to become pastors fully equipped with a seminary education, the wealthiest sections of the church, California and western Michigan, are ordaining pastoral ministers who lack a full seminary education.

the Reverend William Howard, who for a time served concurrently as president of the National Council of Churches, and in that capacity was sent to Iran in 1980 to help negotiate the release of American hostages.

In the relations between black and white, a contribution with little fanfare, but with perhaps the greatest effect, was initiated by the Reverend Dr. Howard G. Hageman as president of New Brunswick Theological Seminary. It was Hageman who recognized the

Resources for Further Study

Black People and The Reformed Church in America, by Noel Leo Erskine. New York: Reformed Church Press, 1978.

Black Manifesto,
http://www.rca.org/images/aboutus/archives/blackmanifesto.pdf

In Remembrance and Hope: The Ministry and Vision of Howard G. Hageman, by Gregg A. Mast. The Historical Series of the Reformed Church in America. Grand Rapids: Eerdmans, 1998.

Report on Response to the Black Manifesto,
http://www.rca.org/images/aboutus/archives/manifestoresponse.pdf

[1] Edwin Tanger Corwin, *A Digest of Synodical Legislation of the Reformed Church of America,* 150-51.
[2] Ibid., 152.
[3] Ibid., 404.
[4] Ibid., 404.
[5] Ibid., 407.
[6] Ibid., 407.
[7] Ibid., 151.
[8] Noel Leo Erskine, *Black People in the Reformed Church in America* (New York: Reformed Church Press, 1978), 70.
[9] February 19, 1913, quoted by Erskine, 71.
[10] Erskine, 75.

10
How We've Worshiped

Celebrating the Lord's Supper in the Oude Kerk, Amsterdam

Copper plate etching, C. Philips Jacobsz, 1784

The earliest Dutch settlers in North America brought with them the liturgy approved by the Synod of Dort in 1618. This liturgy bore little resemblance to that of John Calvin. It consisted of just three items for the Lord's Day: two prayers—one before the sermon and one after—and a benediction. The reason for the very sparse nature of this liturgy was undoubtedly the desire to accommodate both those members of the Dutch church with strong Mennonite sympathies and those sympathetic to the Calvinian liturgy, which, with its prayer of confession and absolution, would

First Reformed Dutch Church, Church of the Green (1728), Hackensack, Bergen County, New Jersey

have horrified those of the Mennonite persuasion. A minimum of explicit requirements gave scope for both groups to worship as they wished.

The Dort-approved liturgy also included an order for the Lord's Supper which could still be found in the 1906 unabridged *Liturgy and Psalms of the Reformed Church in America*. In addition, there was an order for baptism. The Synod of 1574 also made use of a fixed votum, a mandatory beginning to the service. Later editions of the liturgy omit mention of the votum. Perhaps that was because its use had become universal. It was essentially this liturgy, approved by the Synod of Dort, that was brought to America by Dominie Michaelius in 1628. The same liturgy was translated by the Dutch synod for a small classis of seven English-speaking congregations in the Netherlands, and that translation was slightly altered in 1793 by John

Events referenced in the chapter are below the line. Other historical events are above the line.

Above the line:

1685-1750 J. S. Bach

1756-91 W. A. Mozart

1820-1915 Fanny Crosby

1921-1992 Howard G. Hageman

1674-1748 Isaac Watts

1764 First English service in New York Dutch church

1835-1922 Dennis Workman

1936- Brian Wren

1618 Dort decides Law read/sung in a.m., Creed said in p.m.

1707-88 Charles Wesley

1872-1958 R. Vaughan Williams

1962-65 Vatican II

Timeline: 1550 | 1600 | 1650 | 1700 | 1750 | 1800 | 1850 | 1900 | 1950 | 2000

Below the line:

1542 Publication in Geneva of Calvin's liturgy

1618 Liturgy of Dort

1628 Michaelius brings Liturgy of Dort to New Netherland

1793 Livingston brings the Liturgy of Dort in English

1857 Classes fail to approve changes

1878 Optional forms approved, but not those for sacraments

1906 Simplification of sacramental forms approved

1968 Publication of Liturgy & Psalms

1987 Proclamation & sacrament printed together

1958 Committee produces biblical/Calvinian liturgy

Henry Livingston for the newly formed and independent Reformed Dutch Church in America.

Many changes and two centuries intervened between the establishment of this simple liturgy and its acceptance in English by the Reformed Dutch Church. While in the early Dutch usage of that liturgy only psalms would have been sung, some two hundred years later Livingston was commissioned to compile a psalm book in which he included many popular hymns.

In the late sixteenth century, both of the extended prayers of this liturgy were to be read in full each Lord's Day, even as forms for the sacraments were to be used in full. However, in his preface to the English translation, Livingston made it clear that those two long prayers for each Lord's Day were to be understood as models to be used only until ministers developed sufficient skill to compose their own.

Forms for the sacraments fared rather better. Their long descriptions concerning the meaning of the sacraments were judged to be necessary theological bulwarks against false, or at least inadequate, teaching concerning the sacraments. Therefore they were to be used in full, even as they are today (*Book of Church Order*, Chapter 1, Part I, Article 2, Responsibilities of the Consistory, Section 7b, "'The Office for the Administration of Baptism' shall be read" and Section 7c, "'The Office for the Administration of the Lord's Supper' shall be read").

Though we might think that the repetition of the same prayers each Sunday would be cause enough to abandon the practice, Dominie Theodorus Jacobus Frelinghuysen scandalized his clerical contemporaries when he introduced free prayer to North America in 1720. Pietists, Puritans, and Presbyterians, all of whom despised printed prayers, helped bring about the demise of fixed liturgical prayers by the time Livingston introduced his English version of the Dort liturgy in 1793.

In a little more than a half-century, reaction was beginning to set in. When George Washington Bethune left the Presbyterian Church to become a minister in the Reformed Dutch Church, one of his reasons was liturgical:

The Reformed Dutch Church has a liturgy adapted to all offices and occasions of worship. It is perhaps to be regretted that its disuse has become so common among us, perhaps from the weak desire to conform to the habits of other denominations [Congregationalists and Presbyterians]. Certainly there are occasions when the forms of prayer are at least as edifying as many extemporaneous effusions we hear from the desk [pulpit], and it is evident that the wise fathers of the church did not intend that they [liturgical prayers]

Mennonite: A Christian denomination tracing its roots back to the Dutch Anabaptist Menno Simons (1496-1561). Many Mennonites came to Pennsylvania in the early eighteenth century.

Congregationalist: Christians who believe that each congregation is a self-governing unit. American Congregationalists had their origins with the Puritans. Many Congregationalists joined the German Reformed Church in 1957 to form the United Church of Christ (UCC).

Episcopal/Anglican: Episcopal churches of English ancestry are those governed by bishops who are in apostolic succession. The Episcopal Church in the United States is part of the worldwide Anglican family of churches, all of which trace their roots back to England.

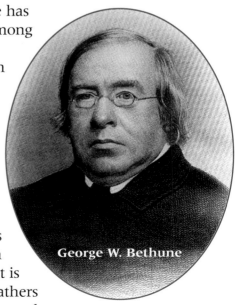

George W. Bethune

Archives of the Reformed Church in America

The tables for Communion in the Old Mud Meeting house, built by the Dutch Reformed in 1800.

The impact of this proposed volume is still evident in the liturgical practice of the Reformed Church today. For example, the invocation (the supplication for God's presence) was far more theologically appropriate to Puritanism or Pietism than it was to the sturdy Reformed confidence that God was present for all of life as expressed in the votum. Also contained in that proposed liturgy was the practice of morning prayers with an Old Testament and New Testament lesson and the insertion of a prayer and a possible hymn between the reading of Scripture and the preaching of the sermon. This form showed the Episcopal

should remain a dead letter in our books.[1]

However, it was not until 1853 that a General Synod committee was appointed specifically to deal with matters of liturgical revision. Even then, it was 1857 before the forms for baptism and the Lord's Supper with their proposed alterations were sent to the classes for approval. (Liturgical forms are part of the constitution of the Reformed Church in America, and its church government requires the approval of two-thirds of the classes to change the constitution.) The classes failed to approve the changes.

Though by 1858 the proposal was declared legally dead, its influence lived on in a ninety-six-page liturgical book (the first liturgical volume produced by the Reformed Dutch Church) that had been circulated within the church as part of the committee's proposal. Up to this time the limited historical forms had been printed only as an appendix to the official hymnal.

St. Nicholas Collegiate Church, Org. 1872, Fifth Avenue at 48th Street, New York.

influence, for when the Reformed read two lessons, it was generally from the Epistles and the Gospels.

The fact that this provisional liturgy of 1857 contained an Order for Public Worship was also a first. The brevity of the prayer following the sermon was also unusual within Reformed practice. That this liturgy should be influenced so heavily by Episcopal usage may perhaps be understood by the constant leakage in the eighteenth and nineteenth century from the Reformed to the Episcopal Church.

Within a decade of the defeat of the revision of the liturgy in 1858, yet another committee was appointed, led by Dr. Mancius Smedes Hutton. He had an amazing grasp of the historical origins of Reformed liturgy for that period and sought to move the church back in the direction of Calvin. To

Calvin's Liturgy

In the sixteenth century, as Geneva underwent reform under Zwingli, the people used his simple liturgy, which eliminated music from worship, focused on a service of the Word, and celebrated the Lord's Supper only four times a year. In 1542 Calvin published a liturgy based on the practices of the early church. But when he tried to introduce the confession of sins and assurance of pardon into the service, people showed their displeasure at this "innovation" by shuffling and muttering, and by the third Sunday they began to leave. Calvin was forced to back down and drop the offending items from the service. At the same time the city council refused to approve a weekly Lord's Supper—another element of Calvin's biblical liturgy.

Donald J. Bruggink

The pulpit in St. Pierre, built for Calvin to help entice him to return to Geneva

Eight years after John Calvin published this edition of his liturgy, London found itself host to four thousand Dutch who had fled Spanish persecution in the Netherlands. Some of these refugees spoke French and some spoke Dutch. Vallerand Pullain, Calvin's successor at Strasbourg, became pastor of the French speakers and used Calvin's liturgy. A Polish nobleman of Reformed persuasion, John a' Lasco, a follower of Zwingli, became pastor of those who spoke Dutch. The Dutch did not stay long in London.

With the death of the Reform-minded Edward VI and the ascension to the throne of Roman Catholic Mary, the Dutch fled to the German cities of Frankfurt and Frankenthal. The Zwinglian liturgy of a' Lasco was published in both cities, and by 1563 it was used in part in Heidelberg by the authors of the catechism, church order, and the liturgy.

Three years later this Heidelberg liturgy (which was influenced more by Zwingli than by Calvin or Luther) was translated by Petrus Dathenus into Dutch and ultimately adopted by the first Dutch synod at Emden. This same service, with minor alterations, was accepted by the great synod of Dort in 1618 as the liturgy of the Reformed Church of the Netherlands. It was this liturgy that was brought to the New World by the earliest Dutch settlers.

Not until 1950 was the fullness of Calvin's liturgy (which includes confession and the assurance of pardon as described in Calvin's *Institutes of the Christian Religion*) brought to the attention of the Reformed Church in America in 1968 in *Liturgy and Psalms*. But only in 1985 was Calvin's liturgy published as a complete Lord's Day liturgy in *Rejoice in the Lord* and, in 1987, in *Worship the Lord*.

return to the tradition of Calvin's Genevan liturgy would provide for a larger degree of congregational participation, as well as restoring the Reformed Church to its traditional standing as a liturgical church. When the proposed liturgy was presented to the synod, it was a 128-page volume with hard covers and gold-edged pages! Ultimately, all of the optional forms contained in the liturgy (ordination, funerals, and so on) were approved, whereas the changes in the forms for baptism and the Lord's Supper were rejected (1878).

It might be noted that when this liturgy was published on no authority except that of the Board of Publication, a psalter, arranged for responsive reading, was included. This compromise with the Anglican chant of the psalms, which was favored by some and rejected by others, was a variant of the monastic antiphonal chanting of the psalms but was completely new in a Reformed context, where psalms by the congregation had always been sung.

The rejection of the alterations to the two principal liturgical forms left the denomination in a continued state of dissatisfaction, and the 1902 synod mandated a new committee to simplify and abbreviate those two sacramental forms. By 1904 the classes had voted and rejected the revisions, with the result that the synod of that year appointed a new committee to deal with the

The Liturgy of the Church

One who worships with a pure heart worships best, whatever the liturgy. But, over the centuries, the church has found certain structures to be most satisfying. Thus the liturgy of the Reformed Church in America looks much like that of Calvin, which looked much like that of the ancient church.[1] This liturgy, common to much of Christ's church, is meaningful because it includes the elements of biblical worship in a coherent, emotionally satisfying progression.

The Approach to God

Votum: An ancient word meaning desire—our desire is to live as the psalmist declared: "Our help is in the name of the Lord who made heaven and earth."

Sentences: Sentences from Scripture spoken by the congregation as the tone is set for worship.

Salutation: The minister greets the congregation in the name of Christ, with the ultimate promises of the gospel: grace, mercy, and peace.

Hymn of Praise: In response to these promises, the congregation raises its voice in a hymn of praise.

Confession of Sin: Having praised a worthy God, we now admit who we are and confess our sin before almighty God.

Declaration of Pardon: The minister, with the promises of Scripture, declares the forgiveness of Christ for those who confess and repent.

The Law: A life of gratitude for forgiveness is a life of obedience. The law is read as a guide to Christian living.

Hymn: We sing a hymn, psalm, or anthem in praise to God for pardon and leading.

The Word in Proclamation and Sacrament

Lessons: Scripture is read from the Old Testament, Epistles, and Gospels.

Members of the 1950 committee to revise the liturgy (l. to r.): Howard G. Hageman, M. Stephen James, Gerrit T. Vander Lugt, and Richard C. Oudersluys

problem. In 1906 the revisions of that committee were accepted with twenty-four of the thirty-five classes voting to approve. This liturgy remained the liturgy of the Reformed Church until 1968.

In the half-century following the 1906 decision to adopt the new liturgy, committees for its revision came and went. In 1950, General Synod appointed a committee of four to begin anew the task of liturgical revision. The composition of the committee was stellar: M.

Sermon: The sermon is a proclamation of God's Word found in Scripture for living the Christian life in the present.

Confession of Faith: Having heard God's Word, the congregation confesses its faith in the words of Christianity's most widely recognized statement of faith, the Nicene Creed, or in the baptismal creed, the Apostle's Creed.

The Peace: Having confessed their faith, members of the congregation now express their peace with one another in the gesture of a handclasp or kiss.

Offering: In the early church, the offering consisted of the bread, wine, and other food used to celebrate the Lord's Supper. After worship, the food was taken to the sick and poor. In many churches today, the bread and wine for the Eucharist are brought forward along with our contributions of money.

The Meaning of the Sacrament: The sacrament of the Lord's Supper is celebrated in remembrance of our Lord's passion and death, in communion with the risen Christ, and in the hope of Christ's return.

The Communion Prayer: We give thanks (*eucharistoumen*) for God's creation, and for our redemption in Christ and the presence of the Holy Spirit, so that the bread and wine may be for us the communion of the body and blood of Christ.

The Response to God

Thanksgiving after Communion: Thanksgiving after Communion usually begins with Psalm 103, followed by intercessory prayer.

Intercession: we pray for others as an expression of the communion of the saints.

Hymn: We sing a hymn of thanksgiving for Holy Communion and all that it promises.

Benediction: Benediction literally means a "good word"—the grace of our Lord Jesus Christ, the love of God, and the communion of the Holy Spirit—given to us as we go forth to live as Christians.

---

[1] A complete description of the meaning of the liturgy can be found in *Understanding Worship in the RCA: The Lord's Day Service with the Directory for Worship* (New York: Reformed Church Press, 1988).

Stephen James, president of New Brunswick Seminary; Richard C. Oudersluys, professor of New Testament at Western Theological Seminary; Gerrit T. Vander Lugt, president of Central College; and Howard G. Hageman, pastor of North Church in Newark, New Jersey. After their first year of meeting, the committee asked permission of the synod "to provide within the liturgy a more adequate expression of the living tradition and teaching of the Reformed faith as a guide to our corporate and private worship."[2]

It was 1958 before the committee provided the denomination with a provisional liturgy that then took another eight years of educative effort before it was finally approved by the classes and published as the *Liturgy and Psalms* in 1968. It was with this liturgy that the Reformed Church found itself at the forefront of liturgical renewal by recapturing not only its Reformation roots but also its continuity with the apostolic church. In its order of Lord's Day worship it now contained all of the elements of worship that one finds scattered in the New Testament: salutation, praise, confession, forgiveness, the Law, Scripture, sermon, creed, offering, Lord's Supper, prayers of thanksgiving and intercession, and benediction.

The difficulty in getting the necessary votes for this liturgy in 1966 were such that the compilers did not make the move of putting the order for the Lord's Supper as a part of Lord's Day worship, despite the fact that the rubrics clearly indicated its necessity for a full diet of worship for the Lord's Day. It was not until the publication in 1987 of the Reformed Church hymnal, *Rejoice in the Lord*, that, for the first time since Calvin's *Form of Prayers after the Custom of the Early Church*, the Lord's Day order of worship was printed in its entirety. *Worship the Lord* (containing the liturgies of the Reformed Church), published two years later, repeated this full diet of Word and sacrament for the Lord's Day. While the majority of the churches in the Reformed Church in America still celebrate the Lord's Supper only four times a year, a very substantial number celebrate monthly, with a few having a weekly service. However, at long last, we now have before us the full Lord's Day worship that Calvin so long ago advocated in his *Institutes of the Christian Religion* of 1536 on the basis of the biblical worship of the early church.

Resources for Further Study

In Remembrance and Hope: The Ministry and Vision of Howard G. Hageman, by Gregg A. Mast. The Historical Series of the Reformed Church in America. Grand Rapids: Eerdmans, 1998.

Liturgy and Confessions, Reformed Church in America. New York: Reformed Church Press, 1990.

Understanding Worship in the RCA: The Lord's Day Service with the Directory of Worship, illustrated by James R. Esther. New York: Reformed Church Press, 1988.

[1] Howard G. Hageman, "A History of the Liturgy of the RCA, Three Lectures," in Gregg A. Mast, *In Remembrance and Hope*, The Historical Series of the Reformed Church in America (Grand Rapids: Eerdmans, 1998), 122. The major content of this essay is a synopsis of Hageman's lectures, to which the reader is referred for a more adequate treatment.
[2] Ibid., 168-69.

11

An Irascible Spirit

The National Synod of Dordrecht, 1618-19. Its decisions constituted theological orthodoxy and right church order in contrast to the Enlightenment and the church order of William I.

In the early nineteenth century, political pressures and tensions from within the church bred a spirit of irascibility in the Reformed Church of the Netherlands. These tensions eventually developed into a schism that profoundly influenced the size and character of the Reformed Church in America.[1]

Before Napoleon made the Netherlands a dependency and then a subject nation, the ideas of republican government imported from France and the tension between the States General of the Netherlands and the royal House of Orange resulted in a nation in conflict. Then came Napoleon's disruption of Dutch maritime trade, which cut off the country from its colonies and, in 1809, resulted in half the population of Amsterdam needing some sort of public relief. This was followed both by heavy taxation to support French armies and by conscription to man those armies, especially for the disastrous invasion of Russia. These conditions added to the human loss, poverty, anger, and conflict within the Netherlands.

After the defeat of Napoleon, the Congress of Vienna, acceding to Britain's desire for a strong sentinel on the French border, ceded Belgium to the Netherlands in 1815 under King William I. Unlike his predecessors, King William I intended to rule as an absolute monarch, and by 1816 he had completely reorganized the Reformed Church of the Netherlands.

This reorganization of the church led to further irascibility within the church. Since the church had become essentially a department of state, the king was able to effect virtually whatever measures he pleased. Initially, he had gained the support of the clergy

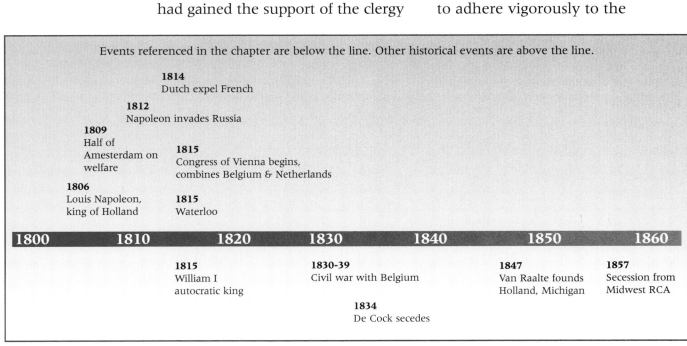

William I, King of the Netherlands

by paying back salaries that had not been paid during the Napoleonic occupancy. But when William replaced the church's venerable psalter with a new hymnal, that support gave way to dissatisfaction. The usual dissatisfaction arising from the adoption of a new hymnal was compounded by the fact that the more conservative element within the church felt it appropriate to sing only the psalms, while the more progressive party wished to sing hymns as well. Irascibility and distrust arose between these two groups.

Further tensions were caused by the government's policy of tolerance. This was, after all, the Age of Reason, and it was reasonable to be tolerant. As this worked itself out in government policy, however, it meant that teachers even in private church schools had to be tolerant; if they weren't, government officials could block their appointment. To those who wished the Reformed Church to adhere vigorously to the

Events referenced in the chapter are below the line. Other historical events are above the line.

1814
Dutch expel French

1812
Napoleon invades Russia

1809
Half of Amesterdam on welfare

1815
Congress of Vienna begins, combines Belgium & Netherlands

1806
Louis Napoleon, king of Holland

1815
Waterloo

| 1800 | 1810 | 1820 | 1830 | 1840 | 1850 | 1860 |

1815
William I autocratic king

1830-39
Civil war with Belgium

1847
Van Raalte founds Holland, Michigan

1857
Secession from Midwest RCA

1834
De Cock secedes

Trouble in Paradise

The Reformed Church of the Netherlands had its own troubles long before King William I began his interference. The Synod of Dordt (1618-19) had witnessed a division between strict Calvinists and moderate Arminian Calvinists. Even within the strict Calvinist party, divisions subsequently grew between Voetians and Coccejians—fundamentally on methods of biblical exegesis, but finding popular expression in Sabbath observance and even in haircuts and dress. Over the years these divisions widened. On the left were ministers like Balthasar Bekker (1634-98), who wished to add reason and scientific discovery to the Reformed worldview. On the right were ministers who, like Jean De Labadie (1610-74), felt competent to distinguish between those of the congregation who were saved and those who were unsaved and sought to drive out the latter.

In the midst of all this, a small groups movement developed. These groups, known as conventicles, had as their basic concern a deeper religious life within the Reformed Church. The conventicles developed distinct characteristics: some emphasized a rational examination of Scripture and its meaning, while others emphasized sharing the personal religious experiences of each member. While the conventicles allowed for a wide range of religious expression within the one Reformed Church of the Netherlands, it was all too easy for those who emphasized faith experience to see their counterparts as putting reason above God's Word, while the latter saw the former as putting personal experience above God's Word. Reason and heart came to stand over against each other.

standards of Dort, this seemed to be interference with doctrine. At this point the elder Albertus Van Raalte made his protest to the authorities, despite a lifelong obedience to those authorities as appointed by God.

If the policies of this authoritarian Protestant king didn't always find happy acceptance in the Protestant north, they were even less well received in the Roman Catholic south. There, the policies concerning education affected every aspect of the Catholic church. For these reasons the conservative church made common cause with political liberals for whom the government of William I was not democratic enough. These combined forces were strong enough in 1830 to start a revolt that ultimately brought independence to Belgium.

Nevertheless, William I was not one to give up power easily, and the civil war went on for nine long years, exhausting north and south

both economically and emotionally. After the Netherlands lost the Belgium market, grain prices in the province of Groningen dropped even as taxes to pay for the war increased. There were other troubles besides. A deadly cholera epidemic was preached by some as God's punishment for the nation having fallen away from God. Not only the people but also the government grew increasingly irascible. The editor of a Gronigen newspaper critical of government policies was branded publicly and given a ten-year prison sentence.

In the midst of all of these tensions, the Reverend Hendrik De Cock began to play an important role for the future of the Reformed Church in America. De Cock had finished his theological education at the University of Gronigen without ever having read either Calvin's *Institutes* or the Canons of Dort. In his parish at Ulrum, he encountered parishioners who

Schism: A separation or division within the church.

Secession: When schism results in a group leaving a church (congregation or denomination). Seceders are those who leave.

Archives, Calvin College

Hendrik De Cock

adhered steadfastly to the Reformed theology of Calvin and Dort. De Cock began a reading of those documents that resulted in his theological conversion.

De Cock's education at Gronigen had been one of optimism and tolerance, as well as pastoral concern. The *Institutes* and Canons of Dort presented a much more sober view of human ability to make things right. De Cock also came under the influence of those who saw the revolt of Belgium and the cholera epidemic as evidence that the Netherlands had fallen away from the Reformed faith. True to his new convictions and encouraged by the crowds that came to hear his call to national repentance and return to the old order, in 1833 De Cock published his first pamphlet.

The pamphlet, like his preaching, was decidedly immoderate in tone. He accused the Reformed Church of being a false church and its ministers of being false teachers. Hearers from other parishes began to question whether such false teachers should baptize their children. Against the advice of trusted friends, De Cock began to baptize children from other parishes. Not even an argument from Calvin's *Institutes* could persuade him to desist. When the appeal was taken up by the provincial synod, De Cock was found guilty of slandering fellow ministers and disturbing the peace of the church. He was suspended for two years without salary—he had, after all, called his colleagues "wolves, thieves, murderers, Pharisees, hypocrites, and devils."

De Cock was also charged before the provincial synod with writing an introduction to a pamphlet against the singing of hymns, calling the practice both unlawful and heretical. This time, he was deposed. An appeal to the General Synod brought a repeal of the deposition, and De Cock was given six months in which to confess that his introduction to the pamphlet on hymns had been harmful to the peace of the church and to promise to obey church order strictly. De Cock denounced this requirement as "an absolute rejection of truth and Christ."

During the six months he had been given to think over the General Synod's demands, De Cock was visited by a kindred spirit, H. P. Scholte, who would ultimately become the leader of the Dutch colony in Pella, Iowa. Scholte had intended to preach and baptize in De Cock's church, but he was prevented by orders of the classical supervisor, who was then kicked and beaten by the crowd that had assembled to hear Scholte. The police found it necessary to close the church in

Donald J. Bruggink

De Cock's church at Ulrum.

order to prevent violence. On the day following Scholte's visit, De Cock decided to secede.

It is very difficult for someone living in the United States to appreciate what secession meant in the Netherlands. Although the Netherlands was one of the most religiously tolerant states in Europe, the Netherlands Reformed Church was still the state church. The law permitted one to be a Lutheran, a Mennonite, or a Catholic. But under the Napoleonic Code that was still in effect, it was illegal to gather in groups larger than twenty unless recognized by the State, and the State only recognized those religious groups established prior to 1810. That meant that anytime more than twenty of De Cock's parishioners met together for worship, they risked incurring fines and imprisonment. To the magistrates, this was the price to be

Hendrik P. Scholte

paid for breaking the law. For the religiously convinced seceders, it was a form of persecution.

Another form of perceived persecution was through the billeting of soldiers in private homes. It was no small imposition for a poor family in an already overcrowded house to provide bed and board for one or more soldiers. The seceders were convinced that they were required to suffer a far greater portion of this imposition than the rest of the citizenry.

Secession itself had other financial repercussions. Financial aid to the poor was dispensed through the deacons' funds of the Netherlands Reformed Church. Thus, to secede from the church was to secede from the possibility of welfare. This was no small matter at a time when 25 percent of the entire population was

De Cock on Hymns

In 1834 a layman, J. Klok, a dyer by trade, wrote a pamphlet against the singing of hymns. Seizing the opportunity to "demonstrate that a layman as 'the child taught by God stands far above the learned of this age in spiritual knowledge,'" De Cock added a preface supporting Klok's argument. In it, De Cock also expressed his own views, for he held "that hymns were contrary to the Word of God, a clamor displeasing God,...in which out of blindness of perfidy the truth necessary to salvation is concealed: a collection of siren lovesongs fit to draw the Reformed believers away from the saving doctrine."[1]

The official Dutch psalter of 1777.

---

[1] tenZythoff, *Sources of Secession*, 124-25.

dependent on some form of welfare.

Seceders from the officially recognized churches of the Netherlands also faced social ostracism. Needless to say, not everyone, even in De Cock's Ulrum, agreed with the seceders. They saw the seceders as disturbers of the peace; as disobedient to church and state; as slanderers of the church, its pastors, and their neighbors.

To the seceders, living out their convictions seemed to mean facing fines, imprisonment, exclusion from the welfare system, social ostracism, and deteriorating financial conditions. Is it any wonder, then, that the glowing reports of freedom to worship as they pleased, together with a bountiful land and limitless financial opportunity, drew the seceding segment of the Dutch church irresistibly toward North America?

Napoleon had affected indirectly and unintentionally the size and character of the Reformed Church in America—positively, as the seceders emigrated with their Reformed faith to the United States, but also negatively, for the seceders brought their irascible spirit with them.

Resources for Further Study

Family Quarrels: The Dutch Reformed Churches of the 19th Century, by Elton J. Bruins and Robert P. Swierenga. The Historical Series of the Reformed Church in America. Grand Rapids: Eerdmans, 1999.

Sources of Secession: The Netherlands Hervormde Kerk on the Eve of the Dutch Immigration to the Midwest, by Gerrit J. ten Zythoff. The Historical Series of the Reformed Church in America. Grand Rapids: Eerdmans, 1987.

[1] This chapter owes much to, and is dependent upon, the research of the Reverend Gerrit J. tenZythoff, which is found in full in his magisterial *Sources of Secession: The Netherlands Hervormde Kerk on the Eve of the Dutch Immigration to the Midwest*, The Historical Series of the Reformed Church in America (Grand Rapids: Eerdmans, 1987).

An Irascible Classis

The Classis of Middelstum was composed of men who largely held to the moderate theology of the University of Groningen that emphasized the teachings of Jesus and a loving God. However, that did not mean that they appreciated De Cock's practice of baptizing the children of their parishioners. Despite the fact that they could find no specific rules in the constitution of the church that forbade such baptisms, De Cock was nonetheless called before the classis to discuss this issue. However, De Cock, while under investigation concerning the baptisms, had also authored a pamphlet entitled, *Defense of True Reformed Doctrine and of the True Reformed Believers, Attacked and Exposed by two So-called Reformed Teachers, or the Sheepfold of Christ Attacked by Two Wolves and defended by H. De Cock, Reformed Teacher at Ulrum*. The two wolves were ministerial colleagues of De Cock. The language used against them in the pamphlet was so derogatory that when De Cock came before the classis on the issue of baptism, the discussion soon turned to his pamphlet. Moderate ministers were of no mind to be so immoderately attacked.

The irascibility of the times, and of the classis, became evident in its proceedings:

The Classis of Middelstum was in more than one respect out of order. First, only five members of the required quorum of eight were present. Second, the only charge being investigated by the classis was that concerning baptism. According to ecclesiastical law, no question should have been asked about De Cock's brochure until a committee of three had investigated and submitted a report. Finally, the classis dismissed De Cock without hearing his defense. On the same day, the classis arrived at a verdict of guilty. . . [and] suspended De Cock.[1]

[1] tenZythoff, *Sources of Secession*, 122-24.

12

The Reluctant Seceder—
The Reverend Albertus Christiaan Van Raalte

Hope College Collection of the Joint Archives of Holland

I n Centennial Park in Holland, Michigan, stands a bronze
statue of the Reverend Albertus Christiaan Van Raalte, founder of
the Holland colony, Hope College, and Western Theological
Seminary and seceder from the Reformed Church in the
Netherlands.

Secession from the Reformed Church in the Netherlands places
Van Raalte alongside the Reverends Hendrik De Cock and H. P.
Scholte. Yet one finds in Van Raalte none of the rash invective so
common in De Cock. And while Scholte also led a group of

Netherlanders to Pella, Iowa, he never joined the Reformed Church in America. When Van Raalte arrived in the United States, he was embraced by the Reformed Church, embraced it in return, and led his followers into its embrace. And yet he was a seceder.

The irascibility prevalent on all sides in the Netherlands offers an explanation.

Beneath all of the conflict chronicled in the previous chapter was a church divided both in polity and theology. In polity some wished to return to the Dortian establishment, to give the church a greater degree of freedom from government, but less theological freedom (i.e., more strictly enforced adherence to the doctrinal standards). Van Raalte's father, a minister of the Reformed Church of the Netherlands, adhered to the older theology of Dort. The nineteenth-century's confidence in reason, augmented by scientific discovery, resulted in a broad optimism among the upper classes. Thus, for example, the Gronniger school of theology, while never denying the traditional doctrines, nonetheless put far more emphasis upon Christ as teacher and saw God's teaching as gradually perfecting humankind. This theology was more believable for the affluent than for the poor.

Van Raalte had been interested in medicine initially, but the cholera epidemic moved him toward the ministry. As a student at Leiden, where the prevailing theology was optimistic, Van Raalte felt drawn to a small group of students known as the Scholte Club, named after its leader, Hendrik Scholte—the same Scholte who made the crucial visit to De Cock before his secession and later led the group of emigrants who founded Pella, Iowa. Even Scholte's friends spoke of his "natural arrogance." His disdain for his professors was reflected in his remark, "No need for the profs to teach me how to lie. I can lie

Anthony Brummelkamp

Simon Van Velzen

Events referenced in the chapter are below the line. Other historical events are above the line.

1830 Civil war with Belgium begins

1839 War with Belgium ends

1840-49 William II

1845-46 Potato blight

1848 Revision of Dutch constitution in favor of greater parliamentary power

1848 "Revolution" in Amsterdam

1861-65 American Civil War

1862 Slavery abolished in Dutch West Indies

| 1825 | 1830 | 1835 | 1840 | 1845 | 1850 | 1855 | 1860 | 1865 | 1870 |

1834 De Cock secedes

1835 Van Raalte rejected by examiners, leaves the Netherlands Reformed Church

1840 First Reformed Grand Rapids organized

1846 Van Raalte arrives in New York

1847 Van Raalte decides on Michigan (Holland)

1850 Classis Holland joins RCA

1857 Van Vleck Hall built

1866 Hope College incorporated. Beginning of Western Theological Seminary

Grand Rapids' First Reformed Church

The first Reformed Church congregation in Grand Rapids, Michigan, did not begin with the Dutch immigration that began to flood west Michigan in 1848 but rather with George Young, a descendent of New Netherland.

Young, who had been living in the Hudson Valley, moved his family to Grand Rapids in the late 1830s. It was Young's desire for a Reformed church in Grand Rapids that led him to appeal for financial assistance from friends back in New York. The Ladies Missionary Society of the church in Ithaca responded with three hundred dollars to support a missionary pastor.

In 1840, the Reverend Hart Waring organized the First Protestant Reformed Dutch Church (now Central Reformed) with twelve members—including three families drawn from the Congregational church nearby. They met initially in the village schoolhouse.

English was the language of worship at First; the next eight Reformed congregations that sprang up between 1849 and 1892 worshiped in Dutch.

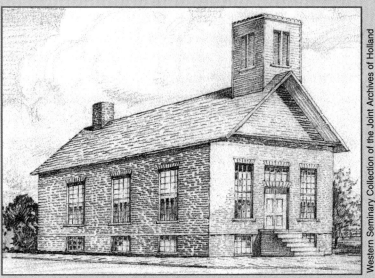

First Reformed Church, Grand Rapids, Michigan

---

perfectly well myself." Of the seven members of the Scholte Club, Van Raalte was the youngest.

Three members of the Scholte Club—Simon Van Velzen, Antonie Brummelkamp, and Albertus Van Raalte—all married sisters of the De Moen family, a household committed to the piety of the Reveil (a piety exemplified by Dina Van Bergh). It is unfortunate that we do not know

Christina Johanna De Moen Van Raalte

more about the influence the De Moen sisters exerted on their husbands. Certainly there was a pervasive piety, albeit the subsequent careers of their husbands took very different turns. Antonie Brummelkamp was the first to receive a pastorate, but within a year he had been deposed for refusing to sing hymns, for demanding of the General Synod that the old liturgical forms be followed, and for declaring that he would follow church order only insofar as he interpreted it to agree with the Word of God. Simon Van Velzen lasted fourteen months in his parish, making similar demands of the General Synod and demanding that all

Depose: To remove a minister or other church office bearer from office.

Christian Reformed Church: This American denomination traces its origins to 1857, when a group of seceders left the Reformed Church in America.

pastors not adhering to the three confessions (the Heidelberg Catechism, the Belgic Confession, and the Canons of the Synod of Dort) be deposed. The classis suspended him for six weeks, but before the period was up he too seceded.

After the ecclesial examiners had encountered two members of the Scholte Club who in their first year in the pastorate made demands of the General Synod and seceded from the Reformed Church without appeal, it is little wonder that they questioned the youngest of the club, Van Raalte, rather carefully. It is interesting to note that he passed his theological exam without difficulty, but he refused to agree to obey the church order on the basis that he was not familiar with it. His examiners then required that he study the order and return for reexamination. Such treatment was not exceptional. That same day, of four candidates being examined, only one passed. Two others (in no way connected with the seceders) were also sent back for more study, while a fifth, previously sent back to improve his Greek and Hebrew, was reexamined.

Van Raalte went to his beloved Professor Clarisse, who wrote a letter to Donker Curtius, the president of the General Synod, on his behalf. Curtius agreed that Van Raalte should have been accepted, but he could not overrule the examiners. It was perhaps indicative of the temper of the times that Van Raalte remembers Curtius telling him, "Preach what

you want, and allow us to preach what we want, but obey the regulations."[1]

To a serious, pious young man like Van Raalte, that could not have seemed like good advice. But Van Raalte went before the examiners once more, this time with an example of the kind of church law he could not follow (he would not exclude a gifted person from teaching the catechism just because he was not yet twenty-five years of age).

The examiners, perhaps judging Van Raalte by his brothers-in-law rather than assessing his spirit properly, refused to accept him for the ministry. With great personal pain, Van Raalte left the church of his father and joined the seceders.

Van Raalte was a successful pastor. Despite the king's offer to legitimize seceding churches (an offer that Scholte accepted), Van Raalte refused and suffered the legal penalties of the Napoleonic Code. However, it was not the laws

Donald J. Bruggink

According to local tradition, Van Raalte was once jailed in this building under the strictures of the Napoleon Code.

Donald J. Bruggink photos

According to local tradition, Van Raalte and other seceding pastors used this barn in which to preach.

Local tradition attributes this windmill as having been built by Van Raalte in Ommen to ease the economic hardship of his followers by giving them a place to grind their grain.

of Napoleon, enforced by William I, that drove Van Raalte to America. Instead it was a lack of potatoes, the staple of the poor. The potato blight of 1845 and 1846 resulted in the literal starvation of the agricultural community. (It was at this same time in Ireland, even more dependent upon potatoes, that over a million people died of starvation.)

Van Raalte saw emigration as a way out for his people. The Dutch East Indies were considered but rejected when the authorities reminded Van Raalte and his flock of strictures upon worship in the colonies. The freedom of worship in the United States and the promise of financial opportunity, together with inexpensive transatlantic travel, settled their resolve.

Initially, Van Raalte intended simply to facilitate the emigration to the United States, but a bout with typhus in 1846 led him to conclude that his sheep would be scattered if he were not there to give them leadership. He decided that he and his family would accompany the people to America.

In that same year the Reverend Dr. Thomas De Witt of New York City traveled to the Netherlands, where he learned of the possibility of Dutch emigration, especially by the seceders. Thus, when the immigrants arrived in New York in November 1846, De Witt and his elder, James Forrester, came to the dock to welcome Van Raalte, his family of seven, and his fifty-three followers. (Just as De Witt welcomed the Dutch immigrants, the church in Manhattan named after him welcomed minorities by its ministries a century later.)

De Witt helped get the seceders to Albany, where they were

Thomas De Witt

welcomed by the Reverend Isaac Wyckoff, pastor of the Second Dutch Reformed Church. Wyckoff found temporary housing for the immigrants and solicited funds to distribute to them. This was only the first of many groups of Dutch immigrants that Wyckoff would help on their way via the Erie Canal to the "West"—Michigan, Ohio, Indiana, Illinois, Wisconsin, and Iowa.

Having brought his little group as far as Detroit, Van Raalte found lodging for them and work for the men in a shipyard; he then headed west to find land. Van Raalte was determined to found a "colonie," a

Isaac Newton Wyckoff

place where his people could maintain their religious identity. To that end he chose a sparsely settled spot on the shores of Lake Michigan, midway between mouths of the Grand and Kalamazoo Rivers. Van Raalte bought land there from the government for $1.25 per acre.

The first colonists arrived in February, the heart of winter. The lead-gray skies of western Michigan must have been of some comfort, for they looked like those in the Netherlands. But the land was different, covered by heavy forests that would have to be cleared if crops were to be planted, but that would furnish material for shelter. Until then, the newcomers were

Classis Business

The Classis of Holland was organized April 23, 1848, in Zeeland, Michigan. Three ministers and four consistories were present: the Reverend Albertus C. Van Raalte and consistory (First, Holland), the Reverend Martin A. Ypma and consistory (Vriesland), the Reverend Cornelius Van der Meulen and

Settler's log church

consistory (Zeeland), and the consistory of the church in Allegan County (Graafschap).

They sang Psalm 103, prayed, elected Van Raalte president and Van der Meulen clerk, and proceeded with several items of business: the frequency of classis meetings, the length of terms for consistory members, festive days in the church calendar, the confessional standards, and church order. The classis also dealt with two items pertaining to marriage:

Art. 7. In the congregation of Rev. Ypma, there is a widow who wishes to get married; but since her former husband died only three months ago, some of the brethren object, and wish her to wait a while.

Answer: Whereas the assembly knows of no regulations on the subject in the word of God, it can not place any obstacle in the way of this marriage; but advises that the parties who contemplate it be instructed; in order that we may seek that which is lovely and of good report; and

George N. Smith

Arvilla A. Powers Smith

(The Indians, who had been converted by the Roman Catholics, had requested a priest but instead got the Congregationalist Smith.) These four were the only whites in the area. The colonists were ill prepared for what awaited them. Even felling trees was a new experience. Several settlers were injured and a few killed before they learned proper techniques. The number of trees a settler could fell eventually increased from one to twenty or thirty a day. By spring, some colonists had

taken in by Isaac Fairbanks, the government agent for Indian affairs, and his wife, Ann, and by the Reverend George Smith and his wife, Arvilla.

that no offense be given to decency, honor and natural human feeling.

Art. 11. The consistory of the Allegan County church asks consideration of a marriage that it is proposed to contract in that congregation. A member of the church wishes to get married to the wife of his deceased brother, who had children by this woman, the said children being still living.

Answer: The assembly judges that such marriages cannot be permitted in the church of God, inasmuch as it is incest, according to Leviticus 18:16 and 20:21.

This last item came back to the classis at its next meeting on September 27, 1848.

Art. 7. The man who wished to get married to his brother's widow, in the congregation of Allegan County, concerning which affair action was taken in Art. 11 of the previous meeting, was present in person at this meeting, because he could not acquiesce in the judgment which the assembly had pronounced. The 18th chapter of Leviticus is read to him. The said person is unable to refute this from

the scriptures, but has only certain arguments, which have no basis in the word of God.

The brethren of the consistory ask what is to be done in case this man, so warned, refuses to listen, and the unanimous judgment is: in case of contumacy, he is to be excluded from the church, because we cannot look upon such a marriage in any other way than as incest.

At its third meeting on April 25, 1849, Elder Dunnewint from the Allegan County congregation announced that he could not support the action of the others in excommunicating the man and woman who went on to marry and asked that the case be reconsidered. "After mature consideration, the unanimous judgment is: The meeting of Classis judged rightly, and the Consistory of the Allegan County church has acted, in the excommunication of these persons, in the spirit of the Classical Assembly."

—*Classis Holland: Minutes 1848-1858.* Translated by a Joint Committee of the Christian Reformed Church and the Reformed Church in America. Grand Rapids Printing Company, 1943.

A log house in the "colonie"

cleared four or five acres.

While the Van Raalte party that came to West Michigan on the ship, *Southerner*, totaled only sixty, by November of the following year, two thousand Dutch had arrived in the colony. The mortality rate was high due to sickness and privation, but conditions were also bad in the Netherlands, and people kept coming. The future of the colony seemed secure.

In 1850, only four years after the seceders had set sail from the Netherlands, Van Raalte led the little Classis of Holland into union with the Reformed Church in America. For those early settlers, the members of the churches in the East had seemed like "angels of mercy." It's not surprising that the Reformed Church in America befriended Van Raalte's immigrants. Because

that church had remained theologically conservative, and because it had thrown off the controls of the Classis of Amsterdam only a half-century earlier, there was great sympathy for these compatriots who were fleeing persecution for freedom of religion. Conversely, the same characteristics that made the immigrants attractive to the Reformed Church in America made that church attractive to Van Raalte.

However, as other settlers flooded in, few of whom had such close ties with Van Raalte as had the original settlers, dissension began to arise. The seceding spirit was much more virulent in some than in Van Raalte. The issue of singing hymns troubled many seceders. Allowing other Protestants to share the Lord's Supper was also an issue. While some members and ministers did secede, beginning what ultimately became the Christian Reformed

Model of the *Southerner*

Van Vleck Hall, completed in 1857 and still in use in the center of Hope's campus. In 1867 theological instruction began and was conducted in the building at the far left.

Church, the main body of the seceders never left the Reformed Church in America.

While Van Raalte had founded his colony in the wilderness to enable it to create its own religious ethos, he was equally concerned that its citizens become Americans. Already in 1848, schools were on the classis agenda. The first schools were Christian schools, paid for by the church. But as soon as they became eligible for state support, they became public. As was the case in most predominantly Protestant communities of the time, Christian teaching was part of the curriculum. Teaching was, of course, in English. Despite the fact that Van Raalte continued to preach in Dutch, he was determined that his people become English-speaking Americans as soon as possible.

As the school grew, an academy was added; then it became a separate school in 1853. At that time Van Raalte gave five acres of land to be used as a campus for the college, while Eastern benefactors donated funds; the largest gift, $7,000, came from Samuel Schieffelin (a dealer in pharmaceuticals, advocate of parochial schools, and friend of Van Raalte). The college's first building, Van Vleck Hall, was completed in 1857, and the school was officially incorporated as Hope College in 1866.

Western Theological Seminary also claims its inception from 1866, as the theological department of Hope College. By that year Hope College had already graduated its first class, among whom were seven who wished to enter the ministry. They successfully petitioned the General Synod of that year to pursue their theological education at the college. In 1885 the seminary separated from the college and set up its own board, faculty, and curriculum. Van Raalte's educational dreams had been fully realized.

If John Henry Livingston is the father of the Reformed Church in America, Albertus Christiaan Van Raalte is the father of the western portion of the denomination. Strikingly similar trials and accomplishments characterize these two men. Livingston entered a factious church and promoted the healing of the division between the Coetus and Conferentie parties. Van Raalte attracted factious seceders from the Reformed Church of the Netherlands but did all he could to promote healing within the colony

as well as union with the Reformed Church in America.

Both men were great preachers. Livingston's sermon, "The Everlasting Gospel," gave impetus to the foreign missions movement in the RCA. Van Raalte's sermons brought people to America, inspired the creation of a colony, and supported the fledgling missionary movement.

Both were figures of their age in promoting education. Livingston, the church's first professor of theology, was instrumental in founding Queens College, now Rutgers University, and New Brunswick Theological Seminary. Van Raalte began by establishing a primary school, then a college, and finally a seminary.

Today, Western Theological Seminary offers a Master of Theology degree primarily for foreign nationals, a Doctor of Ministry for pastors, an Master of Religious Education for Christian educators, and the Master of Divinity for women and men preparing for ministry, as well as being the Center for the Continuing Education of the Church. Hope College continues as a prestigious private college with strong ties to the Reformed Church in America. The heirs of Van Raalte's colony and its institutions continue to play a vital role in the ongoing life of the Reformed Church in America.

Resources for Further Study

Albertus C. Van Raalte: Dutch Leader and American Patriot, by Elton J. Bruins, Jeanne M. Jacobson, and Larry Wagenaar. Holland, Mich.: Hope College, 1996.

The Americanization of a Congregation, by Elton Bruins, 2nd ed. The Historical Series of the Reformed Church in America. Grand Rapids: Eerdmans, 1996.

Family Quarrels In the Dutch Reformed Churches in the Nineteenth Century, by Elton J. Bruins and Robert P. Swierenga. The Historical Series of the Reformed Church in America. Grand Rapids: Eerdmans, 1999.

Vision for a Christian College, by Gordon J. Van Wylen. The Historical Series of the Reformed Church in America. Grand Rapids: Eerdmans, 1988.

Albertus and Christina, The Van Raalte Family, Home and Roots by Elton J. Bruins, Karen G. Schakel, Sara Fredrickson Simmons, and Marie N. Zingle. Grand Rapids: Eerdmans, 2004.

[1] Gerrit J. ten Zythoff, *Sources of Secession*, The Historical Series of the Reformed Church in America (Grand Rapids: Eerdmans, 1987), 133.

13

Room for Everyone— Almost

The Church of Van Raalte, known as "Pillar Church"

People who move from one Reformed church to another may sometimes be amazed that both belong to the same denomination. It is not only that some congregations are predominately African-American, Hispanic, Native American, or Asian, but that even among the mostly Anglo churches, including those still of markedly Dutch descent, there are distinct differences.

The story of why this is begins with the church that took shape in the seventeenth century, which included immigrants from several nations. The first settlers in the colony of New Netherland were Walloons from France and what is now Belgium. The early congregations also included people of German ancestry. In the following centuries, ministers of the German Reformed, Presbyterian, and Congregational churches frequently crossed denominational lines, as is evident in the *Historical Directory of the Reformed Church in America*. This openness to other communions also extended to the professorate of New Brunswick Theological Seminary.

When the second wave of Dutch immigrants arrived in the nineteenth century, they found a denomination that continued to adhere to their doctrinal standards but that was open to Calvinists of other communions. However, while Van Raalte's seceders were initially of a similar mind, the economic conditions in the Netherlands resulted in the emigration not only of a variety of seceders, but of many members of the Netherlands Reformed Church.[1]

While the Reformed Church in America, thoroughly Americanized by the mid nineteenth century, could make room for these diverse immigrants of similar Reformed faith, not all of the seceders were comfortable with the church that welcomed them. Those who had seceded from the Netherlands Reformed Church had suffered much for their decision: they had been taken off the welfare roles, fined when too many gathered for unauthorized worship, and had soldiers billeted in their homes (a common practice, but one which was experienced as persecution). Even those who were not seceders had suffered the transatlantic journey, often a harrowing experience accompanied by sickness and death. Was it any wonder that having suffered so much, they had a hard time assimilating in a strange new land?

Among the seceders were men like Hendrik P. Scholte, who, with his French wife, led his followers to

Events referenced in the chapter are below the line. Other historical events are above the line.

Above the line			
1861-65 Civil War	**1871** Holland fire	**1883** Anti-Saloon League organized	**1896** Spanish American War
1853 New York & Chicago connected by rail	**1871** Chicago fire	**1881** American Red Cross organized	
1846-48 U.S. attacks Mexico to gain NM, AZ, & CA	**1861-65** Abraham Lincoln president	**1873** Financial panic	**1886** American Federation of Labor organized

1850	**1875**	**1900**

Below the line			
1847 Van Raalte establishes Holland, MI	**1856** Christian Reformed Church dates its beginning,		**1885** Christelijke Gereformeerde Kerk advises emigrants to join CRC
1847 Zonne establishes Cedar Grove, WI	**1853** Classis Holland condemns Freemasonry	**1868** Classis Holland & Wisconsin overture General Synod re Freemasonry	**1892** CGK joins Doleante
1848 *Phoenix* disaster off Sheboygan	**1856** First Reformed, Pella, IA, established		**1886** Kuyper's Doleantie leaves the Nederlands Hervormde Kerk **1893** Pleasant Prairie Academy established

The *Phoenix*

The *Phoenix* steamed out of Buffalo, New York, on the morning of November 11, 1847, with a crew of twenty-three; a heavy load of coffee, sugar, and molasses; and an unknown number of passengers, among whom were 175 Dutch immigrants. The ship was destined for ports on Lake Michigan. After riding out rough seas and seeking harbor in Manitowoc, Wisconsin, the prior day, the *Phoenix* headed south for Sheboygan, the final twenty-five-mile leg for the Dutch families.

Around 4 a.m. Sunday, November 21, smoke poured out of the boiler room, and soon flames engulfed the ship. Two small lifeboats carried forty-three survivors and the ship's Bible to shore. The Hollanders—now only twenty-five in number—joined the small Dutch settlements, which were gearing up for their second wilderness winter. Eight Reformed churches clustered together in Sheboygon County, Wisconsin, claim descendents of those who survived this tragedy.

Pella, Iowa. Scholte, who had been present at De Cock's decision to secede, never joined the Reformed Church in America, although as early as 1856 the First Reformed Church in Pella was organized, with Pieter J. Oggel becoming its pastor in 1860.

A smaller group, following the

The First Reformed Church in Cedar Grove, Wisconsin, org. 1854. The present structure was built in 1905 at a cost of $13,468.

Reverend Pieter Zonne (who had been tutored by Scholte and Van Raalte), settled in the Cedar Grove area of Sheboygan County in Wisconsin. The settlers arrived in 1847, and within five years two hundred family farms were in operation. Zonne founded the First Presbyterian Church in Cedar Grove, which has since had a continuous ministry. The First Reformed Church in Cedar Grove was organized in 1853, and in 1854 it was served by a missionary pastor from the East, the Reverend Fred P. Beidler, followed by the Reverend K. Vander Schuur, 1855-56, who had served in South Holland (Graafschap), Michigan, from 1849-51 and was subsequently dismissed to the Associate Reformed Church. The next pastor, the Reverend William Van Liewen, was received from the Classis of Amsterdam (obviously not a seceder). He served in Cedar Grove from 1857-59 and then is lost to the records of the Reformed Church in America. The Reverend Jacob Van de[r] Meulen, straight out of seminary, served from 1861-63. Some pastoral

Communions: A term used frequently as the preferred synonym for denominations. The intent is to underline that the group is more than just a name, but is a communion of people who are Christians together sharing the same beliefs and governance.

That Garden Spot of Iowa

"In Sioux County, that garden spot of Iowa, there is a little town called Boyden, and there we have a church. I am glad to show it because it marks a new departure in church architecture in the West; at least, in Dutch churches in the country districts. Boyden people have proved that a church need not be expensive to be attractive. Inside, it is even more tasteful, both in the finish of the wood and coloring of the walls.

"Boyden stands second on our list of appropriations last year. We gave $800 toward this church, and you who helped to make up that sum will be glad to see how well your money was invested."

—"Women's Work," *The Mission Field*, 1894-95, 162.

The First Reformed Church of Boyden, Iowa

continuity was gained with the Reverend H. Stobbelaar, who ministered from 1864-73. These mostly short pastorates, with movements between denominations and disappearances from the records, all speak of a very unsettled and fluid ecclesial situation, quite unlike the image of religiously cohesive groups of a single mind. Unfortunately, the specific points of theological or personality difference that led to division or very brief pastorates are usually missing from the records.

Having suffered for their secession from the Netherlands Reformed Church, many new immigrants were wary of joining the Reformed Church in America, despite the conservative nature of that church. The nineteenth-century historian Philip Schaff described the Reformed Church as "the most rigid and unmovable of all churches in America."[2] For those seceders who had come in contact with Reformed churches on their way west, the singing of hymns (instead of only psalms) must have raised questions. The government of William I had forced a hymnbook on all the Netherlands congregations and demanded that at least one hymn be sung each Sunday—even in congregations where only psalms had been sung. The singing of hymns had become for some the symbol of all they disliked in the Netherlands Reformed Church—and it was certainly easier to identify than theological heresy.

Another point of issue for the seceders was the failure of the Reformed Church in America to keep the festival days, especially Pentecost (which is still a holiday in the Netherlands). The ecumenicity of the denomination was also called into question; those of a secessionist mentality objected to inviting all Christians but Roman Catholics to the Lord's Supper.

In 1856, individuals like Gijsbert Haan, after protesting the union of Classis Holland with the Reformed Church in America, left the church. By the following year, three congregations (Noordeloos, Graafschap, and Polkton), as well as the Reverend H. G. Kleijn of Grand Rapids, seceded. Only Graafschap offered specific reasons, including all of the above. Professor M. Eugene Osterhaven notes that at heart the reasons for secession were not theological, but attitudinal and emotional. A totally new environment, the rapid disappearance of traditional Dutch ways (Americanization), the difficulty in handling a new language, and the threat of the

Gijsbert Haan

disappearance of the native language in which they could communicate and worship with precision exacerbated those of a naturally contentious spirit. The Reformed Church had room for everyone—but many were uncomfortable in its socially unfamiliar embrace.

The real wonder is that the numbers of those who left in 1856-57 were so small (Haan and Kleijn later returned to the Reformed Church). Undoubtedly the leadership of Van Raalte and those of like spirit played a part. For the great majority, the unity of the church (and the kindness experienced from the members of the Reformed Church in the East) was more important than the issues. Van Raalte was a reluctant seceder. Of the internal divisions within the seceders he later wrote: "The alienation among the faithful in the Netherlands was for me a continuous tearful and heart-rending sorrow. This made me more fearful than all the persecution."[3]

Van Raalte had not encouraged union with the Reformed Church in America lightly. He had visited New Brunswick Theological Seminary and listened to the teachings of the professors and pronounced them good: "I blessed my God that I there found the faith, the faith of my father—the historical church of the Netherlands—and because I found it and loved it, I determined to bring the immigrants into intimate connection with the Dutch Reformed Church of America."[4]

However, with the death of Van Raalte and the loss of his leadership,

Graafschaap Christian Reformed Church (built in 1852, the building was torn down in 2001)

The Peter Hertzog Theological Hall at New Brunswick Seminary, erected within a few years of Van Raalte's visit. This centerpiece of the campus was torn down in the 1960s during the presidency of Wallace N. Jamison.

Enlightenment: A philosophical movement of the eighteenth century that critically evaluated the beliefs of the past from the perspective of rationalism. The Enlightenment was the Age of Reason.

Freemasonry: An international secret fraternity that became a major force during the Enlightenment. In Europe it was often hostile to the church, while in America not only was that hostility lacking, but the participation of many of the founding fathers, including George Washington, gave it wide patriotic acceptance.

an issue of long-smoldering import once again came to the fore. The issue was Freemasonry. The Dutch were not the only recent religious immigrants for whom Freemasonry was a problem. Lutherans and Roman Catholics alike steadfastly refused membership to Freemasons. In Europe Freemasonry, born in the rationalism of the Enlightenment, was virulently anticlerical. Freemasonry was experienced as antithetical to the church. In the United States, Freemasonry and the Enlightenment also had much in common, but the fact that many of the founding fathers, especially George Washington, were masons, cast the movement in a very different light. Not only were such men as Washington not against the church, the euphoria of nationhood had virtually apotheosized Wash-

ington. Freemasonry as experienced in America was not anticlerical but seemed supportive of the church, and to be a Freemason was to be quintessentially patriotic, standing as one with the father of the country.

The nineteenth-century European immigrant, whether Lutheran, Calvinist, or Roman Catholic, understood Freemasonry in its European form, not as it was practiced in America. Thus, when the Dutch in the West learned that not only church members but even ministers in the East were Freemasons, it seemed like a theological impossibility. How could those who deny the church be in it—and even lead it? Would not their presence and their teaching corrupt the church? Overtures were sent to synod demanding the purification of the church.

The issue first arose in 1853 with the Classis of Holland's thorough condemnation of Freemasonry. Overtures to synod began in 1868 and were offered by the classes of both Holland and Wisconsin. The synod replied that this was a matter for consistorial discipline. The overtures were repeated, and the 1870 synod replied graciously but again insisted that this was a matter for the consistory, and that synod should add no "new and unauthorized test for membership in the Christian Church."[5]

There the matter rested for a number of years until it surfaced again with other issues of distress: the irritations of poverty caused by the great fire of Chicago in 1871, the economic recession of the 1870s, the financial difficulties of Hope College, and the cessation of theological teaching in Holland due to lack of funds (for this some blamed Freemasonry). In addition, an incendiary itinerant lecturer,

Edmond Ronayne, himself a former Freemason, excoriated his former associates. Overtures to synod from the Classis of Holland followed and were joined by additional overtures from the classes of Wisconsin, Grand River, and Illinois and the Particular Synod of Chicago. The 1880 synod responded courteously, defending liberty of conscience and declaring that "no communicant member, and no minister of the Reformed Church in America ought to unite with or to remain in any society or institution, whether secret or open, whose principles and practices are anti-Christian, or contrary to the faith and practice of the Church to which he belongs."[6]

Even that was not enough. Holland Classis lost four hundred families in the next two years, including a majority of the members of its first congregation, which occupied the Pillar Church. At the same time there were those congregations who declared, "As long as

Accident in Grand Rapids

"The daily press of January 9th reports a sad accident as having occurred at the Seventh Church of Grand Rapids [Michigan] on Sunday, January 8th. It was Communion Sunday, and Rev. A. J. Van Lummel served the wine to the elders. One after another of them collapsed to the floor. The congregation was in an uproar immediately. A doctor was secured who succeeded in reviving six of the stricken men, but two were taken to the hospital in an extremely serious condition. It was discovered that some one unaccustomed to the task had filled the goblet with a painting mixture containing a poisonous stain, instead of the sacramental wine."

—*Christian Intelligencer and Mission Field*, January 11, 1922

we are not hindered in our leading of our congregation according to our conviction, we consider the threatened schism as a sin with which we can have nothing to do."[7]

While a relatively small number of people left the Reformed Church during the secession of 1856 (to which the Christian Reformed Church dates its birth), the issue of Freemasonry was seen by European Reformed, Lutheran, and Roman Catholic adherents as a clear-cut issue; it was anti-Christian and an evil to be opposed. Thus in 1885 the Christelijke Gereformeerde Kerk in the Netherlands asked the consistories of all of its congregations to advise members immigrating to America to join the Christian Reformed Church. When in 1892 the Christelilijke Gereformeerde Kerk joined the Doleantie of 1886 (the "sorrowing secession" of minister, theologian, prime minister, Abraham Kuyper), it meant that the vast majority of emigrants were predisposed to the Christian Reformed Church. The theological encouragement of their native secessionist churches was augmented by the fact that the Christian Reformed Church, initially formed by those who clung most tightly to their Dutch secessionist roots and whose ranks were swelled after 1885 by new immigrants, offered a context more familiar to subsequent new immigrants than the rapidly Americanized Reformed Church in America.

However, God works in wondrous ways to bring good even out of secession. The infusion of new immigrants from the Doleantie brought not only numbers to the new Christian Reformed Church, but the highly sophisticated and powerful theological structure of Abraham Kuyper. The result has been not only a remarkably literate denomination theologically, but a philosophy department at Calvin College that has seeded many colleges and universities throughout the United States and Canada with a strong Christian witness.

Resources for Further Study

Albertus C. Van Raalte: Dutch Leader and American Patriot, by Elton J. Bruins, Jeanne M. Jacobson, and Larry Wagenaar. Holland: Hope College, 1996.

Family Quarrels in the Dutch Reformed Churches in the Nineteenth Century, by Elton J. Bruins and Robert P. Swierenga. The Historical Series of the Reformed Church in America. Grand Rapids: Eerdmans, 1999.

Word and World: Reformed Theology in America, ed. James W. Van Hoeven. The Historical Series of the Reformed Church in America. Grand Rapids: Eerdmans, 1986.

[1] Roman Catholic immigrants founded a colony around St. Ann (just east of Lake Winnebago on the edge of Sheboygan County, Wisconsin), albeit the Dutch Calvinists and Roman Catholics never made contact with one another.
[2] M. Eugene Osterhaven, "Saints and Sinners: Secession and the Christian Reformed Church," *Word and World*, James W. Van Hoeven, ed., The Historical Series of the Reformed Church in America, 1986, 57.
[3] Ibid., 49.
[4] Ibid., 58.
[5] Elton J. Bruins and Robert P. Swierenga, *Family Quarrels in the Dutch Reformed Churches in the Nineteenth Century*, The Historical Series of the Reformed Church in America, 1999, 115.
[6] Ibid., 125.
[7] Osterhaven, "Saints and Sinners," 72.

14

The Rightful Role of Women

Sara Doremus

The history of the Reformed Church in America has often reflected movements in American society. Around the time that the United States became independent of Britain, the Dutch church became independent of the Classis of Amsterdam. As eastern populations began to move westward, the church moved into western New York State, Ohio, and Illinois. As America grew as a result of immigration in the nineteenth century, the church welcomed Dutch and German Reformed immigrants. As the United

States fought the Civil War, the Reformed Church in America continued to engage in a civil war of its own.

The conflict in the Reformed Church centered on the rightful role of women—a matter that also arose in American society. The abolitionist movement leading up to the Civil War offered women new opportunities to fill leadership roles and claim greater civil rights. The Reformed Church did not play a large role in the abolition movement prior to the Civil War; its women did not participate in the movement's leadership or its work for civil rights. However, women of the Reformed Church had even earlier broken new ground. In 1799 Sarah Van Doren had organized a Sunday school class at the First Reformed Church in New Brunswick, New Jersey, which became the oldest Sunday school in America with a continuous history.

In the area of benevolence, Sarah de Peyster in 1804 became the first Dutch Reformed person, man or woman, to leave a legacy to the church.[1]

Although Reformed Church women were not active in the movement to abolish slavery, concern for the unsaved touched their hearts. In 1810 Sally Thomas,

John Scudder and Harriet Waterbury Scudder

Events referenced in the chapter are below the line. Other historical events are above the line.

1909
Ford Model T

1848
First Women's Rights Convention, Seneca Falls, New York

1914-18
World War I

1903
Wright brothers fly at Kitty Hawk

1920
19th Amendment, Women's Suffrage

1836
Mt. Holyoke College for Women founded

1919
Prohibition

1939-45
World War II

| 1825 | 1850 | 1875 | 1900 | 1925 | 1950 | 1975 | 2000 |

1825
First Church, New Brunswick, women organize to support missions

1870
Mary Kidder begins Ferris Seminary, Japan

1900
Woman's Board begins work in Kentucky

1918
Classes Albany & Montgomery seek to open the office of elder and deacon to women

1972
Offices of elder and deacon opened to women

1844-1925
245 women serve as missionaries in RCA

1855
Sarah Scudder, Chittoor Female Seminary, India

1900
Ida Scudder begins medical work in India

1945
Sara M. Couch returns to Nagasaki

1979
Women ordained to Word & sacrament

1847
Eleanor Doty founds Amoy Girls School, China

1922
Classis of Philadelphia seeks to open all offices to women

Exemplary Beneficence of Reformed Church in America Women*

1804   Sarah de Peyster is the first person, man or woman, to leave a legacy for the benevolent purposes of the church.

1810   Sally Thomas, a domestic servant, bequeaths her modest savings to missions.

1815   Rebecca Knox is the first woman to bequeath funds to New Brunswick Theological Seminary.

1855   Ann Hertzog gives $30,000 to New Brunswick Theological Seminary to enable the construction of Hertzog Hall.

1907   Elizabeth R. Voorhees is a major contributor for Voorhees Hall at Hope College. She and her husband, Ralph, contribute generously to Reformed Church causes, including Voorhees College in Vellore, India, the Amoy mission, New Brunswick Theological Seminary, and the Ralph W. Voorhees School for the Blind in India.

1984   Florence Charavay bequeaths over one million dollars to New Brunswick and Western Theological Seminaries.

—*Some Unique Contributions of RCA Women, A Brief Historical Chronology, 1624-2004,*
by Mary Kansfield. Privately published, 2003.

*With appreciation for the thousands of women, single and married, who have given from their poverty and wealth many millions of dollars to the cause of the Reformed Church in America over the centuries. The above are but a very few examples of the generosity which has funded the church and its institutions.

a domestic servant, bequeathed her savings of $345.38 to the American Board of Commissioners for Foreign Missions—its first legacy. Harriet Waterbury Scudder went to India to serve with her husband in 1819— the first Reformed Church woman to serve in a foreign field.[2]

Nonetheless, social constraints limited their activity. In 1829 Sarah Doremus, a staunch and generous supporter of missions (she was the wife of Thomas Doremus, a wealthy New Yorker), was on the dock to bid David Abeel farewell as he left for Borneo. Upon his return, she invited him to address a group of friends in her home. Abeel pled with the women to organize to support missions to the lost. The

secretary of the American Board of Commissioners for Foreign Missions, Dr. Rufus Anderson, was there; he asked the women to defer. "What!" exclaimed Joanna Bethune, "Is the American Board afraid the ladies will get ahead of them?"[3] Mrs. Bethune's objection notwithstanding, the women did not organize at that time.

In New Jersey, the women were well ahead of the group David Abeel addressed in New York. The women of the First Church in New Brunswick and the Reformed Church in Bedminster had organized for the support of missions as early as 1825.

A church-wide Woman's [sic] Board of Foreign Missions wasn't

Reformed Church in America Women in Education

1799   Sara Van Doren organizes first Sunday school at the First Reformed Church, New Brunswick, New Jersey.

1815   Rebecca Knox is the first woman to bequeath funds to New Brunswick Theological Seminary, which funds were designated for indigent students.

1834   Sarah Doremus from the South Dutch Church in New York organizes the Society for Promoting Female Education in China and the Far East.

1847   Eleanor Doty begins the Amoy Girls' School in China.

1855   Ann Hertzog gives $30,000 to New Brunswick Theological Seminary to enable the construction of Hertzog Hall, which will serve the seminary for over one hundred years until torn down under the presidency of Wallace Jamison.

1870   Mary Kidder founds Ferris Seminary for girls in Yokohama, Japan.

1882   Frances Phelps (Otte) and Gertrude Alcott (Whitenack) become the first women to graduate from Hope College.

1918   Dr. Ida Scudder founds the Vellore Christian Medical College and Hospital.

1938   Frances Beardslee is elected the first woman member of the Hope College Board of Trustees.

1962   Elaine Lubbers becomes the first full-time woman professor at Western Theological Seminary.

Sonja Stewart

1970   Sonja Stewart begins a teaching career at Western Theological Seminary, the first woman to earn a doctorate and become a full professor.

1979   Joyce Borgman de Velder becomes the first RCA woman to receive the degree of Master of Divinity from Western Theological Seminary.

Bernita Babb

1988   Bernita Babb becomes the first Reformed Church in America African American woman to be ordained.

Carol Bechtel

1998   Carol Bechtel becomes the first woman to hold the fourth office as General Synod Professor of Theology.

—Some Unique Contributions of RCA Women, A Brief Historical Chronology, 1624-2004, by Mary Kansfield. Privately published, 2003.

Dr. Ida, India

Archives of the Reformed Church in America

The family can easily be described as incredible. When Dr. John Scudder left a successful medical practice in New York City in 1819 to become the first medical missionary in India, little did he and his wife, Harriet, know that generation after generation of Scudders would follow their lead. Seventeen Scudders, including John Scudder himself, were ordained. Forty-three Scudders—twelve of them doctors—served in India. Others worked in Arabia, Japan, New York, New Jersey, and elsewhere. Their combined years of service—well over a thousand and still counting!

Ida S. Scudder's call to mission work came one memorable evening in India. A granddaughter of the pioneer missionary, Ida had returned home after six years of schooling in the United States. Her intention was to spend time with her parents, prior to enrolling in college back in the States. That evening, a Brahmin came to their door seeking help for his wife, who was dying in childbirth. Unwilling to accept the help of Ida's father, who was a physician—Hindu law forbade another man to look upon a woman—the Brahmin left. That same evening two other men—a Muslim and another Hindu—came to the Scudder home seeking medical care for their wives, who were also in labor. They, too, left, unable to accept the male doctor's assistance. When Ida learned that all three women had died, she said to her parents: "God has taken very drastic means to show me what I must do. He has made it clear that I am to study medicine and come back to care for the women of India."[1]

Completing her medical studies at the Women's Medical School in Philadelphia and Cornell Medical School in New York City, Ida returned to India January 1, 1900. She carried with her a $10,000 donation to construct the Mary Taber Schell Memorial Hospital for women and children. Later, she founded the Christian Medical College and Hospital in Vellore, opening the door for women to study nursing and become physicians and surgeons.

When Ida heard of the dire need for medical care in surrounding villages, she acquired the first motorcar in the district. Although the one-cylinder Peugeot arrived in a crate needing assembly, it soon enabled Ida to open her first outlying dispensary at Gudiyattam, twenty miles away. On Wednesdays, Ida would pack the two-seater with medicines and head off toward Gudiyattam, stopping every few miles along the way to treat those in need.

Efforts like these made Ida a well-known figure in India, so well known that a letter addressed simply to "Dr. Ida, India" found its way to her in Vellore.

---

[1] Dorothy Jealous Scudder, *A Thousand Years in Thy Sight: The Story of the Scudder Missionaries of India* (New York: Vantage Press, 1984), 187.

established until a half-century later. Indicative of the social attitudes of the time, at the board's first meeting all the reports were read—and all the remarks were made—by men. However, the women soon overcame that barrier and, taking greater ownership in their own board, gave generous support to women in missions. Between 1844 and 1925, 245 women served as missionaries for the Reformed Church. These women did not go overseas merely as companions to their husbands. Eleanor Ackley Doty (Mrs. Elihu) founded the Amoy Girls' School in 1847. In 1855 Sarah Tracy Scudder (Mrs. Ezekiel) began to teach orphaned Indian girls (societal

Eleanor Ackley Doty and Elihu Doty

Reformed Church in America
Women in and for Mission*

1819   Harriet Waterbury Scudder is the first Reformed Church in America woman to serve in a foreign field.

1834   The Society for Promoting Female Education in China and the Far East is organized by Sara Doremus, the very first women's foreign missionary society to support independent missionary work in foreign lands.

1836   Azubah C. Condict is the first Reformed Church in America single woman missionary. She serves in Borneo under the auspices of the American Board of Commissioners for Foreign Missions.

1859   Caroline E. Adriance is the first single woman to serve under the Reformed Church in America Board of Foreign Missions. She serves in China from 1859 to 1864.

1860   Women's Union Missionary Society is founded by Sarah Doremus.

1875   Woman's Board of Foreign Missions is established by the General Synod.

1882   Women's Executive Committee of the Board of Domestic Missions is established.

1883   The *Mission Gleaner*, a periodical of the Woman's Board of Foreign Missions, is established to keep women informed.

1884   Emily M. Bussing, president of the Women's Executive Committee of the Board of Domestic Missions, secures the services of the Reverend Frank Hall Wright, who serves Native Americans.

1896   After serving four years as a missionary nurse in Baghdad, Amy Wilkes becomes the first single woman to serve in the Reformed Church in America's Arabian mission. She becomes Mrs. Samuel Zwemer.

1897   The Women's Board of Domestic Missions is established.

1946   The Woman's Board of Foreign Missions merged with the denominational Board of Foreign Missions.

1951   The Women's Board of Domestic Missions is merged with the denominational Board of Domestic Missions.

1955   Ruth Stafford Peale is elected president of the Board of Domestic Missions, the first woman to serve as president of a denominational board composed of men and women.

—*Some Unique Contributions of RCA Women, A Brief Historical Chronology, 1624-2004*, by Mary Kansfield. Privately published, 2003.

*While everyone baptized into the triune name is to be in mission for the gospel, of those specifically described as missionaries, from 1819 to 2000, the *Historical Directory of the Reformed Church in America, 1628-2000*, lists the names of 1,209 women who have served in the various mission fields.

expectations were such that reputable parents would not allow their daughters to be educated); this school eventually developed into the Chittoor Female Seminary. In Japan in 1870, Mary Kidder began teaching young Japanese women. Ferris Seminary at Yokohama developed out of her efforts.

These accomplishments notwithstanding, male chauvinism continued to permeate the church at home and abroad. In both China and India, medical missions were only for men—both as doctors and patients, as male American doctors were not allowed to treat women. The death of women in childbirth was common in both fields. Yet when in 1884 the Woman's Board found a woman doctor to respond to the pleas of Abby F. Woodruff (Mrs. John Van Nest) Talmage of Amoy, the all-male board of General Synod overruled the actions of the Woman's Board as "contrary to good policy and inexpedient." Nonetheless, a decade and a half later, the combination of gradual social change and the powerful impact of the Scudder missionary dynasty resulted in the appointment of Dr. Ida Scudder.

Amelia Lent Van Cleef

Women were so successful at raising money for foreign missions that in 1882 the General Synod called for similar societies to support work at home. The first project was to raise money to build parsonages for churches in the West. The leadership of these boards was totally in the hands of women, though chauvinism set up barriers to cooperation. When Amelia Lent Van Cleef (Mrs. Paul) of Jersey City and Cornelia Anderson of Fordham Manor, the Bronx, wrote to ministers asking them to organize the women in their congregations into auxiliaries for home missions— as requested by the General Synod—many ministers were "neglectful" of the request, while others "refused on the ground that women's place was in the home and not out attending meetings." These resourceful women wrote to women instead, held a convention, and organized sixty-six groups within a year.

While women were advancing in leadership in both the mission field and in mission support, in the secular world women were seeking the right to vote. Interestingly, the denominational paper, the *Christian Intelligencer*, supported women's suffrage, making the argument that women's votes would strengthen the movements for temperance and for peace. Evidently, most Reformed men believed they had enough support for temperance and peace within the church, for when the Classes of Montgomery and Albany overtured General Synod in 1918 to omit the word "male" from the requirements of the *Book of Church Order* (*BCO*) for elders and

Abby F. Woodruff Talmadge and John Van Nest Talmadge

Suffrage: The right or privilege of voting.

Temperance: Strictly speaking, moderation. The "Temperance Movement" was directed against the widespread abuse of alcohol, and its usual goal was abstinence. The hardships of the frontier, and later those of unregulated industrialization, resulted in widespread alcoholism, much as in our day poverty and unemployment has resulted in a higher incidence of drug addiction.

Church offices: In the Reformed Church in America the office holders are ministers of Word and sacrament, elders, deacons, and professors of theology.

deacons, the overture was "not entertained since it would mean friction and division out of proportion to any possible good that might accrue to any portion of the church." However, two years earlier the Reverend Anne Allebach, an ordained Mennonite minister, began a highly successful pastorate at the Sunnyside Reformed Church in Queens, New York.[4]

The question of opening the ordained offices to women turned into the next battle over the role of women in the Reformed Church. The question would remain a matter of contention for the next fifty years and more.

In 1921 three classes made similar overtures to General Synod, asking that the offices of elder and deacon be opened to women; the synod again refused to entertain the overtures. In 1922 the Classis of Philadelphia raised the stakes by asking synod to "remove all restrictions regarding holding of office by the female members of the church." The synod acknowledged that "the issue cannot be ignored" but maintained that "the time is not ripe for this action." Overtures requesting that "male" be stricken from the requirements for elders and deacons were presented to synod by a growing number of classes in 1923, 1932, 1936, 1941, 1945, and 1951. The 1952 synod, rather than rejecting the proposal unilaterally, sent it to the classes, where it was rejected. The 1955 synod voted to appoint a committee to study the matter of the ordination of women to the offices of elder and deacon. Two years later, synod voted that the report of

the committee be printed and distributed to the church. The committee recommended in 1958 that classes vote that "the offices in the RCA be open to men and women alike." It was defeated by the classes. A similar overture to the 1964 synod was not approved.

The 1967 synod again sent an overture for the deletion of the word "male" to the classes. This time, the vote was twenty-six for, nineteen against. The classes voting for the ordination of women as elders and deacons were now clearly in the majority, but the number still fell four classes short of the two-thirds required for a constitutional change. Overtures continued to be sent to synod in 1969, 1970, and 1971. In 1972 the classes approved the ordination of women to the offices of elder and deacon by a margin of thirty to fourteen, and women were at last allowed to be members of consistories.

The same synod of 1972 received an overture to ordain women to the office of minister of Word and sacrament. The synod adopted this overture and sent it to the classes, which rejected it with twenty-seven votes for and fourteen against, with three abstentions. Synods dealt with overtures concerning the issue again in 1973, 1974, and 1975. Again, the synod sent the overture to the classes; the vote this time was twenty-nine for, fifteen against, with a tied vote in one classis! The following year, there were again twenty-nine classes that voted yes, but this time sixteen classes voted no—one of those classes voting no by a single vote.

Our Kentucky Mountain Work

In 1900 the Women's Board of Domestic Mission sent Cora A. Smith, a Bible teacher and nurse, and Nora L. Gaut, a teacher, over the Boone Trail by horseback and wagon to Jackson County, Kentucky. Their work expanded rapidly:

> Most of the readers of the *Intelligencer* are aware that our own Women's Board has for ten years carried on an extremely successful mission work in Jackson county, Kentucky, where we have three missions, at McKee, at Gray Hawk and at Annville.
>
> At McKee we have a minister and his wife and three teachers, and an Academy with about one hundred and fifty pupils enrolled. In connection with McKee there are three outlying Sunday schools. At Gray Hawk we have a minister and his wife, the Rev. Benjamin De Young, a church, and all the activities growing out of it. We also have a little Sunday school at Adkin, back of Gray Hawk, and we are hoping to open others when our force at Gray Hawk is increased by the addition of a trained nurse. At Annville we have just opened a most promising school, with Mr. De Hollander as principal and two teachers. There are more than one hundred pupils enrolled, although the school has been in operation only a few months. We could bring this number up to the hundreds if we were able to care for the pupils. We are also conducting a fine mission work there. Large Sunday schools

Archives of the Reformed Church in America

Lincoln Hall, Annville Institute, Annville, Kentucky

> are maintained both in Annville and outlying districts.
>
> We are the only organization working in Jackson County, and we have a parish of ten thousand souls. There are, of course, occasional mountain preachers going through the county and working in a desultory way, and here and there are a very few resident preachers in the county, self appointed, uneducated men, but behind them there is no organization.
>
> There is no school work but our own in the county except the little public schools which are opened only a few months in the fall and are inadequate to provide even a good elementary education. This is the barest outline of what we are doing.[1]

Today the Reformed Church in America's mission partners in Appalachia are Jackson County Ministries and the Coalition for Appalachian Ministry (CAM). Jackson County Ministries works with young people, and a major component of CAM's ministry is its volunteer program, which focuses on building and renovating homes along with medical, educational, and community development services. The congregations in McKee, Gray Hawk, and Annville are members of Lake Erie Classis.

---

[1] "Our Kentucky Mountain Work," *Christian Intelligencer*, April 12, 1911, 234.

Archives of the Reformed Church in America

Daily Vacation Bible School at Adkins Chapel, Gray Hawk, Kentucky (1936)

In its wording for the offices of elder and deacon, the *Book of Church Order* had specified "males." To refer to the office of minister of Word and sacrament, however, the *BCO* used the neutral word, "persons." Until this point synod, in deference to the fact that only men had been ordained to that office, had taken the position that there would have to be a specific change in the *BCO* for women to be included. The classes would have to vote, by a two-thirds majority, to change the wording from "persons" to "men and women" or a gender-specific equivalent. However, knowing that two separate votes by the forty-five classes had each failed by a single delegate vote to attain the required two-thirds majority of classes, the patience of the majority was growing short. In 1974, the Classis of Rockland-Westchester ordained Joyce Stedge as a minister of Word and sacrament on the basis that she was a "person" as specified by the *BCO*. The synod did not respond to overtures that the ordination be declared null and void, because no complaint had come from the classis doing the ordaining. The synod did adopt a recommendation asking classes to refrain from ordaining women until such time as the *BCO* was amended.

In the government of the United States, changes in policy can be made either by legislation or by the courts, and each branch checks and

Donald J. Bruggink

Joyce Borgman (de Velder)

balances the other. The government of the Reformed Church in America followed a similar process in the matter of ordaining women as ministers of Word and sacrament. Since the will of the majority had been thwarted in the legislative process, some sought a judicial decision.

The classes of Brooklyn and Albany ordained Valerie De Marinus Miller and Joyce Borgman de Velder as ministers. Some members of those classes voted against the action and brought their complaint to the Committee on Judicial Business for adjudication. The committee declared that the term "persons" included by definition women as well as men, and it refused to overturn the ordinations of Miller and de Velder. As required by the *BCO*, the decision of the Committee on Judicial Business had to be referred to the General Synod to be sustained or denied. The General Synod of 1979, after a lengthy debate, voted by a wide margin to sustain the decision of its judiciary body that "persons" did include women. Women could now be ordained to the office of minister of Word and sacrament.

The struggle over the rightful role of women in the Reformed Church in America was by no means over. The Reformed Church is a biblically conservative community. During the period of intense debate on the subject, the conviction of many in

Sara M. Couch—To Love and Suffer with Them

Archives of the Reformed Church in America

Reformed Church missionary Sara M. Couch served in Japan from 1892 to 1946. She spent nearly three of those years in an interment camp in Tokyo during World War II. No one heard from her during those years.

When Japan surrendered in August 1945, Couch returned to her home in Nagasaki, the city devastated by one of two U.S. atomic bombs. Here's some of what she reported in an October 5, 1945, letter to friends back in the States:

Here I am in devastated Nagasaki, in a badly damaged house, but so thankful that peace has come and that I am at home again. O Jun san has been through a good deal, but is remarkably well, tho very thin. I did not know for a time whether she was living or whether the house was standing or not. The experiences of long internment have done much to fit me for living under present conditions.

O Jun san's third story room is probably hopeless, at least for the present. My study and bedroom and some other places leak very badly and we have had two typhoons in the three weeks since I returned....Our goods are in a mixed up mess, but practically no furniture, dishes or clothing were damaged....It is said that there is not one undamaged house in the city.

Urakami, the Mitsu Bishi munitions works, hospital, station and all that section are completely gone. So many people were killed. Two of our elders, the head of the hospital, and most of the doctors and nurses, and so many Middle School students, and many whole families were wiped out. Chnizei Gakuin, Akunoura church, Seikokwai and Greek churches are gone, but our church still stands, as does Kwassui.

...Just now active Christian work does not seem feasible. I have not yet been to church, no trams yet and I am not strong enough for the long walk. We have no pastor, only a very few attend the service. Some have left the city, some are ill, some have grown cold. We certainly need your prayers. Beyond praying, I believe just now the most I can do for the people of this city is to love them and suffer with them. We do not yet know the fate of many of our friends.[1]

---

[1] *Historical Highlights: Newsletter of the Historical Society of the Reformed Church in America*, vol. 6, No. 3, September 1985.

its minority that the Bible opposes the ordination of women was respected by those who were equally convinced that the Bible supports the ordination of women. The 1980 synod voted to add a "conscience clause" to allow any member of a classis who believed the Bible to be against the ordination of women to abstain from voting on or participating in any action involving a woman's ordination. At the same time, it forbade any minister or consistory member to vote against such action. In this way the Reformed Church guarded the right of the minority to follow their consciences while upholding the will of the majority. For such a policy of mutual respect, the members of the Reformed Church may justly be proud.

[1] From Mary Kansfield, *Some Unique Contributions of RCA Women: A Brief Historical Chronology, 1624-2004*, privately printed, 2003.
[2] Ibid.
[3] Mary Eleanor Anable Chamberlain, *Fifty Years in Foreign Fields: China, Japan, India, Arabia: A History of Five Decades of the Woman's Board of Foreign Missions, Reformed Church in America* (New York: Woman's Board of Foreign Missions, RCA, 1925), 7.
[4] Judith Nelson Gorsuch, "Rev. Anne Jemima Allebach (1874-1918)," *HEHP Quarterly*, vol. 3, no. 4, Winter 2000.

Resources for Further Study

Clarity, Conscience, and Church Order: Reflections on the Book of Church Order, http://www.rca.org/images/aboutus/archives/bcoreflections.pdf

Constitutional Theology, by Allan J. Janssen. The Historical Series of the Reformed Church in America. Grand Rapids: Eerdmans, 2000.

Hands, Hearts, and Voices: Women Who Followed God's Call, by Una H. Ratmeyer. New York: Reformed Church Press, 1995.

History of Women's Involvement in the RCA, http://www.rca.org/lead/women/history.php

Letters to Hazel: Ministry within the Women's Board of Foreign Missions of the Reformed Church in America, by Mary Kansfield. Historical Series of the Reformed Church in America. Grand Rapids: Eerdmans, 2004.

Patterns and Portraits: Women in the History of the Reformed Church in America, ed. Renee S. House and John W. Coakley. The Historical Series of the Reformed Church in America. Grand Rapids: Eerdmans, 1999.

The 'Conscience Clause,' 1980

The Book of Church Order, The Reformed Church in America, 2002 edition, Part II, Article 2, Section 7, reads:

The classis shall examine students of theology for licensure, and licensed candidates for the ministry for ordination. If individual members of the classis find that their consciences, as illuminated by Scripture, would not permit them to participate in the licensure, ordination, or installation of women as ministers, they shall not be required to participate in decisions or actions contrary to their consciences, but may not obstruct the classis in fulfilling its responsibility to arrange for the care, ordination, and installation of women candidates and ministers by means mutually agreed upon by such women and the classis.

15

Justice on Earth

Parade for women's suffrage, New York City, May 6, 1912.

Library of Congress

Concerning the role of church and magistrate (government and state), Calvin taught that the church was to instruct the magistrate in the ways of God, and the magistrate in turn was to support and protect the church. This position became part of the Belgic Confession, and thus part of the constitution of the church in the Netherlands.

In its early years in America, the Dutch church was so enthusiastic about the new nation, and so preoccupied with its own needs, one might have thought that it had turned its back on its historic responsibility to be a teacher to the state. In fact, the church gradually did come to fulfill this role.

At the beginning of the twentieth century, the General Synod's Committee on Public Morals spoke to two major issues of social concern: temperance and Sabbath observance. The weight of these issues is lost on those unfamiliar with the times. An influx of more than twenty-eight million immigrants between 1860 and 1920 meant cheap labor, with workers forced to toil under incredibly harsh conditions just to survive.[1] The result was pandemic alcoholism, in many ways similar to the scourge of drugs in our own day. The church was, in fact, far more involved in social action with reference to alcoholism in the first quarter of the century than it was with reference to drugs in the last quarter of the century.

The position of the church against alcoholic beverages and saloons carried it into the political field as prohibitionists worked to ratify the Eighteenth Amendment, which became part of the U.S. Constitution in 1920. From 1922 onward, recommendations in support of the Eighteenth Amendment were before the synod. In 1932 the report of the Committee on Public Morals and Industrial Relations concerned itself entirely with the government's failure to enforce prohibition and the possible alternatives. The position of the church for over half a century was voluntary total abstinence, which was seen as an ethical rather than a legal

President Herbert Hoover surrounded by the Women's Christian Temperance Union

Events referenced in the chapter are below the line. Other historical events are above the line.

1900	1925	1950	1975	2000

Above the line:

1920 18th Amendment

1927 Lindbergh flies NY to Paris

1933 Barmen Declaration

1933 Hitler becomes German chancellor

1935 U. S. Social Security Act

1938 Germany annexes Austria & Czechoslovakia

1939 Nazi Germany attacks Poland

1945 Peace in Europe & Pacific

1973 Peace in Vietnam

Below the line:

1924 Synod chides Senate on failure to support Court of International Justice

1929 Middle Collegiate Church Education for World Peace

1934 Synod offers moral support to Christians in Germany

1940 Church World Service organized

1940 Overtures opposed to Social Security

1950-69 Everett Dirksen, senator

1953 Synod reverses itself on Social Security

1965 CAC urges political solutions in SE Asia

1967 Right of conscientious objection

1979 Arie Brouwer, "Choose Life"

1981 El Salvador White House protest

War-Time Service

Eighty young men were inducted into Hope College's Student Army Training Corps in October 1918. It was wartime, enrollment was down—more than eighty men had left the college for military service during the previous school year—and the campus had been offered as a training ground for new recruits.

Under the command of Lt. Jacobsen of the United States Army, the corps took over Carnegie Gymnasium as barracks and officer's quarters. Van Vleck Hall served as a dispensary and infirmary, and the third floor of Van Raalte Hall became the mess hall. Army officers taught military

Hope College Collection at the Joint Archives of Holland

Hope Women's Patriotic League in downtown Holland, WWI

courses; college faculty taught the academic subjects. Uniformed corps members marched to chapel and to classes.

A year earlier, Hope women had organized the Patriotic League. Under the supervision of the dean of women, the league organized a letter-writing campaign that kept in touch with Hope servicemen. It also set up a booth in downtown Holland, collecting more than $15,000 by selling government bonds.

World War I ended in November 1918. A month later Hope bid farewell to the Student Army Training Corps. Of the 150 students who left campus for military service, 147 returned to pick up their studies where they left off.

---

imperative. This position was reaffirmed in 1957, although it was then openly recognized that not everyone was of the same mind on the subject.

The concern for Sabbath observance was twofold. First, it represented a continuance with the Puritan portion of America's past—a setting apart of the Lord's Day for worship, biblical instruction, and rest. That tradition was believed to be under attack by the waves of immigrants from Ireland and southern Europe, whose concept of keeping the Lord's Day was very different from that of Protestant America. Secondly, Sabbath observance served the social purpose of guaranteeing a day of rest for people at the bottom of the social structure, who often worked sixty hours per week.

However, the issues that occupied

the synod perhaps more than any others in the twentieth century were issues concerning peace. Peace issues were the first to move synod to address government directly, rather than simply to urge action upon individuals. In 1924 the synod chided the United States Senate for its dilatoriness in affirming the Court of International Justice. It addressed Presidents Coolidge and Hoover with appreciation for their efforts on behalf of peace and disarmament. While the enthusiasm for disarmament may seem strange in this time of multibillion-dollar armament budgets, this was the post-World War I era. The memory of the millions who had died in the trenches of France was still fresh. Many people still held to the idealism of America's entry into "the war to end wars," and plans like the Kellogg Peace Pact were proposed to

Conscientious objectors: Those who refuse to serve in armed forces based on moral principles.

Eighteenth Amendment: The amendment to the Constitution of the United States outlawing the manufacture, transportation, and sale of alcoholic beverages (1919-1933).

Kellogg Peace Pact: A treaty (1928) signed by seventy-two nations renouncing war as an instrument of national policy. The treaty retained the right of self-defense, along with commitments to previous alliances. It contained no mechanism for enforcement.

reduce armaments. In 1929 four meetings were held in the Middle Collegiate Church in New York City under the auspices of the synod's Committee on Education for World Peace. Several resolutions were proposed and all were adopted, except for the one on the League of Nations.[2]

The international scene continued to concern synod. In 1934 it expressed support for Christians in Germany. The 1938 synod adopted a resolution renouncing war. The 1940 synod passed a resolution to stay out of war. On December 7, 1941, Japan attacked Pearl Harbor. While the church and its members supported the nation throughout World War II, the church did not fall into the rhetorical excesses of WWI, and it also supported conscientious objectors, albeit without overwhelming enthusiasm.

It's also interesting to note social issues of the early twentieth century that the Reformed Church did not address. For example, in 1932, in the depth of the Depression, the Committee on Public Morals and Industrial Relations had nothing to say about the economic situation or widespread unemployment. And while the Reformed Church in America was a charter member of the Federal Council of Churches in 1906, synod said nothing about its

The Four Chaplains—Comrades in Heroism

The story of the four chaplains is more about grace than justice. On February 3, 1943, the SS Dorchester was 150 miles off Cape Farewell, Greenland, with 902 soldiers and crew on board. With enemy U-boats on the prowl, the captain had ordered servicemen to sleep in their clothes and life jackets. Many, because of discomfort, disobeyed orders.

The four chaplains included John P. Washington, a Roman Catholic; Alexander Goode, a Jew; George L. Fox, a Methodist; and Clark V. Poling, from the Reformed Church in America. Poling attended Hope College and graduated from Rutgers in 1933 and from Yale Divinity School in 1936. He was ordained in the Reformed Church in America and, in 1938, became pastor of the prestigious First Reformed Church in Schenectady, New York. With the advent of America's entry into World War II,

Poling felt called to enter the chaplaincy.

The ship captain's fears were well founded. At 12:55 a.m. a torpedo hit the Dorchester amidship below the water line, knocking out all power and lights. Pandemonium ensued. The chaplains reached the deck, did what they could to calm the men, offer prayers, and comfort the dying. They opened a locker of life jackets and began distributing them to those without. When the life jackets were gone, engineer Grady Clark witnessed an amazing act. The chaplains stripped off their own life jackets and gave them to the next men in line.

The chaplains were last seen on the slanting deck, arms entwined, offering prayers. In the water, with a life jacket, private William B. Bednar later remembered, "I could hear the chaplains preaching courage. Their voices were the only thing that kept me going."

By 1:24 a.m. the Dorchester had slipped beneath the icy waters. There were 230 survivors.

The four chaplains were awarded a Special Medal for Heroism, a postage stamp was issued in their honor, and the First Reformed Church in Schenectady honors its former pastor with the Poling Chapel.

efforts to establish a minimum wage, to reduce the work week to forty hours, or to eliminate the abuse of women and children in the workplace. (However, the 1910 synod did endorse the council's efforts furthering peace.) In 1934 the Committee on Social Welfare found the synod willing to pass its resolutions on temperance, gambling, and race relations but failed to find support for its protest against child labor. (Two years later, the synod had a change of heart and adopted a resolution against child labor.) In brief, the Reformed Church, along with most of Protestantism, was not inclined to become involved in issues involving economic structures.

A case study on the ambivalence the church felt in its relation to governmental involvement in economic life can be seen in its reaction to Social Security. The Social Security Act was created during the Depression to protect the laboring classes and provide for their retirement. As the act began to be expanded to cover more wage earners, the question arose as to whether clergy were also to be

Church World Service

Archives of the Reformed Church in America

In 1944 the Committee on the Reformed Church Emergency Fund recommended a denominationwide appeal for $175,000 for the "vast and varied needs created by the war."[1] In 1945 the classes responded with $158,296, increasing that amount to $271,719 the following year. The money was channeled through the World Council of Churches.

The Committee has adopted the principle not to administer any relief directly, but to clear every appeal through the Geneva office of the World Council of Churches. Numerous appeals have come to us from individuals and organizations. We, however, at this far distance, are in no position to judge the legitimacy of these appeals....Working in this way we are assured that our contributions for both physical and spiritual needs will be administered where they are most needed.[2]

In 1946 the Reformed Church in America joined several other denominations through the Federal Council of Churches to establish Church World Service to coordinate overseas aid. Its initial program assisted churches to reestablish themselves after the war by supplementing minister's salaries, constructing wooden structures to serve as places of worship, and providing Christian literature and material support.

In 1947 Church World Service created the Christian Rural Overseas Program (CROP). Friendship Trains began crossing the United States, picking up corn, wheat, rice, and beans to be distributed around the world by CROP Friendship Food Ships.

---

[1] *Minutes of General Synod of the Reformed Church in America*, 1944, 164.
[2] Ibid., 1946, 172.

included. The 1940 synod received sixteen overtures utterly opposed to including ministers or lay workers. The reason given was that this would break down the barriers between church and state. That position was reaffirmed by the synod of 1941. However, by 1943 the Committee on the Minister's Fund began to question the synod's stand.

In 1951 the Classis of Schenectady overtured synod requesting that the Federal Council of Churches represent its member churches before Congress to seek enactment of legislation that would allow the voluntary participation of clergy in Social Security. Synod rejected the overture. However, before that synod adjourned, it appointed a special committee to study the matter. The committee reported in 1953 that there had been a substantial shift in opinion. The committee rejected the contention that voluntary participation would break down the barriers between church and state and lead to state control of the church. By 1955 a poll of Reformed Church ministers, to which 392 responded, indicated that 342 had

A.J. Muste—One of Our Own

Time magazine named him "The Number One U.S. Pacifist."[1] J. Edgar Hoover labeled him a "Communist fronter."[2] Martin Luther King, Jr., and other prominent black civil rights leaders considered him a trusted friend and supporter.[3] He was one of the great leaders for peace and justice in the United States in the twentieth century, and he was a product of the Reformed Church in America.

Born in the small town of Zierikzee in the Netherlands in 1885, Abraham J. Muste immigrated with his parents to western Michigan at the age of six. Four uncles had preceded them, started small businesses in Grand Rapids, and paid their way to follow.

Muste's uncles belonged to a Christian Reformed church, but elders at that church refused to accept the family by transfer of membership from the *Hereformde Kerk* in the Netherlands, requiring instead a new confession of faith. Rather than provide the new confession, the Mustes turned to the Fourth Reformed Church, which accepted their letter of transfer.

Muste attended preparatory school in Holland, Michigan, and went on to Hope College. At Hope he captained the basketball team to two championships, was editor of the *Anchor*, and delivered the valedictory address at his graduation in 1905 on the subject of discontent and doubt (Hope College continues to host the A. J. Muste Peace Lectures each year). After teaching Greek and Latin for a year at Northwestern Classical Academy in Orange City, Iowa (where he pursued his college romance with future wife Anna Huizenga, daughter of the Rock Valley Reformed Church minister), he enrolled at New Brunswick Theological Seminary.

While at New Brunswick, Muste's spiritual search and quest for knowledge led him to take courses at New York's Columbia University and after graduation to pursue a masters degree at Union Theological Seminary. Muste's only Reformed Church pastorate was at the Fort Washington Collegiate Church in Washington Heights, New York. He served that congregation for five years, resigning after growing restless under the

Hope College Collection of the Joint Archives of Holland

A.J. Muste arrested for peaceful protest of the Vietnam War outside the induction center on Whitehall Street, New York, December 15, 1966

elected Social Security, 45 had not, and the rest were undecided. The Reformed Church had done an about-face, and even as it had lost its fear of control by the state, it was simultaneously emboldened to carry out its responsibility of speaking to the state.

World War II brought a transition in the involvement of the Reformed Church in America in issues of social action. A theologian of the church, the Reverend Dr. Eugene P. Heideman, has suggested that the doctrine of justification by faith for salvation came to be seen with the added dimension of justification by faith for salvation and for justice. He notes that in the church's twentieth-century confession of faith, *Our Song of Hope*, the doctrine of the atonement continues to insist that God's righteousness be satisfied. "But," Heideman adds, "it also insists that in Christ's death 'the justice of God is established.' By using the word 'established,' it links the atonement of Christ to the righteousness and peace of God in the Old Testament."[3] "Justification by faith cannot be separated from justice on earth."[4]

confines of traditional Reformed theology.

According to a Sunday *New York Herald* report of the time, some church leaders reacted to Muste's action with anger. The senior pastor of the [Marble] Collegiate Reformed Church, Dr. David J. Burrell, blamed Union Theological Seminary "for the whole trouble," telling the *Herald* reporter that he was "quite satisfied that this institution was the direct cause of Mr. Muste's loss of faith." On the other hand, the eminent Henry E. Cobb, senior pastor of the West End Collegiate Church, did not accept this view. While he mourned the loss of Muste from Dutch Reformed life, he acknowledged that the dissident "would work more happily...in a body freer theologically than our Reformed Church."[4]

On the eve of World War I, Muste became pastor of a Congregational church in Newtonville, Maryland, where he became an outspoken pacifist. From there Muste was drawn to the Quakers and to the Fellowship of Reconciliation, an international movement opposed to war. For two years he was the executive director of the union of textile workers, and he participated in many of the strikes in the mining, automobile, and textile industries in the 1930s. For a short period from December 1934 to

Hope College Collection of the
Joint Archives of Holland

July 1936, he was affiliated with the Trotskyist Workers Party of the United States. Disillusioned, Muste returned to his religious roots, spending the rest of his life putting faith into action— supporting opponents of conscription during World War II, denouncing the nuclear arms race, and mobilizing protests against the war in Vietnam.

I am a Christian believer. I was brought up in the Christian church. After some years during which I was a thorough-going Marxist-Leninist, renouncing all religion as [the] "opiate of the people" and the church as nothing but a bulwark of a reactionary status quo, I returned to the church and to faith in the love of God as revealed in Jesus Christ as the one means of salvation for the individual and for mankind. I must find a sanction for my pacifism, therefore, in my Christian faith, and it is at this point that I naturally begin the argument.[5]

[1] *Time*, July 10, 1939.
[2] *New York Post*, March 20, 1957.
[3] Jo Ann Ooiman Robinson, *Abraham Went Out: A Biography of A.J. Muste* (Philadelphia: Temple University Press, 1981), xv.
[4] Ibid., 17.
[5] A. J. Muste, *Non-Violence in an Aggressive World* (New York: Harper & Bros., 1940), 11.

Everett Dirksen—Senator from the RCA

Everett Dirksen, long-time Republican congressman from Illinois, was a member of the Second Reformed Church in Pekin, Illinois. He served in the United States House of Representatives from 1933 to 1949, and in the Senate from 1950 to 1969, where he was minority leader for ten years. A skilled legislator and a theatrical speaker, Dirksen was one of the most influential senators during the turbulent 1960s. In February of 1964, the House passed a sharp civil rights bill, HR7152. Because Dirksen questioned certain aspects of the bill and reacted strongly when pressured by a Chicago civil rights group, he was perceived by many to be opposed to passing a civil rights bill.

On April 29, 1964, five members of the Christian Action Commission of the RCA met Dirksen in his Senate office to urge passage of that crucial civil rights legislation. The meeting had been arranged by the Reverend Charles Ausherman, then pastor of the South Branch Reformed Church. It took place the day before Ausherman's birthday.

When the delegation arrived, Dirksen asked for Ausherman by name. He said he had received word that Ausherman's pregnant wife had been in a serious car accident on her way to purchase him a birthday gift. "I have brought up my car and driver to take you to the airport," Dirksen said. "My secretary has held the New York Air Shuttle, which is waiting for you. A private plane at Kennedy will take you to your local airport. I am very sorry for you and your family."[1]

Ausherman's son, born two months premature, survived the accident. His wife died. Senator Dirksen, involved in a titanic struggle over civil rights, found time to send a personal note of condolence.

Opponents at the end of March had begun a lengthy filibuster to prevent passage of the civil rights bill. Dirksen, using his considerable influence and skill, proposed modest changes in the bill to sway moderates to vote for cloture. On June 10, after fifty-seven days, the filibuster ended, and on June 19, after a total of eighty-seven days of debate, the Senate passed the Civil Rights Act of 1964—landmark legislation in which Everett McKinley Dirksen played a crucial part.

* * * * * * * * * * *

Other Reformed Church members in national public service include:

Martin Van Buren, the eighth president of the United States, was a life-long member of the Kinderhook Reformed Church in Kinderhook, New York.

Theodore Roosevelt, the twenty-sixth president of the United States, was a member of St. Nicholas Collegiate Church in New York City. As governor of New York, Roosevelt had his own pew at the First Church in Albany.

Joseph Bradley, a member of the United States Supreme Court, was an elder in the Reformed Church. He was chosen to be the neutral member of the commission that decided the presidential contest between Rutherford Hayes and Samuel Tilden

Frederick Frelinghuysen, also a Reformed Church elder, was secretary of state during President Arthur's administration.

---

[1] "Time Can't Erase the Tears We Shed," *Church Herald*, March 1989, 16.

More and more the synod entered into direct correspondence with presidents, prime ministers, and legislatures. A myriad of issues were addressed. The Christian Action Commission (CAC) produced a plethora of position papers. Most of the papers failed to produce debate because they were never brought to a vote, other than simply to "be received." Perhaps the purpose of the CAC was only to present its papers for information and edification, but the frequent result was that the papers were considered by too few, and so never fulfilled their educative purpose.

One major issue about which the Christian Action Commission reached a conclusion (unlike abortion or homosexuality) was the conflict in Vietnam. An overview of the role of the CAC gives insight into the commission's usefulness and limitations.

Already in 1965 the rising conflict in Southeast Asia caused the CAC to issue an "Addendum to the Report of the Christian Action Commission to the 1965 General Synod," which urged upon the United States the participation of the international community in reaching a political solution (*Minutes of General Synod*, 1964, 220-22). The following year it continued to decry the conflict, supporting the National Council of Churches study that urged the parties to keep trying to reach a political solution (*MGS*, 1966, 227-29). In 1967 the emphasis was on "The Right of Dissent and Conscientious Objection," with the CAC endorsing the right of such objection to military service.

In 1968 the CAC statement on Vietnam (*MGS*, 1968, 202-204) was followed by "The War, the Draft, and Conscience" (204-205), which called on churches to support both those in the armed forces and conscientious objectors, and "Ethical Aspects of Compulsory Military Conscription" (205-208). However, lest the impression be left that Vietnam was the only concern of the CAC, as usual it considered a variety of other issues. Its 1968 reports also include "Response to the Urban Crisis," "Fair Housing and the Law," "International Olympic Games," "A Christian Concern for the Poor," "Church Property as an Expression of Christian Social Concern," a "Proposed Policy Statement on Withholding Consumer Patronage to Secure Justice," "Conventions on Abolition of Forced Labor, Abolition of Slavery, and the Political Rights of Women," and "Abortion Law Reform" (208-18).

In 1969 the "Statement on Vietnam" was tenth on the list of issues of the CAC; it consisted of an affirmation of the beginnings of a peace process in Paris (*MGS*, 1969, 247-48). In 1970, following the CAC's four-page "Statement on Vietnam," the synod adopted the commission's resolutions urging the withdrawal of American troops (214-17). However, a motion that the General Synod become the repository of the draft cards of conscientious objectors was defeated 190 to 50, with 14 abstentions (218).

In 1971 the issue of Vietnam was treated in a paper entitled, "Military-Industrial Complex," which included resolutions to

Arie R. Brouwer—
Advocate for Social Justice

While A. J. Muste is certainly the most widely known pacifist with Reformed Church origins, his position at the time of World War I was sufficiently unpopular that his stay in the denomination was short. In contrast, the Reverend Arie R. Brouwer advocated for social justice in many areas and remained throughout his life an active member in the Reformed Church in America.

Born in Northwest Iowa, Brouwer was a Hope College graduate and a member of a highly intellectual and conservative cadre at Western Theological Seminary. He went on to pastorates in Byron Center, Michigan, and Passaic, New Jersey, and then became general secretary (the highest administrative office) of the Reformed Church in America from 1977 to 1983.

Brouwer then became deputy general secretary of the World Council of Churches, where he was a candidate for the secretariat. Unfortunately, President Reagan's speech calling the Soviet Union "the Evil Empire" made it impossible for the Soviet delegation to vote for Brouwer, and a compromise candidate was sought. However, the National Council of Churches of Christ in America soon tapped Brouwer to be its general secretary, a position he served with vigor until 1989.

Throughout his service, Brouwer's passion for social justice was part of his Christian commitment. In the struggle against apartheid in South Africa, he testified before the Eloff Commission in South Africa in 1983 and was arrested in 1985 for demonstrating in front of the South African Embassy in Washington D.C. Brouwer was also a founder of Bread for the World; he was involved in issues of race, including freedom for Jews in the Soviet Union; and he spoke out on the issues of American intervention in El Salvador, the arms race,

impending nuclear annihilation, militarism, and peace. He was, in short, the preeminent spokesperson for social justice in the Reformed Church in America in the 1970s and 80s.

In 1979, with the cold war at its height, and the threat of nuclear annihilation hanging over the world, church leaders from the Soviet Union and the United States met in Geneva. Brouwer volunteered to do a first draft of the conference joint statement. The following, called "Choose Life," is quoted in part:

I call heaven and earth as witness against you this day, that I have set before you life and death, blessing and curse. Therefore, choose life, that you and your descendants may live.

Deuteronomy 30:19

We make this appeal as servants of Christ gathered from among the churches of the USA and the USSR. We have been drawn together across the differences of language and culture by our common Christian calling to foster life in the midst of a race towards death. We affirm our unity in confessing Christ as Lord and Saviour.

WCC Photo, Peter Williams

Praying for peace in St. Pierre (Calvin's church) in Geneva, Switzerland, November 17, 1985, on the occasion of the Reagan-Gorbachev summit meeting.

Gathered in Geneva during the season of Lent we have been especially conscious of the sufferings of our Lord who offered Himself that we might have life and have it abundantly (John 10:10). From our faith in Christ, the All Powerful, the Conqueror of Death, we have drawn strength to choose life in spite of the spreading power of death.

We're convinced that the arms race cannot be won, it can only be lost. All of us have long been aware of the nuclear terror. Many people have accepted it as an inescapable part of our contemporary world. Numerous voices in the church have been raised against it in both our countries. Our experience in this consultation now compels us to cry out against it with one voice. The existence of forces having the capacity to devastate our planet not once or twice, but many times, is absurd and cannot be tolerated. It must be confronted and overcome in the name of the Christ who lives and reigns forever.[1]

Arie Brouwer leads the Good Friday procession past the White House, accompanied by Robert Neff, general secretary, Church of the Brethren; Kenneth Taegarten, president, the Christian Church (Disciples of Christ); and Avery Post, president, the United Church of Christ.

In 1981 the cold war also affected policies within the Americas. Corrupt governments in Central and South America were supported by the United States as presumed bulwarks against communism. Upon the occasion of the appropriation of another 25 million dollars to be added to the 10 million in military aid already appropriated for the small country of El Salvador—the country in which right-wing death squads had assassinated Archbishop Oscar Romero and had more recently killed four nuns—Brouwer, with other church leaders, participated in a Good Friday demonstration in front of the White House, carrying a cross and reading the following statement in Lafayette Park:

We have come here on this Good Friday to witness to the sufferings of Christ in the sufferings of the people of El Salvador. We remember our brother and father in God, Archbishop Oscar Romero, who during last year's Lenten season was martyred for his ministry to the people of El Salvador. In the midst of these memories, and in the face of violent death rampaging across El Salvador, we are drawn together in the communion of Christ's suffering. We gather to pray to God and to petition the government.

We have come first to protest the sufferings and crucifixion of the Salvadorian people. For decades, the people of El Salvador have endured all manner of injustice, cruelty and barbarism. In this very week we call Holy, they are under the cross. Daily, mothers see their sons stripped, beaten and murdered. Just as the powerful in Jerusalem were prepared to crucify our Lord in order to maintain their positions, so the powerful in El Salvador are prepared to crucify a whole people in order to maintain their power.

We have carried our protest to Washington because our government is increasing the power of the persecutors through new and larger grants of military aid and through military advisors. The crucifixion of our Lord depended finally on the imperial power of Rome. The crucifixion of the Salvadorian people depends finally upon the imperial power of the United States. We are gathered here to say to our government—Stop the crucifixion.[2]

---

[1] Arie R. Brouwer, *Ecumenical Testimony*, The Historical Series of the Reformed Church in America. Grand Rapids: Eerdmans, 1991, 9.
[2] Ibid., 20.

withdraw all U.S. forces from Indo-China as soon as possible and to continue support for conscientious objectors (*MGS*, 1971, 226-28). That synod also heard from Glenn Pontier, a seminarian and conscientious objector, and it adopted recommendations to support a legal defense fund for objectors. A recommendation to designate the Communion offering for the fund was defeated, however, while support for freedom of conscience for Glenn Pontier was adopted. The recommendation to designate an ad hoc committee to receive draft cards on behalf of the synod was also defeated (230).

In 1972, the CAC's opposition to the war in Vietnam continued with recommendations addressing sorrow at death, the government's misuse of $200 billion for war while needs at home were neglected, and the need to "study the effects of amnesty." Synod adopted all of these, but it did not endorse a resolution expressing regret at supporting a repressive regime in South Vietnam. By 1973 peace had at last come, but the conflicted nature of the country, and the church, was evident in the synod's response to CAC recommendations related to its report, "Amnesty" (*MGS*, 1972, 203-207). A weak recommendation to "learn about" was adopted, while one to grant a "broad general amnesty" was not (208). At the same time the report, "A Crisis in Stewardship," which decried the waste of resources in warfare, was adopted with all of its recommendations (208-12).

So what did the Christian Action Commission accomplish? It added its voice to those in the nation who opposed the war. It also offered support and encouragement to those who on conscientious grounds refused to serve in the military and were willing to be jailed for their stand. Obviously it failed to convince even a majority on many issues. It did, however, attempt to offer a specifically Christian viewpoint, which encouraged a certain amount of discussion. In a sense, the commission helped the church return to its theological roots and assume responsibility to instruct civil government.

Resources for Further Study

Clarity, Conscience, and Church Order: Reflections on the Book of Church Order,
http://www.rca.org/images/aboutus/archives/bcoreflections.pdf

Constitutional Theology, by Allan J. Janssen. The Historical Series of the Reformed Church in America. Grand Rapids: Eerdmans, 2000.

Hands, Hearts, and Voices: Women Who Followed God's Call, by Una H. Ratmeyer. New York: Reformed Church Press, 1995.

History of Women's Involvement in the RCA,
http://www.rca.org/lead/women/history.php

Patterns and Portraits: Women in the History of the Reformed Church in America, ed. Renee S. House and John W. Coakley. The Historical Series of the Reformed Church in America. Grand Rapids: Eerdmans, 1999.

[1] Sydney Ahlstrom, *A Religious History of the American People*, 735.
[2] Mildred W. Schuppert, *A Digest and Index of the Minutes of the General Synod of the Reformed Church in America, 1906-1957*, 283.
[3] Eugene P. Heideman, "Heidelberg and Grand Rapids: Reformed Theology and the Mission of the Church," in James W. Van Hoeven, ed., *Word and World: Reformed Theology in America*, The Historical Series of the Reformed Church in America (Grand Rapids: Eerdmans, 1986), 115.
[4] Ibid., 116.

16

Two Nations, One Church

Monarch Reformed Church, Alberta, established 1909

For centuries, churches typically have been circumscribed by political boundaries. The Kingdom of Edessa in the third century was known as the first Christian kingdom. Jumping ahead twelve centuries to post-Reformation times, we find Reformed churches organized by nation in Switzerland, France, Hungary, Poland, the German principalities, Bohemia, England, Scotland, and the Netherlands. Although the Dutch church in America maintained its relationship to the Classis of Amsterdam even after the British took control of New Netherland in 1664, the Revolutionary War resulted in the severing of those ties. Nonetheless, circumstances and faith eventually did create a single church in two nations—Canada and the United States.

The story of the Reformed Church in America (RCA) in Canada is the story of two nations and one church. It is also the story of the third major immigration of Dutch to America. The first was between 1613 and 1664; it gave rise to the Reformed Church in the eastern states, principally New York and New Jersey. The second wave of Dutch immigrants began arriving in 1847 and settled in the Midwest, principally Michigan, Illinois, Wisconsin, and Iowa. The third migration was to Canada after World War II.

This third migration was not, however, the first extension of the Reformed Church into Canada. After the Revolutionary War, many of the Dutch who had supported the Crown found it desirable to continue to live under British rule.[1] In 1784 four townships were laid out in Upper Canada (now Ontario). The township of Kingston included many Dutch who had emigrated from the Hudson and Mohawk Valleys. More than five hundred people of Dutch origin settled in Ernestown and Fredricksburgh townships. The township of Adolphustown included settlers from the Albany area who came under the leadership of Captain Peter van Alstine. Together these four townships covered an area extending almost fifty miles from Kingston to Belleville.

In the years immediately following the Revolution, only one Dutch Reformed pastor ministered in all of Canada. The Reverend John Broeffle was a pastor to settlers to the northeast, near Quebec, and simultaneously served churches in New York State. In

---

Events referenced in the chapter are below the line. Other historical events are above the line.

1945
Peace, Netherlands physically devastated

1945
Dutch gov't encourages emigration

1945
A Bridge Too Far

1783-87
Settlement of Loyalists in Canada: 100 acres to heads of families, 50 acres to each member

1874
Bell's telephone

1907
Financial panic

1940
Nazi Germany conquers Netherlands

1812-14
War of 1812

1834
Cyrus McCormick's reaper

1857
John Deere's steel plow

1890-93
World-wide depression

1914-18
World War I

1776
Revolutionary War

1800	1825	1850	1875	1900	1925	1950	1975	2000

1798
Rev. Robert McDowell appointed missionary to Dutch in Canada

1809-10
Rev. John Beattie, missionary to Canada

1810
Fourteen churches established by McDowell

1818
Without adequate support, McDowell becomes "father" of the Presbyterian Church of Canada

1909
Church established in Monarch, Canada, first of two churches organized 1909-1948

1949
Canadian immigrants seek affiliation with RCA

1962
Classis Ontario formed with 19 churches

1993
Regional Synod of Canada

1953
NHK sends Bons, Heldering, Molenaar, Boekhoven, van Kuiken, & Falkenburg to serve

John Beattie—A Passion for the North

John Beattie kept a detailed diary. He was an early Reformed Church missionary with a passion for the Canadian north. Born in Salem, New York, in 1784, Beattie was ordained by the Classis of New York in 1809.

On May 14, 1810, Beattie left his Long Island home on one of his missionary tours—he was gone five months. He boarded a sloop and made his way to Albany: "Under this adverse providence, during these four days, I have had some gloomy reflections—a long journey before me—an entire stranger in the land to which I am sent—a wilderness to pass through before I reach missionary ground—my horse in the meantime oppressed by standing still on board, and starving for want of provisions. These considerations combined depressed my spirits, and rendered these four days gloomy. But I still enjoyed one consolation, I trusted that God, who called me to the mission work, would conduct me safely through."[1]

On his way between Albany and Lake Ontario in Canada, Beattie gives a vivid description of the bad roads—"the worst road that it is possible for the human mind to form any conception of"— "horrid bridges," and "the mosquitoes were the occasion of more misery to me than all the rest of my difficulties combined." Of his lodgings: "An old weather-worn log house covered with bark—a dismal inn to the weary traveler." He slept on the floor and had to maintain "an arduous contest with an innumerable multitude of little nocturnal beasts which inhabited the place." He found the roads in Canada even worse, causing his horse to lose a shoe and become lame. Of his mission field in Canada he noted: "The morals of the people are said to be very much corrupted, and there is little or no religion in the place."

[1] Quotes from John Beattie's diary are recorded in *A Manual of the Reformed Church in America 1628-1902*, Board of Education of the Reformed Church in America, 1902, 307.

1798 the Classis of Albany sent the Reverend Robert McDowell, the son of a British army officer, to minister in Canada—presumably to Dutch expatriates. His efforts led to considerable success; six churches were organized, numbering more than four hundred families. While accepting calls to three of the churches he had founded, McDowell also traveled as far as two hundred miles west and seventy-five miles north to communities that wanted to hear the gospel. Unable to sustain this pace, in 1806 McDowell solicited the General Synod for ministers to help him in the work. The names of at least seven "missionaries" appear, men who had pastorates in the States but ministered briefly in Canada. McDowell's personal records are missing several pages, but the entries that remain show 1,638 baptisms and 870 weddings, and that by 1810 he had established fourteen churches.

The minutes of General Synod reveal little about how the War of 1812 changed the way the church in the United States viewed its British counterpart in Canada. While as late as 1818 it was reported that there were still eleven Reformed Dutch churches in the Province of Upper Canada, it also was observed that "circumstances prevent us from contributing in the manner that is desirable and that would provide those benefits which we would expect to derive." Also in 1818 McDowell joined the Presbytery of the Canadas; he subsequently became known as the

United Church of Canada: Established in 1925 by uniting Methodists, the Congregational Union of Canada, the Council of Local Union Churches, most Presbyterian churches, and the Canadian Conference of Evangelical Union Brethren.

father of the Presbyterian Church in Canada. The one church that had spanned two nations was torn asunder by a war between those nations. The ties of ethnicity and common faith had been strong enough to bridge the acrimony of the Revolution under the leadership of McDowell. They were not strong enough to survive this second war and the failure of adequate support that accompanied it.

After the War of 1812 and until the years following World War II, the Reformed Church in America was content to serve in the United States, with a few exceptions. Prior to, and continuing with the impact on the Netherlands of World War I and the subsequent worldwide depression, Dutch came to Canada. In Alberta they began to organize churches that joined the RCA. In 1909 a church was established in Monarch that continues to be active today. In 1912 another church was organized in Bottrell, which relocated to Dog Pound in 1923 and survived until 1971. Groups that were never formally organized met in Carlstadt, Alderson, and New Holland. But prior to the flood of Dutch immigrants following World War II, only two churches were organized in Canada.

World War II devastated the Netherlands. At the beginning of the war, Germany undertook saturation bombing of Rotterdam. During the war, the country was stripped of everything the Nazis could use for their war machine. Liberation involved further destruction as bitter battles were fought to dislodge the Germans. By the end of the war the Netherlands

suffered from crucial shortages of material resources, particularly of housing. In order to deal with these shortages, the Dutch government actively promoted emigration. Australia, the United States, and Canada were popular destinations, with the largest number of emigrants traveling to Canada.

Because of its close ties with the Gereformeerde Kerken in Nederland (GKN), the Christian Reformed Church (CRC) was able to respond quickly to the needs of the Dutch immigrants. At that time, both the GKN and the CRC looked with suspicion at ecumenical engagement, especially at the formation of the World Council of Churches. Both the Nederlands Hervormde Kerk (NHK) and the Reformed Church in America, however, were enthusiastic about the World Council and had been members of its predecessors. Committed to ecumenical engagement, the NHK proposed that the Dutch immigrants be assimilated into the United Church of Canada (UCC). For those immigrants fluent in English this was a realistic proposal, and one that would foster the assimilation of the immigrants into the life of the country. To that end, the NHK appointed one of its ministers, the Reverend L. Bruijn, to assist new immigrants in Canada.

Despite the NHK's best ecumenical intentions, many of the immigrants did not have a command of English sufficient to make them feel at home worshiping in a Canadian church. Nor did the UCC have the linguistic resources to minister to the Dutch

Coming to Canada

The following accounts, and those throughout this chapter, are taken verbatim and with permission from *To All Our Children: The Story of the Postwar Dutch Immigration to Canada*, by Albert VanderMey (Jordan Station, Ont.: Paideia Press, 1983).

"Neither of us had ever gone on a long trip before. In Holland, we didn't travel much. So this was quite an outing. The ocean was always a wonderful sight, even when there was a storm. But then, we never got seasick."

—Newlyweds Leo and Boukje Hovius aboard the *Kota Inten*, March, 1948 (97)

Kota Inten

"There are a lot of foreigners on board. 250 Ukranians who were carried off to Germany in 1941....These people have nothing at all.

"We had a very intimate Sunday. The church service lasted over an hour, and the collection was for the Ukranians....There was also an international evening of song. First the Ukranians sang, followed by the Frisians, the Swedes, the French, and the Netherlanders....It was very catching, and in the end nobody could stop singing. So we sang a lot of Dutch songs."

—Mrs. Koob Kollen, aboard the *Kota Inten*, 1948 (100-102)

"I'm as sick as a dog.... lie on my cot, groaning. Our quarters smell abominably of filthy diapers and vomit. Crying babies...worn out mothers with ashen faces. Fathers coming in to check on their women and children pinch their noses shut and grumble 'What a stench!'

"We have to keep our own quarters clean. There is even an inspection to see that it's done! Women scurry back and forth with pails and mops to clean up the vomit from the floors and to mop up the washroom. Do all ships make their passengers responsible for cleaning up their own quarters? I'll ask my brothers the minute I see them...."

—Geertrui Beldman, age 28, aboard the *Beaverbrae*, Feb. 17, 1950 (95)

"I had to pay the full fare—around $725—myself. There were some eighty-five passengers, mostly single people between twenty and thirty-five. It was like a holiday—we had a riot on that plane. We started dancing, and the pilot said: 'Please, calm down a bit. Don't forget you're in an airplane.' The flight took eighteen long hours. First the plane landed in Iceland, where the passengers were treated to dinner—I'm sure it was bear meat—and next it stopped in St. John, Newfoundland, at 4 p.m. That's where I became a landed immigrant."

—Nico De Jong, age 22, aboard the KLM DC-6, June, 1952 (108)

Mrs. Marten Geertsma of Pitt Meadows, British Columbia, explains: "We came to Canada in 1951 on the second emigrant plane. We flew quite by accident; the boat we were supposed to go with was full. It took eighteen hours to fly from Amsterdam to Montreal, with a stopover in Iceland. We put the baby in a net hanging from the ceiling. Our second daughter slept on the floor, and the stewardess offered to look after her."

in their native language. The UCC also ignored the tendency of immigrant ethnic groups to band together for mutual solace and support. At the same time, tensions that arose from the continuing separation of the GKN from the NHK meant that many of the immigrants felt no more comfortable worshiping with the GKN/CRC than they did with the UCC. Bruijn was charged not only with finding church homes for the immigrants, but also with holding services for them in the meantime. In September, 1948, Bruijn was holding seven such services, which meant each of his temporary congregations could worship every third Sunday, at best. This situation was hardly satisfactory, and it led Peter Posthuma, Arend and Gerrit Dunnink, and C. van Staalduinen of Hamilton to contact the RCA.

Lacking addresses for official correspondence, they wrote to the editor of the *Church Herald*. The editor, Louis Benes, asked the Reverend Harri Zegerius to reply to their letter.

While the RCA did not maintain strong ties with the NHK, it did have a firm commitment to the ecumenical movement and therefore a respect for the NHK's position in Canada. Thus, the RCA's Board of Domestic Missions did not respond immediately to the Canadian immigration. Many in the Midwest did not share those ecumenical commitments but were aware of the work of the CRC in Canada. In his reply to the Dutch in Hamilton, Zegerius spoke of the interest in the Dutch immigrants, "first by Classis Grand Rapids of the Reformed Church, and then by our Mission Board."[2] While there is no

Immigrants Arrive

Jacob Hofstee's boss arrived at the train station in Chatham, Ontario, shepherded the entire family into his car, and took them to their new home. The new arrivals walked inside, and then stood there as if in shock. There was nothing in the house—no furniture, no beds, no curtains, no food....

The family spent the first night on the wooden floor under their clothes. The next day, the farmer brought some straw. The small trunk, which had been put on the train, also arrived, yielding some blankets and spreads. And before the day was over, a table and some chairs graced the house, courtesy of the farmer.

—VanderMey, *To All Our Children*, 156.

A bad case of hay fever made life difficult for Rimmer Tjalsma, who had come to a farm at Watford, Ontario, in 1950. On many days, work was next to impossible. When there was no improvement, his sponsor suggested that he move away from the farm....

Tjalsma looked over the pamphlets that various church representatives had distributed on the boat, and he picked a name at random: Rev. Harri Zegerius of the Reformed Church, based in Hamilton. The minister was understanding when the problem was explained...saying "Hop on the earliest train and come and see me. I'm sure we can help you."

Before long, Tjalsma was making $10 a day in the tobacco harvest. His earnings were "terrific," considering he had made only $45 a month at the farm near Watford. There was one big drawback, however, the work was only seasonal.

—VanderMey, *To All Our Children*, 184.

record of involvement by the Mission Board, Zegerius sprang into action, and in the same month traveled to Hamilton with the Reverend Jacob Brouwer. There, Zegerius and Brouwer met with Bruijn, who intended to establish a Dutch-speaking congregation within the UCC. After Zegerius and Brouwer presented the Reformed Church in America and its theological commitment, however, the assembled group voted by a three-fourths majority to join the RCA. As a result of that visit, the recommendation was also made that "the Board of Domestic Missions, RCA, undertake this work among the Dutch immigrants in Canada as a Domestic Missions project."[3]

In February of 1949, the Hamilton group addressed the Reverend Richard Van den Berg of the Board of Domestic Missions, formally seeking inclusion within the Reformed Church in America. Confronted with this ecumenical conundrum, the church did what it often does: it formed a committee to study the situation. The committee's conclusion was more pragmatic than theological; the Reformed Church would assist the recent immigrants, but after the Dutch became acclimated to their new land, they would be free to join any of its churches. For the immediate future, the committee recommended that the RCA "present the Gospel message in their native tongue to minister to their spiritual needs and to organize Reformed Churches for those with a Christian Heritage and theological lineage like our own."[4]

From the moment the Reformed Church in America decided to welcome Dutch-Canadian immigrants, events moved swiftly.

Welkom Imigranten

In February 1950, the Rev. Harri Zegerius and Neil Eelman crossed the border into Canada with a house trailer with "Welkom Imigranten, Reformed Church in America" written on its side. Eelman intended to take it to Nova Scotia to meet incoming immigrant boats.

"In Quebec it ran into difficulties....It got stuck in the snow. Then the police came along and made threatening noises. They said they were against any evangelism preaching. Well, the trailer was

photo from *To All our Children*

pulled free and hidden for the rest of the winter. In the spring, we put it on the road again."—Harri Zegerius

Eelman, who traveled hither and yon to assist immigrants, became known for the little organ he carried along. No matter what the occasion, he would play the familiar heart-warming tunes. And the people would join in song, smile, and feel spiritually refreshed.

—VanderMey, *To All Our Children*, 315.

In July 1949, the request was made to the Nederlandse Synod for permission to join the Reformed Church in America. On October 10 of that year, Chatham officially joined the denomination; Hamilton did so a day later. In the early part of 1950, Zegerius was called to be pastor of the Hamilton church. Another of the early servants of the Canadian mission was the Reverend Jacob Blauw, who, during five years of service, was responsible for the shipment of 720 tons of donated clothing to Canada.

While generous with its used clothing, the Reformed Church in America was ill prepared to serve the Canadian churches with Dutch-speaking ministers. Here the Americanization of the Reformed

A Harried Zegerius

The station wagon was stuffed full of bundles and boxes of used clothing and the man behind the wheel looked a little used himself. He wore a pair of coveralls and an old hat. Beads of sweat stood on his brow,

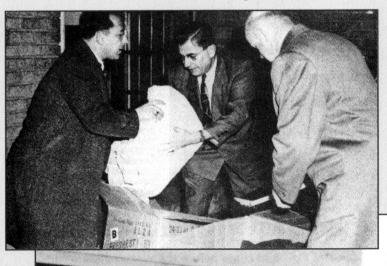

his shoulders sagged with fatigue, and yet his eyes glistened with anticipation.

He was none other than Rev. Harri Zegerius, returning to Canada with another load of clothing donated by Reformed Church groups in the United States and destined for hard-pressed immigrant families. He enjoyed this work. It was rewarding to see the relief in the eyes of a mother who couldn't afford to buy clothes for her growing children or a Sunday dress for herself.

Rev. Zegerius got so involved with his work that occasionally some part of his wardrobe became lost.

"One day, I couldn't find my suit jacket. I looked all over the place. Finally, I concluded that it must have gotten gathered into a bundle of used clothing. When I was in Halifax once, meeting an immigrant boat, I spotted an old man shaking from the cold. He was dressed only in a suit. I said to him, 'Here, take my overcoat. I don't need it back. I'll find something for myself in the bundle.'"

—VanderMey, *To All Our Children*, 333-34.

Church put it at a disadvantage. But despite the fact that the RCA's work with the immigrants had done much to disrupt the ecumenical intentions of the NHK, the NHK cooperated by sending theologically trained, licensed candidates to serve RCA churches in Canada. Among those sent in 1953 were Cor Bons, Johan Heldering, Gerrit Molenaar, Henry Boekhoven, Jellie van Kuiken, and Jan Falkenburg—all with their wives, and the latter two with daughters. The young churches were also providing candidates for ministry.

Farm kitchen, Exeter, Ontario, circa 1950

Ministering to the Dutch immigrants involved much more than providing opportunities for worship. Many immigrants arrived destitute, lacking even clothing appropriate to their new land. Promised employment was sometimes fraught with difficulties, which were acerbated by language barriers. It soon became apparent

Ecumenism in Lethbridge, 1953

"Several members of our [Christian Reformed] congregation always went to the railway station to meet the immigrant trains," recalls Rev. Scholten. "For the night trains, the clergy took turns: For

instance, I picked up the people for Father Verhagen of the Roman Catholic church and for Rev. Karel Hanhart of the Reformed Church. It even happened that members of our Protestant churches slept overnight in the Roman Catholic manse—ecumenical cooperation 1953 style."

There was more of that cooperation when Sinterklaas, the Dutch Santa, made his rounds. A woman on a visit to Lethbridge had brought a surprise— a Sinterklaas costume. So all the immigrants got together for an evening of fun. Rev. Hanhart was the good saint, Rev. Scholten was Zwarte Piet, the Moorish aide, and Father Verhagen was master of ceremonies.

—VanderMey, *To All Our Children*, 323.

The Drayton Reformed Church, Drayton, Ontario. Congregation organized in 1952, building restored and enlarged in 1999.

that more staff support was needed, and "fieldmen" were employed to minister to these needs. These fieldmen worked with ministers to meet a wide range of basic needs, from meeting immigrants' ships or planes to helping them find housing, employment, clothing, appliances, affordable and reliable cars, and, of course, churches.

The work of establishing churches in Canada ostensibly fell under the authority of the Board of Domestic Missions, but in practice different classes typically helped fund different churches. While this promoted a high level of interest and support from the classes, it was not conducive to communication between the various churches in Canada. At the end of ten years of work in Canada, the twenty-one churches in Ontario belonged to nine different classes. Looking back, it may seem obvious that the Canadian churches needed to form their own classis, but for reasons of indecision, support, loyalty, and "ownership," the obvious did not take place until 1962.

The indecision resulted from the initial policy between the NHK and the UCC that "when these settlers have become established and acclimated to the country and language, they will be given the opportunity to unite with other denominations or to continue as Reformed churches."[5] In 1959 the newly appointed director of the Board of Domestic Missions, the Reverend Russell Redeker, called a conference of all Canadian pastors plus one elder from each church. The issue of union with another denomination was openly debated. The Reverend Gerrit ten Zythof, a recent graduate of Utrecht, argued for union with the Presbyterian Church.[6] The Reverend Dr. Eugene Heideman,[7] pastor in Edmonton, urged that the Canadian churches continue to support the needs of immigrants while helping them unite with other churches, and that extension work be concentrated in the United States. The pastors and elders rejected these positions. Instead, the churches of Ontario wanted their own classis within the Reformed Church in America. In their new land they had established their identity as Reformed within the RCA, but they saw the advantages of forming their own classis within Ontario. (In one instance, however, geographical proximity transcended national boundaries, when the church at Chatham decided to remain within the

Classis of Lake Erie.) While the conference of 1959 established the continued commitment of the Canadian churches to the RCA, and the denomination's continued support and inclusion of the Canadian churches, it took until 1962 to establish the Classis of Ontario.

With that action the unity of the Ontario churches was now assured, but the churches of the Far West in Alberta and British Columbia still felt the tension of being one church in two nations. They were definitely a part of the Reformed Church in America insofar as most belonged to classes in the United States, but their existence within Canada created problems and opportunities that were distinctly Canadian. The establishment of the Council of the Reformed Church in Canada (CRCC) in 1973 was an attempt to

Photo Westdale Reformed

The Westdale Reformed Church, Hamilton, Ontario. Organized 1949, church built in 1956.

solve this problem. However, the ultimate goal for many Canadian churches was a Regional Synod of Canada, which was established in 1993.

The tension inherent in attempting to have one church in two nations has continued and is

An Evangelical Suitcase

When Rev. Harri Zegerius stepped out of the train in Toronto early one morning after a trip from Ottawa, his somewhat bleary eyes spotted a Dutch suitcase—green, wooden, rather battered, with dull brass corners. It belonged to a middle-aged couple, much wrinkled and weary, who had just ended a two-day trip from Saskatchewan.

"A cup of coffee soon loosened their tongues. They had been in the boondocks—way out, really—for sixteen months. In that time, they'd heard many promises, but not once had they been taken to a church service. Now they were looking for spiritual help. They said: 'We'll let you know when we've settled down. Will you

come and hold a service for us then?' I sealed that promise with a prayer."

Some months later, in early 1951, a letter came from St. Catharines, Ontario, signed by eight families, including the couple from Saskatchewan. Fieldman Martin DeVos led the first service. Before long, St Catharines had a thriving Reformed congregation

"When we celebrated the 25th anniversary of that congregation," says Rev. Zegerius, "There were many reasons to be grateful to God. And right on the platform, to remind us of God's providential ways with us, was that old green suitcase that helped start it all."

—VanderMey, *To All Our Children*, 329-30

further illustrated by the change in name desired by the Canadian churches of the Reformed Church in America. For almost three decades, Canadians referred to themselves as the Reformed Church in Canada. The name was approved by the General Synod in 1990.

In 1945 at the close of World War II, there were two organized congregations in Canada. In 1959, as the flow of immigrants subsided, there were thirty-two. As the Reformed Church in America celebrated its 375th anniversary in 2003, the Reformed Church in Canada numbered forty-one congregations, members of one church that transcends national boundaries.

[1] See John W. Beardslee, "The Reformed Church in the American Revolution," in James W. Van Hoeven, ed., *Piety and Patriotism*, The Historical Series of the Reformed Church in America (Grand Rapids: Eerdmans, 1976), 17-33.

[2] Peggy Humby, *The History of the Reformed Church in Canada* (Stoney Creek, Ont.: Privately published by the author, 1993), 41.

[3] Ibid., 42.

[4] Ibid., 44.

[5] Ibid., 82.

[6] Ten Zythof ultimately established and became head of the Department of Religion at Southeastern Missouri State College; he maintained his membership in the Classis of Holland until his death in 2001.

[7] Heideman, after serving as a missionary in India, chaplain at Central College, and dean at Western Seminary, became secretary of program for the General Program Council of the RCA.

Resources for Further Study

The History of the Reformed Church in Canada, by Peggy Humby. Privately published, 1993.

The McDowall Saga: A Story of Three Generations, by Donald R. Baird, http://www.rca.org/images/aboutus/archives/mcdowall.pdf

Piety and Patriotism, ed. James W. Van Hoeven. The Historical Series of the Reformed Church in America. Grand Rapids: Eerdmans, 1976.

To All Our Children: The Story of the Postwar Dutch Immigration to Canada, by Albert VanderMey. Jordan Station, Ont.: Paideia Press, 1983.

17
Westward Ho

The A.C. Van Raalte Church. Pioneers living near Thule, South Dakota, built this sod church shortly before they were officially organized on October 8, 1886. The interior measured sixteen by thirty feet, and its seven-foot-high walls were whitewashed on the interior. The roof was constructed of one-inch boards covered with tarpaper and a layer of sod.

Archives of the Reformed Church in America

A s the people of the United States marched westward, the Reformed Church in America went too—not everywhere, and not always with the first settlers, but it did move westward, ultimately to realize its greatest success in California.

The mid-nineteenth century immigrants from the Netherlands settled primarily in Michigan, Illinois, Indiana, Wisconsin, and Iowa. From Iowa they soon began to move west and to plant churches in Nebraska (1857) and Kansas (1871) and north into Minnesota (1869) and South Dakota (1880). Later in the nineteenth century, churches were established in Montana (1896) and Oklahoma (1898).

Where the Dutch settled in substantial numbers the churches grew and thrived. Where the Dutch population was too small to support a minister, churches were dropped, disbanded, merged, or transferred to another denomination. (The distinction between dropped and disbanded is that dropped congregations just disappear, whereas disbanded churches are officially terminated, decently and in order.) Nineteenth century records show the number of churches in each state and their status as follows: Nebraska 3; Kansas 3—all disbanded or dropped; Minnesota 9—2 disbanded; South Dakota 20—3 disbanded, 7 dropped, and one transferred; North Dakota 1; Montana 1—dropped; and Oklahoma 1—dropped. Of these thirty-eight churches, twenty remain active.

The movement of Dutch in these states from 1900 through the end of World War II in 1945 continued the pattern: Nebraska 3—1 disbanded; Kansas 2—1 dropped; Minnesota 9—2 dropped; South Dakota 18—2

Events referenced in the chapter are below the line. Other historical events are above the line.

1876
Colorado statehood

1867
Nebraska statehood

1869
First state board of health in Massachusetts

1864
Montana opened for settlement

1866
First municipal board of health in New York

1865-73
Epidemics of smallpox, typhus, typhoid, & cholera

1889
Oklahoma opened for settlement

1861
Colorado & Nevada opened for settlement

1861
Kansas statehood

1889
Dakotas, Washington, & Montana statehood

1854
Kansas & Nebraska opened for settlement

1850
California granted statehood

1883
Northern Pacific Railway

1914–18
World War I

1939-45
World War II

| 1850 | 1875 | 1900 | 1925 | 1950 | 1975 |

1847
Holland, MI (first church organized, and below)

1880
Dakota

1910
Lynden, WA

1955
Crystal Cathedral

1854
Cedar Grove, WI

1896
Montana

1921
Denver, CO

1871
Kansas

1854
Chicago, IL

1923
California

1869
Minnesota

1856
Pella, IA

1857
Nebraska

Before and After

From a letter to the Board of Domestic Missions published in the *Mission Field*, 1902-03, 176:

It is a sad duty to report the total destruction of the church building of the Delaware congregation. This region was visited on the night of the 24th of June by the severest windstorm ever witnessed here. Our little church and outbuilding were ground to kindling wood. Our people are now clearing away the debris....The spire in falling struck the corner of our house and crashed through the windows....Doors and windows were broken by flying pieces. The Lord has wonderfully preserved our lives.

—Rev. E.F. Koerlin
Davis, So. Dakota,
July 2, 1902

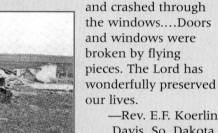

Archives of the Reformed Church in America

dropped, 1 disbanded, 4 merged, and 1 transferred; North Dakota 5—2 disbanded; Montana 2—1 disbanded and 1 dropped; and Oklahoma 13—3 dropped, 2 disbanded, 1 merged, and 5 transferred. Colorado also must be added to the list with 4 churches organized—2 dropped, 1 disbanded, and the State of Washington, which saw 5 churches organized—1 dropped, 1 disbanded. Of sixty-one churches established, twenty-nine remain active.

To this record of enthusiasm and courage (and disappointment when congregations found it impossible to continue) must be added the story of California. If any Dutch followed the gold rush, they did not try to establish a Reformed church. The first Reformed church in California—Hope Community in Los Angeles—was not established until 1923, but it remains active today. In fact, all ten churches established in California before 1945 remain active. When the members of the Reformed Church became involved

Holy Roller

From the *Mission Field*, 1903-04, 168:

They have a habit in South Dakota, when convenience requires it, of moving towns or churches from one site to another over the level prairie, regardless of distance. Some years ago the town of Grand View was picked up, placed on wheels and carried to Armour, the railway station, five miles away. More recently the church of Centerville was hauled over the prairie, nearly twenty miles, to Lennox. And now the Charles Mix Church, for a long time inconveniently far from the growing town of Platte, has been drawn to that place.

in the nation's "Westward Ho!" their major success occurred in California.

In most of the states mentioned above, suitable land for agriculture prompted Dutch settlement. Along with agriculture, settlers developed an entire support system necessary for a community, and of course for churches. But what prompted the Dutch to settle in California? A few may have come for health reasons because of the climate, but, as in the other western states, the majority came to California for agriculture, especially milk production. Some came from the Midwest and some came from the Netherlands (the use of Dutch in worship until well into the 1940s is evidence of the heavily immigrant nature of the church). With them came a new concept for what could justly be called the dairy industry. Instead of pastures, there were feed lots for which feed was purchased, rather than grown by the owner. Milking a multitude of cows occupied a major part of the day. In short, dairying was commercialized, and it was very successful, as was the sale of land as the suburbs encroached upon the dairies— eventually driving some as far away as Idaho.

To the solid record of those committed immigrants from the Midwest and the Netherlands must be added the ministerial leadership of individuals like Henry Beltman,

Good and Faithful Servant

Surely the First Reformed Church in Lynden, Washington, would be among those congregations receiving the Lord's accolade of "good and faithful servant." The Dutch came because the soil and climate of northwest Washington were good not only for agriculture in general, but also for growing tulips commercially. The church began in 1910 with thirty-three members. In 1911 it reported 65 families and 101 communicants. While worship was held in the afternoon, in Dutch, the Sunday school, begun in 1911, numbered a hundred and was conducted in English. By 1918, morning worship was in English, afternoon in Dutch, and a Christian Endeavor Society for young people, organized in 1919, was held in the evening.

By its twenty-fifth anniversary, the church counted 594 souls. In 1944 it spawned the Nooksack church, but five years later the Lynden congregation numbered 834 souls. Another daughter church, Faith Reformed, was organized in 1954.

Over the years the church has sent into full-time service the Reverends Henry Bovendam, Corstian Klein, Wesley Kiel, and Sam Hoffman. By its seventy-fifth anniversary, Lynden was also supporting thirty-six missionaries. Six years later it gave birth to a third church, this time in Bellingham. Nonetheless, by 1995 the church needed three worship services, and three years later a fourth was added on Saturday evening.

Under the leadership of the Reverend D. Marc de Waard, a team of fourteen leads the many ministries of the church, including parish nurses and telecare. First Reformed in Lynden continues to serve.

Photo: Lyndon Reformed Church

Lyndon's pastor from 1911-15, the Rev. J.G. Brouwer, and family ready to enjoy the new sport of motoring.

Edward Fikse, Albert Van Dyke, and Chester Droog, who challenged the church to reach beyond its Dutch boundaries. The influx of workers during World War II occasioned the beginning of that outreach. The Miraloma Community Church in San Francisco was organized in 1942, followed by the Mayfair Community Church in Lakewood in 1944, the first to be started without a Dutch nucleus.

The record of church growth in California after World War II has been notable. On the one hand, the coming of new immigrants from the Netherlands resulted in the organization of the Second Reformed Church in Artesia with

In Sickness and in Health

Photo: First Reformed, Denver, CO

The First Reformed Church in Denver, Colorado, organized 1922.

In the years just prior to World War I, Denver, Colorado, was known as a center of activity for those suffering from the "white plague," tuberculosis. The Bethesda Sanitarium, a joint mission of the Christian Reformed Church and the Reformed Church in America, had opened its doors in 1910.

Almost one hundred years later, most members of Denver's First Reformed Church, founded in 1921, can tell how Bethesda has played a part in their family histories. When a Dutch-American family arrived in Denver and one member of the family checked into the "San," the others, including children, often moved into the basement of someone living on "Dutch Hill." Wives were given doctors' notes to take to prospective employers indicating that a "man's" job could rightfully be offered, as the husband could not be expected to fill his traditional role as breadwinner. Other Dutch-

Americans came to Denver as well, not because of illness, but to work at Bethesda.

The Dust Bowl and Great Depression also contributed to growth. Parts of South Dakota went seven years without harvesting a crop. Folks from Dutch-American enclaves in the Dakotas and Kansas sometimes left for Denver with only the address of the church. There were jobs in Denver, and Gates Rubber Company and Samsonite continued to hire.

First Reformed Church has always confronted the realities of human suffering and the need for Christian service. When children were young, the church, along with local Christian Reformed congregations, started Denver Christian Schools. As parents grew older, those same congregations began the Christian Living Center, a multifaceted home for the elderly. Throughout its history, First Reformed has been involved in Reformed Church world missions, work on southwestern Indian reservations, and the local rescue mission. More than a dozen young women and men raised in the church became missionaries or entered the ministry.

Service frequently finds a personal dimension at First Reformed. Nellie Kats is 101 years old, and she attends worship every Sunday. Nellie let her driver's license expire two years ago, when her mechanic said she needed a new car if she was going to keep driving. A young woman from First Reformed either drives her or makes sure she has a ride each Sunday. She does so because Nellie helped her grandparents when they were young, and she's returning the favor.

services in Dutch. On the other hand, many established churches found themselves with new neighbors, and new churches were organized with the intention of reaching out to their entire communities.

In thirteen states outside the original orbit of mid-nineteenth century immigration in Michigan, Illinois, Indiana, Wisconsin, and Iowa, forty-eight churches were established, of which thirty-five remain active. But in California

All Aboard!

At 8:50 a.m. on June 6, New York City minister and elder delegates to the 1922 General Synod boarded the "Synod Train," a special, running on the Lehigh Valley, Michigan Central, and Rock Island Railroads. The train picked up other delegates and synod visitors at Philadelphia, Bethlehem, Wilkes-Barre, Sayre, Ithaca, Geneva, and Rochester on its way to Buffalo. From there it rambled down the tracks, stopping in Detroit, Jackson, Battle Creek, Kalamazoo, Niles, Michigan City, and Chicago. From Chicago the train went directly to Pella, Iowa, to the campus of Central College.

The clerical fare from New York to Chicago was $16.35, from Chicago to Pella an additional $7.60. The fare for elder delegates and visitors from New York was $44.09. Pullman fares for an upper berth were $10.20, for a lower berth $12.75. Two persons could occupy the same berth without extra charge. Fares from intermediate points were prorated.

This was the first synod meeting at Central College—the school grounds, buildings, and equipment (conservatively valued at $110,000) had been acquired recently from the Northern Baptist Convention on the condition that the Reformed Church in America continue to maintain an accredited Christian college in Pella.

According to the *Christian Intelligencer and Mission Field*, the synod meeting was "one of the most delightful meetings" the General Synod ever held and the "hearts of the whole Synod had warmed

greatly toward Central and Hope [College]."[1] Unfortunately, at the close of the synod, shortly after midnight on Sunday, June 14, fire destroyed "Old Central."

Hopelessly the brethren stood about and saw the building devoured by the fire fiend. Did we say hopelessly? No! For there under the trees even while the fire was doing its worst, the heart of the Reformed Church was lifted to Almighty God in prayer and psalm, and we doubt not, God heard the cry. Almost immediately, irresistibly and simultaneously, it seemed, the thoughts of all turned toward another building.[2]

Those thoughts turned into pledges. On the Synod Train the next morning, passengers raised $12,265 for a new "Old Central."

1 *The Christian Intelligencer and Mission Field*, June 28, 1922, 405.
2 Ibid.

Old Central, before and after.

Emmanuel—God with Us

In 1924 enough recent Dutch immigrants had arrived in southern California, principally to work in the farming and dairy industries, to form the first Reformed church: Hope Reformed in Los Angeles. Just a year later, the congregation that was to become Emmanuel Reformed was organized. Whether its first worship was held in a literary hall or rented tavern seems open to question. Without question has been the church's continuing vitality.

Truly a Dutch church, it was 1940 before the evening service was held in English, and 1948 before all services were in English. In 1960 the church reached its high point as a Dutch-American congregation—and then the Dutch dairy families began to leave the area and the church, and the ethnic mix of the neighborhood became more diverse.

Emmanuel, with its Dutch constituency declining, chose to become a mission church,

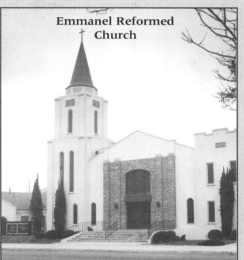
Emmanel Reformed Church

adding an educational building for new programs, even in the face of shrinking membership. The Reverend Harold Korver came in 1971. He introduced programs to fill community needs, and the worship and educational programs grew.

In the 1980s demographics changed again, with the community shifting from Anglo to Latino. Only three decades before, the language of Emmanuel had switched from Dutch to English, now the need was to speak Spanish. Again rising to the challenge, ministry teams, cell groups, and an intense discipleship program prepared many members for personal evangelism, while new programs ministered to new needs (e.g., painting five hundred homes, removing graffiti, and cleaning streets and alleys as well as building for recreational and educational programs for the community). God with us. Amazing grace.

sixty churches were established, of which thirty-three remain active. Part of the large attrition can be attributed to the fact that nine of ten Korean churches have been disbanded or have left the denomination. The insistence that the Korean churches be part of the classis at a time when few of the Korean-born pastors had a sufficient command of the language to feel at home, let alone participate as equals, led to their leaving, along with their congregations, to join other communions. However, there was also attrition among Caucasian churches. While many succeeded because of gifted pastors who could

reach out to others, some failed because of poor placement, either of church or pastor. Sometimes successful church starts failed under subsequent leadership of a different style. Most remarkable, however, has been the continuance of the once solidly Dutch churches that have managed to continue their ministries as the culture of their neighborhoods changed radically.

Evidence of faithfulness is found in the forty-two churches and twelve mission churches in the classes of California and Central California at the beginning of the twenty-first century. Of this number, five are Korean, three

A Long Way to Go to Milk

Photo: Twin Falls Reformed Church

Twin Falls, Idaho, Reformed Church

Twin Falls Reformed Church was born when, in the early 1970s, Dutch dairy farmers from California migrated to Idaho to search for new opportunities. Families in southern California were facing rapid suburban development in Artesia, Chino, and Bellflower, and several dairy farmers and related service providers sold their California property and moved to Idaho to pursue new operations.

In July 1976, the Reverend Chester Droog, then field secretary of the Synod of the Far West, visited a growing cluster of families with Reformed and Christian Reformed backgrounds in the Twin Falls area to provide consultation and support. The group had been gathering in a Grange Hall several miles outside the Twin Falls city limits. Droog urged the interested families to charter a new Reformed Church congregation within the city for the purpose of reaching out to the unchurched, in addition to welcoming Reformed families relocating from out of state.

Following Droog's advice, the core group purchased a building in the heart of the city of Twin Falls, where steady streams of folks from a variety of backgrounds gathered for weekly worship with those Reformed folk new to the area. Twin Falls Reformed Church was officially organized October 28, 1976. Despite the risks of taking an inclusive approach to ministry, the congregation had grown significantly by the time the Reverend Donald Nienhuis assumed leadership as the founding pastor. Most notable was the number of young families with children in attendance.

This led to a second critical decision. The church decided to give highest priority to children and youth, above all other programming options. Without funds in the budget to justify such a move, as a step of faith the congregation added a full-time associate pastor to expand Twin Falls' ministry with young people. The Reverend Brian Vriesman was installed in that position in 1985. By 1989 Vriesman had become the senior pastor, following Nienhuis's retirement.

To this day, the Twin Falls Reformed Church continues to thrive on the dual emphases of diversity and youth as the church commences its third building program. The long tenures of the congregation's senior pastors has added to its stability and appeal, as well as the diverse flavors of worship, congregational life, and creative witness to residents of the greater Twin Falls area. Moreover, Twin Falls Reformed Church has played an active role in spawning additional Idaho congregations.

Hispanic, two Chinese, three African-American, and forty-one Anglo, with a total formal membership of 20,187. It should be recognized that many of the forty-one listed as Anglo contain varying numbers of other races.

It is also in California that the most widely known pastor of the Reformed Church in America, the Reverend Dr. Robert Schuller, built the Crystal Cathedral. The story of Schuller's boyhood in northwest Iowa, his education at Hope College and Western Seminary, a short pastorate in the Midwest, and the beginning of a ministry in an outdoor movie theater in California, is well known. Schuller's astute sense of "find a need and fill it" coupled with a sense of the need for "pre-evangelism" has made him one of America's outstanding evangelists.

Sensitive to the effectiveness of television, Schuller provided a visual context for his message with

Robert H. Schuller

Amazing Growth

In 1967 Al Fikse came to the Classis of California reporting that free land for a church would be given if the classis would build a church structure on the property within two years. The Classis Extension Committee observed that there were only three hundred people in the area, the classis had no money to give, and they did not believe that any pastor of sound mind would come to such a remote place.

A month later the classis received a petition signed by seven families requesting permission to begin the work immediately and assuring the classis of no future burden. In a gesture of good faith, the classis gave them permission. These seven families secured their own financing, built their own facility, and divided the projected budget for

Rancho Community Church

several years among themselves. They called a young graduate from Western Seminary, Steve Struikmans, who accepted the challenge.

Today Rancho Community Church has grown from those seven families to seven hundred families. Crowded out of their fifteen-acre campus, the congregation is moving to a forty-acre site that will include a school (preschool through eighth grade), a family life center, Christian education facilities, and offices. They are keeping their original minister.

The campus of the Crystal Cathedral.

Photos: Crystal Cathedral

ever to receive such an honor. The centerpiece of his architectural cornucopia is undoubtedly the Crystal Cathedral, perhaps the finest creation of Philip Johnson's later career.

In 1970 Schuller founded the Institute for Successful Church Leadership that in three decades produced more than twenty thousand graduates. In 1992 the Fuqua International School of Christian Communications was established, specializing in the art of preaching.

From the Crystal Cathedral, the *Hour of Power* is transmitted through 185 television stations in the United States and Canada, and to 165 countries on seven continents, with a worldwide audience estimated at ten million. In 1989, Schuller was invited by Mikhail Gorbachev to communicate a message of hope to the people of the Soviet Union, with a reported two hundred million viewers.

The Reformed Church in America can justly be proud of Robert Schuller and his ministry to millions. At the same time, we must also be grateful for the manifestation of God's grace in thousands of church members and their pastors who faithfully serve Christ.

a series of structures created by America's foremost architects: Richard Neutra, Philip Johnson, and Richard Meier. So adroit have been his choices of architects, and the buildings commissioned of such quality, that the American Institute of Architects named Schuller to its board of directors, the only minister

Resources for Further Study

My Journey: From an Iowa Farm to a Cathedral of Dreams, by Robert H. Schuller. New York: HarperCollins, 2001.

18

The Limitations of Doing It 'Right'

New Brunswick Theological Seminary, circa 1880

The **Reformed Church in America experienced** explosive growth during the nineteenth century. In just one decade, from 1850 to 1860, it grew by 150 churches. That's one church every twenty-five days for ten years. But other denominations grew at even more phenomenal rates. For example, the Methodists sustained an average growth rate over the eighty-year period from 1820 to 1900 of one new church every forty-two hours. What prevented the Reformed Church from realizing that kind of growth?

Back in 1768, a few years before Livingston's plan for union brought peace to the slightly more than one hundred Reformed congregations, the Methodists only had three lay preachers in the colony, a chapel in New York, and a Bible class in Philadelphia. But by 1820 the Dutch Reformed Church had 180 congregations, while the Methodists had 2,700. Widely different ideas about the "right" ways to provide leaders and organize churches lay behind this disparity. "Right" for the Reformed Church in 1764 meant preaching the gospel in Dutch (even though less than 3 percent of the population spoke Dutch, while more than 80 percent spoke English). It also meant remaining in proper relationship to a judicatory in Amsterdam, where few if any of the people making decisions had ever been to the New World. "Right" also meant maintaining a proper ecclesial relationship with the Classis of Amsterdam, even though ministers had to be educated and ordained three thousand miles away, across the turbulent Atlantic. For the early followers of Van Raalte, it was "right" to unite with the Reformed Church in America. "Right" for that church meant to protect freedom of conscience to belong to any organization as long as Christ came first, even though it meant losing many members. "Right," even for the early immigrants to Iowa and West Michigan, always meant an educated, settled ministry, so, to survive, churches had to grow large enough to support an educated, settled ministry.

Contrast this situation with that of the Methodists. Their ministry did not require formal seminary education, and it was certainly not settled. In fact, the backbone of the Methodist advance was the circuit rider. Charles Wesley himself traveled widely in England, and in America Francis Asbury continued the practice. The circuit rider was sometimes ordained, but often a licensed lay person. His parish was

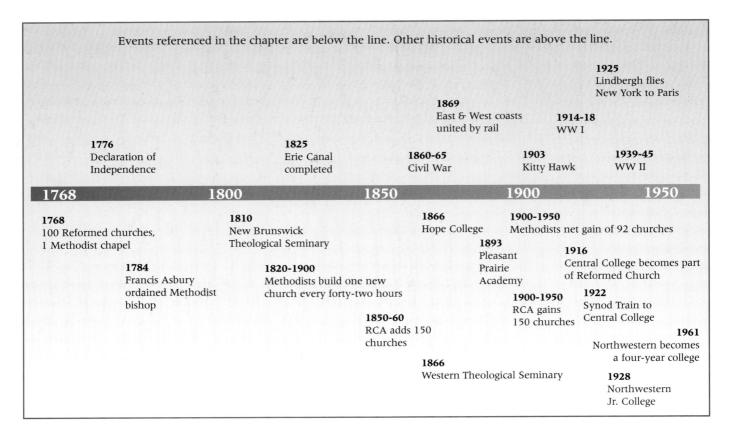

Events referenced in the chapter are below the line. Other historical events are above the line.

1925
Lindbergh flies
New York to Paris

1869
East & West coasts
united by rail

1914-18
WW I

1776
Declaration of
Independence

1825
Erie Canal
completed

1860-65
Civil War

1903
Kitty Hawk

1939-45
WW II

1768   1800   1850   1900   1950

1768
100 Reformed churches,
1 Methodist chapel

1810
New Brunswick
Theological Seminary

1866
Hope College

1900-1950
Methodists net gain of 92 churches

1893
Pleasant
Prairie
Academy

1916
Central College becomes part
of Reformed Church

1784
Francis Asbury
ordained Methodist
bishop

1820-1900
Methodists build one new
church every forty-two hours

1900-1950
RCA gains
150 churches

1922
Synod Train to
Central College

1850-60
RCA adds 150
churches

1961
Northwestern becomes
a four-year college

1866
Western Theological Seminary

1928
Northwestern
Jr. College

Educated Ministry and Missions

There's an interesting relationship between an educated ministry and missions. The church's demand for ministers who are knowledgeable in Hebrew and Greek has often uncovered a fluency in language. Sometimes these students became missionaries who used their gifts to become fluent in the languages of faroff lands. We have already related how Reformed Church missionaries were instrumental in providing China with a Romanization of written Chinese that enabled people of all classes to become literate.

China, however, was but one field. In India, Japan, and the Arabian Gulf, missionaries established churches, hospitals, educational institutions, and worked for the betterment of the conditions of women. Through the tradition of an educated ministry, they carried the gospel to the uttermost parts of the world.

The Circuit Rider

a circuit, sometimes five hundred miles in length and requiring up to six weeks to make the rounds of fifteen to twenty-five preaching stations. Methodist circuit riders preached wherever they could gather people—in barns, houses, taverns (as in Holland, Michigan), or in the open. If people were converted, a class for religious instruction was started, and one of the believers was appointed as the class leader. Members who felt the call to preach were encouraged to apply for a local preacher's license, which entitled them to deliver sermons and organize classes. This was obviously a far cry from what the Dutch perceived as the "right" way of doing things; i.e., where even a Yale man like John Henry Livingston was required to make a six-thousand-mile round trip for continued theological education in Dutch universities, with examination and ordination by the Classis of Amsterdam.

Methodist flexibility was apparent almost from the start, when Francis Asbury, still a lay person, was ordained a deacon on Christmas Day 1784, an elder the next day, and, on the following day, a bishop! Methodist polity allowed for a ready supply of lay preachers who were, nonetheless, under episcopal control. The inept or unworthy did not advance; a licensed preacher who learned and grew could be ordained a deacon, then a presiding elder in charge of a district, and possibly even a bishop. (Further, it

Methodists: Charles and John Wesley may be considered the founders of Methodism. Both were ministers ordained by the Church of England; each had a transforming experience of God's presence (1738). While remaining in the Church of England, they formed religious societies. Particularly effective in education and moral reform were the Methodist "classes" of twelve members, each under a "class leader." The preaching of the Wesleys in the open air to the poor with its attendant "enthusiasm" resulted in hostility from the upper classes. In America, Methodist classes—started by circuit riders who were often lay preachers—proved to be especially effective on a sparsely inhabited frontier.

A Western Seminary in the Midwest

When Western Theological Seminary resumed ministerial training in 1885, classes were conducted in the Oggel House. It was torn down to make room for Phelps Hall.

Like New Brunswick Theological Seminary, which began its life as a result of students not wishing to travel east to the Netherlands for their education, Western Theological Seminary began as a result of students not wishing to travel east from Michigan to New Jersey. Like New Brunswick, which began as a part of Queens College (now Rutgers University), Western began as a part of Hope College. Like New Brunswick, which for a time ceased operation due to a lack of funds, Western ceased operations for six years for the same reason. Like New Brunswick, which eventually separated from Queen's College, Western became an independent institution in 1885.

Seminary instruction began in 1866, as a theological department of Hope College, following a successful petition to General Synod by seven members of Hope's graduating class who wished to prepare for ministry in the Midwest. Hope's president, Dr. Philip Phelps, and the Reverend Albertus Van Raalte supported their desire, and seminary education began. By the time of its temporary closure in 1877, Western had already graduated twenty-nine students.

The Reformed Church established Western as an independent seminary because it recognized the importance of having a seminary in the Midwest

for the Midwest. While theologically conservative, New Brunswick was thoroughly Americanized. In the Midwest, schisms within the church based upon Dutch perceptions indicated that Americanization had only begun. It was highly desirable to have a seminary both sensitive to the Dutch community and able to train students who would become loyal ministers of the Reformed Church in America.

That the seminary was indeed of the Midwest for the Midwest is indicated by its list of professors and students. Nonetheless, its professors all had classical and seminary training, almost all had pastoral experience, and some had advanced degrees. Their attainments were such that, in Western's first century, one professor was called to the faculty of Dubuque Seminary, another to New Brunswick, and a third to Princeton.

By 1966 Western could count 1,066 graduates, 2,210 by the end of the twentieth century. Its graduates have served Reformed, Presbyterian, Congregational, Methodist, and Episcopal churches throughout the United States and have served abroad in India, Indonesia, Myanmar, China, Japan, Taiwan, the Philippines, Egypt, Sudan, Ethiopia, Kenya, Iraq, Kuwait, Bahrain, Pakistan, Cyprus, Lebanon, Mexico, and Venezuela, as well as in specialized ministries and chaplaincies.

should be noted that the Methodists did not discourage membership in fraternal secret organizations, which they identified with patriotism.)

But Methodist polity was not without its difficulties. While there was phenomenal growth, nurture was of necessity often rudimentary. The circuit rider's visit to a preaching station every six weeks could not provide the teaching, preaching, and pastoral care possible from a settled minister. And while it is true that Methodists urged education, it is also true that among the Methodist churches of the South, as late as 1927, only 4 percent of its ministers were seminary graduates.

The grassroots nature of the Methodist church also meant that it tended to reflect the outlook of the dominant culture. For example, while Wesley had been outspoken in his condemnation of slavery, the Methodists of the South were the bulwark of the Confederacy and committed supporters of the institution of slavery. The lack of a strong educational and doctrinal tradition also allowed some portions of the Methodist church to swing wildly from camp meeting evangelism to liberalism within a few decades.

Pleasant Prairie Academy

Archives of the Reformed Church in America

The only requirements for admission were an eighth grade education, a good moral character, and a desire to study. Applicants who were not known to the faculty were to bring a letter of recommendation from their pastor or consistory, or from some other responsible person.

Founded in 1893 by German-speaking churches of the Reformed Church in America, Pleasant Prairie Academy was located on the main line of the Chicago Great Western Railroad near German Valley, Illinois, a village of "sturdy, honest, God-fearing, East Friesian stock."

Tuition for the year was $25. Students coming from west of the Mississippi paid $10 per semester. Students preparing themselves for the ministry had first dibs on dormitory rooms at $10 per year. Girls had to stay at the homes of neighboring families.

The academy believed that public speaking was the greatest of all arts. It encouraged every student to participate in its literary society that performed weekly. Competitions in drama, humor, and oratory were held in each class to identify the best speakers, who went on to compete in an annual event.

By 1930 the academy had "sent forth twenty-eight young men who have become ministers of the gospel, as well as many other young men and young women who have become centers of Christian influence wherever they have gone." In 1951 the Classis of Pleasant Prairie turned the academy over to a local board appointed by members of the Silver Creek Reformed Church of German Valley, who operated the school for another seven years.

Baptists: Baptists believe that an adult conversion experience is to precede baptism by submersion. Their view of the church is that of independent, freely associating Christians. Ordination was given to anyone who felt called by God and sustained by another ordained preacher. This gave Baptists tremendous flexibility, since there were no educational requirements and most preachers did not require congregational support. In contemporary life, while Baptist congregations still retain a great deal of independence, rigid control is exercised over Baptist institutions by Baptist Conventions. Today, most established Baptist ministers have a seminary education.

Christian Churches (Disciples of Christ): Nineteenth-century American in origins, in an attempt at a pure, unitive Christianity they rejected all denominational labels, affirmed the Bible as their only creed and law, and adopted a radically congregational polity with a contractual ministry. Their message was simple: faith, repentance, baptism, remission of sins, gift of the Holy Spirit, and life eternal. Baptism was by submersion, and the Lord's Supper was celebrated once a week. Today some Disciples groups have no denominational offices, while the Christian Churches (Disciples of Christ) formalized a General Assembly in 1968. The assembly meets biennially and is composed of representatives of all congregations.

Methodist polity did allow for tremendous growth. That one chapel of 1768 had grown to 53,908 churches by 1900, while many of the nine hundred Reformed churches organized during the nineteenth century failed through their inability to support an educated, full-time ministry. Many Methodist churches simply continued as part of the circuit. However, the fifty years after 1900 saw a net gain of only 92 churches for the Methodists, while the Reformed Church gained 144.

Many Christians are convinced that the Methodists chose the better path: to use any who were willing to preach, however meager their formal education, and to spread the gospel, however thin the sowing might be. Others, while thanking God for Methodist accomplishments, point to the riches American Christianity gained from settled ministries and educated pastors. The Methodists' flexible polity did enable them to preach in every pioneer settlement and hamlet. But it's interesting to note that the numerically explosive denominations of the American frontier—Methodists, Baptists, and Disciples of Christ—have all moved toward a settled, educated ministry. The Reformed Church in America, throughout the nineteenth and twentieth centuries, insisted upon three years of seminary education, first at New Brunswick since its opening in 1810, and also at Western Seminary since 1866. To the extent that the church looks favorably upon the "commissioned pastor," it would appear that the Reformed Church is poised to follow the path abandoned by Methodists and Disciples.

The body of Christ includes many members with many different gifts. The same is true of the various communions that make up the Christian church. The calling of the Reformed Church has been to provide an educated ministry to lead the church in theology, evangelism, and missions throughout the world.

Resources for Further Study

From Strength to Strength, by Gerald F. DeJong. The Historical Series of the Reformed Church in America. Grand Rapids: Eerdmans, 1982.

Two Centuries Plus: The Story of New Brunswick Seminary, by Howard G. Hageman. The Historical Series of the Reformed Church in America. Grand Rapids: Eerdmans, 1984.

Vision for a Christian College, by Gordon J. Van Wylen. The Historical Series of the Reformed Church in America. Grand Rapids: Eerdmans, 1988.

Vision from the Hill: Selections from Works of Faculty and Alumni, published on the bicentennial of New Brunswick Theological Seminary, edited by John W. Beardslee III. The Historical Series of the Reformed Church in America. Grand Rapids: Eerdmans, 1984.

Northwestern—Academy to College

Academy Hall, circa 1886

Like Hope College, Northwestern started as an academy in 1882. First classes were held in the consistory room of the First Reformed Church in Orange City and in the local public school. Henry Hospers donated a full city block in Orange City for the new academy, and the community was canvassed for funds to build. A two-story frame structure was ready for occupancy in 1884 and was known as the Pioneer School.

Of that first building, the principal, the Reverend James Zwemer, could later say:

> The building . . .was built to stand as a testimony to the importance of higher education; a protest against ignorance and materialism; indeed as a huge ballot box, where the passer-by could cast his vote yes or no on the important question for these parts, whether we would be a people only for hogs and corn, or also for "dedication" and culture.[1]

Students seeking a higher education packed the Pioneer School; soon more space was desperately needed. The board of trustees purchased an abandoned skating rink, two stories, ninety-five by forty-five feet. Officially called Academy Hall, students dubbed it simply the Rink or Noah's Ark. Zwemer was evidently not without a sense of humor, for in 1895, on the occasion of the twenty-fifth anniversary of the founding of the Dutch colony in northwest Iowa and a year after a new classroom building, the brick Zwemer Hall, had been built, he observed, "If the cradle of the Academy was the Pioneer School, it was in the Rink that we learned to walk," adding that it

> Indeed became an ark of salvation. There we were kept; there we grew, and grew from strength to strength; there students came as doves to their windows; from there systematic efforts to self-reliance began; from there, the blessed Providence led us to a permanent place of living, where we wish to remain with the youth entrusted to us.[2]

---

[1] Gerald F. DeJong, *From Strength to Strength* (Grand Rapids: Eerdmans, 1982), 20.
[2] Ibid., 22.

Norman Vincent Peale—
A Positive Preacher

The decade of the 1950s has been described as both placid and stress-filled. Amid outward calm and growing prosperity, the spread of suburbia and increased mobility disrupted social stability by breaking up close communities and cohesive extended families. Ministering within this mix was Norman Vincent Peale—"as important for the religious revival of the fifties as George Whitefield had been for the Great Awakening of the eighteenth century."[1]

Peale was born in Ohio in 1898 and was ordained in the Methodist Church. Marble Collegiate Church in New York City called him to its pulpit in 1932. There, his powers in the pulpit gradually increased, as did his ability to communicate to broader audiences through the mass media.

Peale preached to a people still dealing with the effects of World War II, and "although he by no means brought about the postwar renewal of religious interest, he rode its crest, and more than any other, he set the tone and guided the interests of the popular revival."[2] His book titles display his essential message. *A Guide to Confident Living* was published in 1948, *The Power of Positive Thinking* in 1952. Both sold more than two million copies. The two were undoubtedly the most influential of his forty-six books.

With the pulpit of Marble Collegiate at its prestigious Fifth Avenue location as his base for five decades, Peale was in constant demand as a lecturer. He spoke on radio and appeared on television, he had a newspaper column, and he wrote for mass-circulation magazines, including his own *Guideposts*.

Founded by Ruth Stafford Peale and her husband in 1945, *Guideposts* continues to be published, "committed to communicating positive faith-filled principles for people everywhere to use in successful daily living." The magazine and its web-site (www.guideposts.com) remain faithful to Peale's message. Its archives offer nearly twelve thousand inspirational stories and spiritual how-to articles and the site ends with the assurance, "This site is powered by Positive Thinking."

---

[1] Sydney E. Ahlstrom, *A Religious History of the American People* (New Haven: Yale Univ. Press, 1972), 956.
[2] Ibid.

Norman Vincent and Ruth Stafford Peale, 1952.

19
The Limitations of Being Christian

The global mission conference in Edinburgh, 1910 (held in the assembly rooms of the Church of Scotland), often cited as the birth of the ecumenical movement.

The Reformed Church in America's numerical growth has been and will continue to be limited by a continual "membership leakage" that results from (1) our numerical distribution in a mobile society, and (2) our biblically sound theology.

From the beginning of colonial times, wherever members of the Dutch church were too thinly scattered to support a settled, educated ministry, leakage occurred to other denominations. In more heavily

Dutch communities, churches grew strong as families grew, adding to the covenant community. At the turn of the millenium, as a result of population mobility, we continue to lose members despite the fact that it has been a long time since our congregations were limited to people of Dutch ancestry. One reason is that the average American family changes its place of residence once every four years. When a Reformed Church family moves to another community, the probability is high that the community will not have a Reformed church.

In the mid-twentieth century, when earlier immigration had still left strong pockets of Dutch immigrants, there was only a single county in the entire United States and Canada where 50 percent of the people were Reformed, and that was Ottawa County, which encompasses most of Holland, Michigan. Only five counties had Reformed populations between 25 and 50 percent: Sioux, Marion, and Mahaska in Iowa, and Newago and Missaukee in Michigan. (These figures were achieved by lumping Reformed and Christian Reformed together for statistical purposes.) All of these counties have since suffered further dilution of their Dutch populations. In short, there are very few places in North America to which one can move and still be near a Reformed church.

Being biblical also increases the threat of leakage, since that includes readily admitting that one can be fully Christian in other denominations. While there have been individual exceptions, the denomination as a whole has never seen itself as exclusivist. When in

Events referenced in the chapter are below the line. Other historical events are above the line.

1873
"Blessed Assurance"

1884
"God of the Prophets"

1867
"Immortal, Invisible, God Only Wise"

1771
"Guide Me, O Thou Great Jehovah"

1881
"Come, Let Us to the Lord Our God"

1930
"God of Grace and God of Glory"

1968
"I Come with Joy to Meet My Lord"

1750	1800	1850	1900	1950	2000

1743
Synod of South Holland proposes merger

1876
Presbyterian Alliance today known as the Alliance of Reformed Churches Throughout the World holding the Presbyterian Order

1908-49
Federal Council of Churches

1948
World Council of Churches

1950
National Council of Churches of Christ in the United States of America

1999
Joint Declaration on Justification by Faith

1997
Formula of Agreement

1743 the Synod of South Holland in the Netherlands proposed to the little Dutch Church in America that it unite with its Scottish Presbyterian and German Reformed counterparts, the union failed to take place, not because any group denied that the others were Christian, but in large part because the three groups worshiped with different languages.

Throughout its history, the Reformed Church has seen at least twelve official efforts to seek a more complete union with other denominations. In every case, these attempted organizational or corporate unions failed to muster a sufficient majority to approve the union. Nonetheless, the denomination's perpetual willingness to consider such talks is ample proof that its members do not see themselves as "the only true Christians."

It seems always possible to get a majority of elders and ministers at a General Synod to recognize other denominations as not only Christian, but so similar that they desire to enter into talks seeking a closer corporate union. This is convincing evidence that we see ourselves as one Christian

Why Ecumenism?

The term *ecumenism* is used to refer to the whole church, to the biblical truth that the church as the people of God and the body of Christ are one and must show forth that truth in obedience to the gospel. "The ecumenical vision rests on the conviction that Christians 'are related to one another thanks to actions of God in Jesus Christ which are prior to any decisions they may make. . . . Christ has made us his own, and he is not divided."[1] "The mandate for ecumenical work is . . . to bear witness to the God of peace and justice, the God made known to us in Jesus Christ, through the way we live with one another. It is from this conviction, this vision of wholeness in Christ, that the ecumenical movement gets its energy, purpose and direction."[2]

_____

[1] Michael Kinnamon and Brian E. Cope, eds., *The Ecumenical Movement: An Anthology of Key Texts and Voices* (Grand Rapids: Eerdmans, 1997), 7.
[2] Ibid., 86.

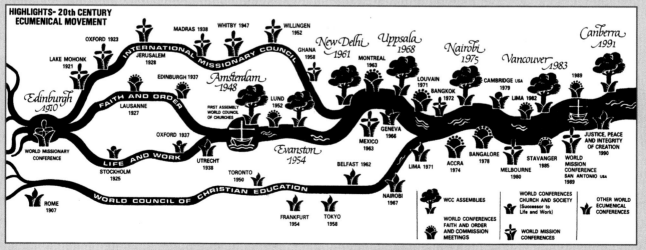

Twentieth century ecumenical streams—graphic hanging in the foyer of the WCC

denomination among many. Further proof of this recognition was seen in 1997, when several Reformed communions and the majority of Lutherans approved the Formula of Agreement, which broke down 450-year-old walls by allowing Lutherans and Reformed to recognize the validity of one another's ministries and sacraments.

Most dramatic of all in our ecumenical witness is our recognition of other denominations as fully Christian through our refusal to rebaptize Christians of other denominations and our invitation to all baptized Christians to share in the Lord's Table. It was that acknowledgment of other denominations as fully Christian that offended some of the nineteenth-century Dutch seceders when they came to this country.

Precisely because of the mobility of today's society, we must ever remind our congregations that throughout Christendom there are many who seek to proclaim God's Word faithfully and celebrate the sacraments. We are not a sectarian group that—by teaching some strange doctrine or by demanding certain peculiarities of behavior beyond the biblical requirement— seeks a claim that sets us apart from all others. Sects grow through the zeal and exclusivist nature of their adherents, but the spiritual carnage that results when those individuals are separated from such groups of "only true believers" is fearful.

The startling growth statistics of some new sect may prompt us to ask, "Why can't we grow like that?" While not seeking to aid or abet complacency or a failure to witness, some of the answer as to why the Reformed Church doesn't grow like the sects is, "Because we are biblical." We recognize that the Reformed Church in America is one Christian denomination among many.

Since we are a part of mainstream biblical Christianity, as people move and find themselves joining other denominations, will members of other denominations who move near our churches also feel comfortable in joining us? Yes and no. Yes, it happens all the time. People find in our settled, educated, biblical ministry good church homes despite the variety of their back-grounds. Most of our congregations include members who have come from just about every conceivable Christian communion. However, the sociological probabilities are against us.

For example, if a member of the

The Alliance of Reformed Churches Throughout the World Holding the Presbyterian Order

The world's oldest Protestant confessional alliance, first called the Presbyterian Alliance and often known as the World Alliance of Reformed Churches, was organized in London in 1875. Its continued intent has been to strengthen Reformed churches throughout the world. That work has included theological discussions with other communions leading to a greater sense of unity. It has also meant using the influence of the alliance to rescue church leaders from persecution. The alliance contributed in some measure to the dismantling of apartheid in South Africa when it declared such racism to be heresy. The Reformed Church in America has been a member of the alliance since its inception.

Reformed Church in Holland, Michigan, moves to San Antonio, Texas, there will not be one Reformed church in the entire city, but there will be plenty of Presbyterian churches in which to feel at home. Conversely, if a Presbyterian moves from San Antonio to Holland, Michigan, there is a Presbyterian church to attend. That same person may nonetheless join a Reformed church because of its minister, congregation, building, programs, preaching, music, or for some other reason. But when all is said and done, the edge, in terms of probabilities, goes to those denominations that have the larger distribution of churches.

That the Reformed Church in America has for so long managed to defy statistical and sociological probabilities that spell imminent dissolution is a tribute to its people and pastors. Together they have provided a fellowship that has reflected a settled, educated, biblically sound ministry and with that ministry have engaged in careful Christian nurture. The result has been a church that has been attractive to many when familiar denominational labels have not been as satisfying.

Having acknowledged that we have been defying the laws of statistical and sociological probability, we nonetheless need to acknowledge that "leakage" is one of the reasons we do not grow more than we do. We nurture many in the faith who then go on to become good members of the churches of other denominations. Many churches in highly mobile

areas must feel more like schools than traditional parish churches— places where people receive education for a time rather than where they are born, baptized, nurtured throughout life, and finally buried.

But if, because of small size, we suffer more than many from leakage and are not exclusivist but acknowledge a common Christian heritage, and as well have striking similarities of theology and polity to other communions, then why do we remain separate? The question has remained with us since 1743, when the Synod of South Holland suggested that we join forces with the Presbyterians and the German Reformed. That question will not go away, but it remains because we are a denomination with almost four hundred years of history as one of the family of Reformed churches, originally Dutch but now American and Canadian.

Because our biblical Christian life has been lived within the main-stream of Christ's church, the question will be raised again and again: Can we best serve Christ in union with another denomination or as a distinct communion? If we seek to follow the latest fads in church growth to the point that we no longer teach or preach our confessions of faith or use them in worship, bear a clear biblical witness, or care about the content of hymnody, then there is no serious reason for a separate existence. On the other hand, if we wish to build on our experience as a communion committed to a biblically and theologically educated ministry, which in turn educates its

United Church of Christ: The UCC was formed in 1957 through a union of Congregational Christian Churches (going back to the Puritans) and the Evangelical and Reformed Churches (primarily German in origin). The UCC has a unique combination of congregational and Presbyterian polities in which decisions are made at synods, but the conscience of each congregation is respected.

Evangelical Lutheran Church in America: The ELCA was formed January 1, 1988, of the Lutheran Church in America, the American Lutheran Church, and the Association of Evangelical Lutheran Churches. It comprised Lutherans of German, Swedish, Norwegian, Finnish, and Danish backgrounds. It is the fifth largest denomination in the United States.

membership in Holy Scripture, theology, hymnody, and the confessions, then perhaps there is a reason for our continued existence even as we acknowledge other Protestants as well as Orthodox and Roman Catholics to be likewise Christian in their confessions and commitments.

Resources for Further Study

Concord Makes Strength: Essays in Reformed Ecumenism, edited by John Coakley. The Historical Series of the Reformed Church in America. Grand Rapids: Eerdmans, 2002.

The Ecumenical Movement: An Anthology of Key Texts and Voices, edited by Michael Kinnamon and Brian E. Cope. Grand Rapids: Eerdmans, 1997.

Ecumenism and the Reformed Church, by Herman Harmelink III. The Historical Series of the Reformed Church in America. Grand Rapids: Eerdmans, 1968.

Introducing the World Council of Churches, by Marlin Van Elderen and Martin Conway. Geneva: WCC Publications, 2001.

A Formula of Agreement

In 1998 the Evangelical Lutheran Church in America, the Reformed Church in America, the Presbyterian Church in the USA, and the United Church of Christ signed the *Formula of Agreement*. This historic document rescinded mutual anathemas from the era of the Reformation. It indicated agreement among the churches in the essentials of doctrine and recognized each other's ministries and sacraments. In short, these churches, after four centuries in which Lutherans and Reformed were separated, at last reached full communion.

October 4, 1998. For the first time since the Reformation the sacrament of Holy Communion is mutually celebrated by Lutherans and Reformed, marking the *Formula of Agreement*.

The National Council of Churches of Christ in the United States of America

M. William Howard served as president of the National Council of Churches while executive secretary of the Black Council/African American Council of the Reformed Church in America. He became president of New York Theological Seminary.

The National Council of Churches was established in 1950, and the Reformed Church in America was a charter member. As the voice of mainline Protestantism in America, the council's activities include Bible translation (the Revised Standard Version, and more recently the New Revised Standard Version); educational work, including the standardized Sunday school lessons; social action issues; and issues of faith and order.

The National Council's work attracts media attention only when it's controversial; for example, several years ago a subgroup of Faith and Order published a translation of the lectionary with a strong feminist bias that received extensive media coverage. When Faith and Order published an affirmative commentary on the Nicene Creed, the oldest and most widely accepted creed in Christendom, it received no media coverage.

Church World Service is perhaps the best known division of the National Council. Two members of the Reformed Church have given extensive service to the council. The Reverend William Howard served as its president, and the Reverend Arie Brouwer served as its general secretary.

Arie Brouwer, as general secretary of the NCCCUSA, presents a crayola birthday card from church school children in Grand Rapids on the occasion of the millennial celebration of Christianity in Russia. On the platform of the Bolshoi Theatre in Moscow are church leaders from around the world. Raisa Gorbachev is seated just behind Brouwer, to the left.

The World Council of Churches

WCC headquarters in Geneva, Switzerland

The World Council of Churches, meeting in Amsterdam, sends this message of greeting to all who are in Christ, and to all who are willing to hear:

We bless God our Father, and our Lord Jesus Christ Who gathers together in one the children of God that are scattered abroad. He has brought us here together at Amsterdam. We are one in acknowledging Him as our God and Saviour. We are divided from one another not only in matters of faith, order and traditions, but also by pride of nation, class and race. But Christ has made us His own, and He is not divided. In seeking Him we find one another. Here at Amsterdam we have committed ourselves afresh to Him, and have covenanted with one another in constituting this World Council of Churches. We intend to stay together. We call upon Christian congregations everywhere to endorse and fulfill this covenant in their relations one with another. In thankfulness to God we commit the future to Him.

—Amsterdam, 1948[1]

The World Council of Churches came into being in Amsterdam after World War II, in 1948. The Reformed Church in America voted its intent to join in 1937, but war intervened. One of the members of the Reformed Church, the Reverend A. Livingston Warnshuis, helped write its constitution.

The World Council grew out of three earlier ecumenical movements. In 1910 the **World Missionary Conference** was held in Edinburgh, Scotland. There, representatives of many of the world's Protestant churches discussed how their missionary work in foreign lands might be carried out most effectively. The Reformed Church in America was there.

Out of that Edinburgh conference the **International Missionary Council** was formed, which in 1961 became integrated into the World Council of Churches. At its beginning and integration, the Reformed Church in America was there.

The obligation to take the Gospel to the whole world, and the obligation to draw all Christ's people together, both rest upon Christ's whole work and are indissolubly connected. Every attempt to separate these tasks violates the wholeness of Christ's ministry to the world.

—International Missionary Council 1951[2]

In 1925 a conference of many of the same churches met in Stockholm to discuss the **Life and Work** of the church. Many believed that divided Protestantism could work together to meet the needs of the world, even if it couldn't agree on items of doctrine. The Reformed Church in America was there.

However, it was soon recognized that churches had to come to grips with what they believed, and it began to be recognized that the churches had much more in common than that which divided them. Thus **Faith and Order** was born in a conference in Lausanne in 1927. The Reformed Church in America was there.

Today the World Council is composed of

approximately 330 communions, including the Orthodox churches. While the Roman Catholic Church is not officially a member, its representatives participate on many levels, especially that of Faith and Order.

The most notable achievement of the World Council of Churches has been to enable the member communions to recognize one another as the church of Christ. This has led to doctrinal discussions between churches (bilaterals) that have resulted in areas of large consensus, as in *Baptism, Eucharist and Ministry* and the *Joint Declaration on Justification by Faith*. The council has also assisted churches undergoing persecution. While it has made strides in common worship (the *Common Lectionary* and the *Lima Liturgy*) and in recognition of full communion

Donald J. Bruggink photos

Donald J. Bruggink, 1969.

Herman J. Ridder, then president of Western Theological Seminary, admires the statue of St. Paul in the library of the WCC, given by Pope Paul VI to commemorate his visit to the council in 1967.

Chapel of the WCC

between Lutheran and Reformed, the inability of Protestant, Orthodox, and Roman Catholic Christians to sit at the same Eucharistic table is a painful reminder of the work that remains to be done to manifest the unity we already have in Christ.

---

1 Kinnamon and Cope, *The Ecumenical Movement*, 21.
2 Ibid., 343.

Lutherans and Catholics Reach Doctrinal Agreement

The *Joint Declaration on the Doctrine of Justification* (adopted in Augsburg, Germany, October 31, 1999) is one of the most remarkable ecumenical documents of our time. In it Lutherans, represented by the Lutheran World Federation, and the Roman Catholic Church came to consensus on the doctrine of justification, the principal doctrine of conflict at the time of the Reformation. At that time, the conflict resulted in mutual condemnations between the two churches that continued in force until 1999, when they were withdrawn in light of the new consensus. The following paragraphs from the declaration (with original numbering) provide a glimpse into the substance of the agreement.

The Common Understanding of Justification

The Reverend Ishmael Noko of the Lutheran World Federation and Bishop Kasper, secretary of the Pontifical Council for Promoting Christian Unity, two of the signers of the Joint Declaration of October 31, 1999.

14. The Lutheran churches and the Roman Catholic Church have together listened to the good news proclaimed in Holy Scripture. This common listening, together with the theological conversations of recent years, has led to a shared understanding of justification. This encompasses a consensus in the basic truths; the differing explications in particular statements are compatible with it.[1]

15. In faith we together hold the conviction that justification is the work of the triune God. The Father sent his Son into the world to save sinners. The foundation and presupposition of justification is the incarnation, death and resurrection of Christ. Justification thus means that Christ himself is our righteousness, in which we share through the Holy Spirit in accord with the will of the Father. Together we confess: By grace alone, in faith in Christ's saving work and not because of any merit on our part, we are accepted by God and receive the Holy Spirit, who renews our hearts while equipping and calling us to good works....[2]

Explicating the Common Understanding of Justification

19. We confess together that all persons depend completely on the saving grace of God for their salvation. The freedom they possess in relation to persons and the things of this world is no freedom in relation to salvation, for as sinners they stand under God's judgment and are incapable of turning by themselves to God to seek deliverance, of meriting their justification before God, or of attaining salvation by their own abilities. Justification takes place solely by God's grace.[3]

---

[1] "Joint Declaration on the Doctrine of Justification," in Jeffrey Gros, FSC, Harding Meyer, and William G. Rusch, eds., *Growth in Agreement II, Reports and Agreed Statements of Ecumenical Conversations on a World Level, 1982-1998* (Grand Rapids: Eerdmans, 2000), 568.

[2] Ibid., 568-69.

[3] Ibid., 569.

20
What's Next?

Middle Collegiate Church

Dave Cross photo

As rumors of his death circulated, Mark Twain quipped, "Reports of my death have been greatly exaggerated." In the nineteenth century, Nietzche reported the death of religion. In the counterculture decade of the 1960s, God was declared dead. Recently mainline denominations, including the Reformed Church in America, have also been described as on their way out.

   Predictions of the demise of the Reformed Church are not limited to the twentieth century. In 1845 the classes of the Synod of New

York reported, "Pastor after pastor has been heard putting forth the melancholy exclamation: 'Who has believed our report,' and church after church has been heard complaining that citizens of the heavenly Jerusalem have too much forgotten their character as denizens of that holy commonwealth."[1] In 1847 they reported, "The Word of God seems to fall like rain on the rock, and spiritual barrenness prevails."[2] And in 1861, "Nothing cheery to report."[3]

It is true that in the last four decades of the twentieth century mainline denominations suffered massive losses. Reformed Church losses, however, were considerably smaller than those of other mainline communions—strange, because losses should have been much greater because of its small size. Time and time again, the Reformed Church, by grace alone, has survived when to all appearances it should have died.

However, the Reformed Church's smaller percentage of loss is hardly cause for either complacency or optimism. Why have mainline denominations lost so many members? Some have offered the following reasons: ecumenism, secularism, failure to hold the young, lack of theological nurture, and at least some losses have resulted from being in the forefront of proclaiming the gospel to our age.

Moving forward has always resulted in losing people who are convinced the old ways are best. In the nineteenth century, the Reformed Church in the Midwest lost many members when recent seceders objected to singing hymns and offering the Lord's Supper to Christians of other communions. It lost more members by refusing to add the exclusion of lodge affiliation as a test for church membership. The Reformed Church in America also failed to acquire an entire German classis because of its stand against slavery—despite the scriptural citations in favor of slavery advanced by Dr. How.

In the twentieth century, issues that troubled the church and resulted in a shrinking membership

Events referenced in the chapter are below the line. Other historical events are above the line.

2,000
Celebrations of a new millenium

| 2000 | 2025 | 2050 | 2075 | 3000 |

2000
RCA Mission 2000: Discerning the Spirit, Engaging the World

By Grace Alone!

2,003
Reformed Church in America celebrates its 375th year of God's grace!

Hispanic Harvest

A million-dollar radio outlet for a dying church? Well, yes, but it's not dying anymore.

The Corona (California) Community Church "has been transformed into Iglesia La Senda, a thriving Hispanic RCA congregation. Eighty-five percent of La Senda's members first heard about the church on pastor Adres Serrano's radio broadcast.

"In 1997 Serrano went on the air at a local station with his first broadcast. He asked listeners to respond to his message, and scores of people did. So many that 'the station manager told me I needed to get a studio and get my own telephone line,' says Serrano.

"In 1999 Serrano became pastor of Corona Community Church, where the surrounding community is 92 percent Hispanic. He bought an FCC license and began looking for land to build his own transmitter. A former Corona elder offered to help back Serrano's radio outreach. Serrano also mortgaged his home and sent a proposal to RCA

Andre Serrano

Mission Services' Urban Innovation Grant Program (starter grants for new programs), which netted him an additional $30,000 over three years. Serrano purchased his station for $1 million and began broadcasting in November 1999.

"Thanks to pre-recording and automation, Serrano's programming runs 24 hours a day, and his 50-watt broadcasts have the potential to reach 90,000 listeners. He airs the four sermons he preaches each week, plus news, interviews, traffic reports, and lots of music. 'We have no commercials and lots of prayer,' he says. 'We invite people to know the Lord. . . . Our ministry comes to life when we see people confess Jesus Christ as Lord and Savior.'"

—From *Mission Today, Reformed Church in America*, May 2003

included the ordination of women and participation in ecumenical organizations such as the National Council of the Churches of Christ and the World Council of Churches. In the twenty-first century, issues associated with homosexuality will also likely result in losses. Like the issue of slavery, some will cite Scripture as a permanent condemnation, while others will see the love of Christ as transcendent—especially as scientific discovery leads us in the direction of seeing homosexuality not as a chosen lifestyle, but as a genetic disposition.

Some of the reasons suggested to account for the Reformed Church's shrinking numbers might also be understood as keys for future growth.

Ecumenism as a Source of Growth

Ecumenism, as understood here, is the awareness that we are one in Christ. It is the response to Christ's will, expressed succinctly in John 17:11, "that they may be one, as we are one." The result is that much of the interdenominational hostility of the nineteenth century has given way to awareness of our unity in Christ, which is far more important than many of the things that divided us. While ecumenism has resulted in openness to other communions, making it easier for members of the Reformed

Michaelius to Middle

Gordon Dragt

Jacqueline Lewis

The Middle Collegiate Church in New York City stands in a direct line of descent from Dominie Michaelius, who held the first Dutch service in America in 1628. Three hundred seventy-five years later, the church of which Michaelius was the first pastor still exists—not only the Reformed Church in America, but also his more immediate ecclesial offspring, the four Collegiate churches of New York: Marble, Middle, West End, and Fort Washington.

Organized as a congregation in 1729, Middle's present building was constructed in 1891. The church had a glorious history of ministering to solid, committed white Reformed people, but by 1985 most of its constituency had moved away. The East Village had seen an influx first of eastern Europeans, and more recently many aspirants to the arts community. Life in the East Village was vibrant and raw. Attendance at Middle varied from twelve on a low Sunday to twenty-seven, tops. Of those who refused to stop worshiping, the median age was probably in the seventies. The Collegiate consistory considered closing this venerable offspring of Michaelius.

Enter the Reverend Gordon Dragt, brashly assuring the consistory that the church could be turned around. Unlike Michaelius, he cast no aspersions on those around him, he did not see the "natives" as incorrigible, and, also unlike Michaelius, he did not leave. Like Michaelius, he found the task before him daunting. Dragt tells of early days of self-pity, of leaving the church after a near-empty service and crossing the street to Moshe's bakery to indulge himself in the sweetest, most sugary pastry he could find. Looking across 2nd Avenue at Middle, the great

rectangular stones became, in his vision, doors. "On each door was a sign that said welcome, and another sign that had a person's name, or talent, or race, or sexual orientation, or age, or human condition, or gender. . . . I believed God was saying to me in that vision, 'Gordon your mission here is simply to keep opening more doors and welcoming more people, no matter who, no matter what, no questions asked, simply a ministry of opening doors and welcoming people.'"[1]

Because many in the East Village are engaged in the arts, the arts are also given a large place in the life of Middle Church. On frequent Sundays, a jazz band, either on the sidewalk or in the church, begins a concert of familiar gospel songs forty minutes before the service. As the *New York Times* described it, "An Old-Time Religion Gets Some New Twists." As a part of the service, the regular choir offers new and classical anthems, while the sixty-five-voice ethnically diverse Jerriese Johnson East Village

Gospel Choir can bring the service to ecstasy. Four other choirs spanning all age ranges also contribute to the worship celebration. On some Sundays the resident dance company contributes to the service, at other times nine-foot-tall puppets—and almost always a biblical sermon by Dragt or his African-American associate, the Reverend Jacqueline Lewis. But the sermon of God's love is embodied by the ministry team. Before the service, Dragt can be seen and experienced, a warm handshake for newcomers, a hug and a kiss for the familiar—up one aisle and down another, reaching, touching—welcome, welcome, welcome.

While Middle Church fields the usual ministries,

church school for all ages, Bible studies, family events, Sunday brunches following worship, the annual reading through the Bible challenge, Crop Walks, and even a Strawberry Social, it also engages in outreach to its specific East Village community. It offers a children's five-day after-school arts center, as well as children's summer arts programs and day trips. It also offers a Monday Celebrate Life meal for people with Aids, a community senior adult center, social worker and supportive services, a clothes closet, a food pantry, Alcoholics Anonymous and other self-help groups, a women's ministry council, use of facilities by the community, OASIS (Open to All Singles in the Spirit), GLAM (Gays and Lesbians At Middle), which constructs a float sponsored by Middle for an annual parade, the Second Avenue Street Festival, and the Seventh & Second Photo Gallery for artists of the community.

The result? Despite a constantly changing community, Middle now has two to four hundred attending worship, with standing room only for special festivals, and more than 750 members, with weekly program contacts of a thousand.

A *Village Voice* writer has this to say: "Middle Collegiate Church is the best church to worship at when the others won't have you back." *Time Out New York* reaffirms, "Amen to That! From jazz jams to free grub, this church offers more than sermons and song – Middle Collegiate Church – Eclectic celebrations at this East Village pillar offer everything from jazz to current-events. Post-celebration activities include social brunches, art exhibits and children's art workshops." The *New York Daily News* describes the Easter program: "There, jazz musicians will perform with a brass quartet and gospel choir. And, yes, the bill includes the Hallelujah Chorus!"

The *New York Times* (Nov. 8, 1996), reported: "Dr. Murray J. Berenson, a physician who has been

attending Middle Collegiate on and off for five decades was like most of two dozen or so old-timers who continued to worship at the church during its nadir in the mid-1980s. He has remained there through the subsequent changes wrought by Mr. Dragt, through the sudden appearance, he says, of 'a lot of people with all kinds of earrings.' And Dr. Berenson has wondered, in flickering moments, about the propriety of the dancers and the jazz band as methods of spurring membership. He said, 'But then I thought, What did the missionaries do?' He added, 'they got people into hospitals, cured their broken bones or wounds, and then sold them the faith. We're just using music instead of medicine.'"

The medicine of music and art would have seemed strange to Michaelius, but there is a far older testimony to its appropriateness for worship, as is pointedly obvious in Dragt's free paraphrase of the psalmist: "Praise God! Praise God in this place of worship in the middle of this great city! Praise God for the loving things God has done! Praise God with horns and guitars! Praise God with harps and flutes! Praise God with the piano and the organ! Praise God with drums and dancing! Praise God with tambourines and cymbals; with clapping hands, tapping feet, and moving bodies! Praise God with sermons, poetry, drama, and stories! Praise God with singing and with laughter! Praise God through the dying of the old and the rising of the new! Praise God with justice and with peace on earth and goodwill to all! Praise God for God's extravagant and amazing grace! Praise God, all living creatures! Praise God!"[2]

Dave Cross photos

---

[1] Gordon Dragt, *The Middle Collegiate Church Story*, unpublished mss., March 21, 2003.
[2] Ibid.

Church to join other denominations, it similarly means that members of other denominations find it easier to become members of the Reformed Church in America.

While the Reformed Church can no longer count on denominational loyalty to keep churches growing, ecumenism makes others more open to the Reformed Church. Reformed congregations appeal to people searching for Christian nurture for their children; clear and relevant preaching of the gospel; and a community characterized by Christian fellowship, love, and care. Ecumenism helps counter the Reformed Church's small size by allowing individual congregations to attract new people on the basis of Christian witness and nurture. The experiences of such churches as Paramount in California and Twin Falls in Idaho are examples of such growth.

Secularism

Secularism can hardly be considered an impetus for church growth. But neither must it mean the death of the church. The erosion of religious commitment is hardly new. One has only to read the Old Testament to be aware that time and again wealth and prosperity corroded Israel's commitment to God. It is interesting that in what are arguably the most secular areas of the country—affluent Orange County in California and the wealthy northwest suburbs of Chicago—pastors of Reformed background (the Revs. Robert Schuller and Bill Hybels) have achieved outstanding evangelistic successes. In countless churches large and small, the proclamation of the gospel and the expression of Christianity in love, acceptance, witness, action for justice, and hope has proven stronger than secular forces. The Middle Collegiate Church on the lower east side of New York City is a good example. In a congregation that had lost most of its constituency, the Reverend Gordon Dragt and his growing congregation have lived Christ's message of love and acceptance in a community of marked diversity, and they have filled the church.

Failure to Hold the Young

Infant baptism is almost universally practiced among Reformed Church members. Studies have found that church and church school attendance are most positively influenced by the example of parents and grand-parents. Seemingly, at this level, any secularizing tendencies are the result of a failure of parental example.[4]

However, a disturbing finding in recent studies of mainline denominations is that, in general, higher levels of education lead to higher levels of church dropouts. At the same time, these studies indicate that in both mainline Protestant and Roman Catholic churches, the level of biblical and theological literacy is relatively low. Perhaps the church has stressed such good things as fellowship and social action while neglecting to constantly rebuild the foundations

The New Church of Greater New York

Hak Kwan Lee

The church that bears this unusual name can tell an amazing story of God's grace and of the faith and determination of an immigrant Korean community. The Reverend Hak Kwan Lee is a graduate of Princeton Theological Seminary and Columbia University. He began the church with three families, totaling eleven people. In Flushing, Queens, they rented space from a church, but when the rent became exorbitant, they were forced to find a new location within two months. Unable to locate appropriate, affordable space, the congregation spent one week worshiping outdoors in a public park. But Lee had heard of a former synagogue school building for sale in Roslyn Heights, a Nassau County community east of New York. He and his wife investigated, even though they knew there was no money in the treasury. They were impressed with the building and location and negotiated. There was already a bid on the property for $1.6 million. Lee offered $1.5 million with a vision statement, and his bid was accepted.

When asked how they would make payment, Lee replied that they had no money, but he proposed a method of payment that included a mortgage assumed by the former owners. In the process of moving, the congregation looked for a responsive denomination with which they could affiliate. It found openness to ethnic congregations in the Reformed Church in America and became a member of the Classis of Nassau-Suffolk in 1994.

The church continues to thrive, now served by a staff ministry, as well as a number of seminarians. Membership has grown to more than five hundred, including more than two hundred young people. Since its establishment, the church has been working on its ministry of mission. Originally supporting work on four mission fields, the church increased its involvement to thirty-seven sites by the end of its first seven-year ministry term.

Presently, the church supports twenty-six overseas mission bases, four domestic opportunities, and four campus and young generation fields. As a special project, the church took a main role in supporting "Manna Mission," the chief task of which is to build bread factories in North Korea, as well as developing hospitals and a stationery factory. The church also has helped establish schools and dormitories for Koreans in China. Another effort is "Yucatan Mission" for the minority indigenous people of Mayan descent, as well as some Korean immigrants who went there as laborers at around the end of the Chosen Dynasty in the early twentieth century. The mission for Mexico includes planting churches, supporting seminaries, running mission centers, providing medical services, and cooperating with and supporting local churches.

Liturgy: Literally, the service of the people, their action in the worship of God. Liturgy refers to the service of worship, its structure and its parts.

Biblical preaching: Preaching that explains the original meaning of the passage in the Bible and applies it to life today, preferably with positive examples of what life looks like when lived in accordance with the biblical teaching.

Theology: Literally, the study of God. Theology involves giving structure to the biblical message. Theological synopses of the faith are found in the Apostles' and Nicene creeds, and the doctrinal standards and confessions of the church (for the Reformed Church) are contained in the Heidelberg Catechism, Belgic Confession, and Canons of Dort.

of biblical and theological understanding. And nowhere does this seem more prevalent than in youth fellowships, even as it continues to be true among adults.

While the emotions are one avenue to religious commitment, it would appear that such is not enough to stem the tide of dropouts among the more highly educated. The church has perhaps depended too much on fellowship and emotions when it should also have been educating its young rigorously in the truths of the faith. The abandonment of catechetical training is not a little to blame for a poorly understood faith. The great twentieth-century Scottish theologian, Thomas F. Torrance, observed that people do not of themselves know the truth about God; they do not even know how to ask the right questions. The catechetical method has for centuries been a staple of the faith precisely because it does frame the right questions, thereby enabling the right answers. If the church would hold its increasingly educated young, it can no longer substitute a "good time" for good knowledge of the faith. Young people must be given tools to help them account for the hope that is in them (1 Peter 3:15).

In some instances the church also is failing to prepare its members intellectually in the area of singing. Emotional appeal should not be seen as a substitute for biblical content when it involves the hymnody of the church. The theology (i.e., the faith content) of many congregants is expressed in the words of what is sung. If we are

to retain the educated, we should nurture faith through hymns of biblical and theological substance.

Theology as a Source of Growth

Frequently, leaders in a congregation, including the pastor, have almost unconsciously assumed that other members share their biblical, theological, and liturgical understanding. But church membership is constantly changing, necessitating the constant rebuilding of biblical, theological, and liturgical foundations. Practically speaking, this can mean biblical preaching through the books of the Bible in the sequence of the lectionary. Theological understanding comes through familiarity with such confessions as the Heidelberg Catechism, which contains such basics as the Apostle's Creed, the meaning of the sacraments, the Ten Commandments, and the Lord's Prayer. Because congregants worship every week, church leaders, especially pastors, often take for granted that they understand the structure and purpose of the elements of the service. In all of these areas, congregants are entitled to have their pastors educate them.

The Role of Immigrants in the Growth of the RCA

One of the heartening signs for the future is the accession of nationals from other countries into the Reformed Church in America. The Synod of New York has been especially successful in including immigrants from what were once mission lands. The endeavors of an educated clergy who went abroad to share the gospel have now resulted in nationals from those countries joining the Reformed Church even as Dutch immigrants did in the nineteenth century, and for largely the same reasons—a conservative, biblical theology and a warm, accommodating, and helpful welcome.

In the Synod of New York there are twenty-three Asian congregations, including a Taiwanese congregation in Boston, the first congregation the Reformed Church has been has been able to start and sustain in that city in over three hundred years. In addition, current work includes one Taiwanese, one Indonesian, one Tamil Indian, and one Korean church, with hope for developing relationships with a Fugianese church from China and an African church from Ghana. The Classis of Queens has been particularly successful in welcoming Asian

Shin Kwang Church, Bayside, Long Island, New York

immigrants. Due in large part to this openness, the Classis of Queens increased the number of its congregations by fifty percent between 1950 and 2000.

There was a time when the Reformed Church found itself unable to assimilate people of different ethnicities and economic status within its North American congregations even while sending its highly educated ministers and women overseas to spread the gospel. In the mid-twentieth century, this racial and economic provincialism began to change. Highly respected voices, such as that of Howard G. Hageman, pastor of North Church in downtown Newark and later president of New Brunswick Theological Seminary, began to chronicle church flight from

Shin Kwang Church, Bayside, Long Island, New York

Iglesia del Consolador, Chicago

neighborhoods that were no longer predominantly Anglo. He challenged congregations to stay put and minister to new neighbors. This is precisely what many churches in the Synod of New York have done. Churches such as Elmendorf Reformed and DeWitt Reformed in Manhattan; Mott Haven and Fordham Manor in the Bronx; First Reformed in Jamaica, Newtown, and Bowne Street in Queens; the Community Church in Cambria Heights; and New Lots Reformed in Brooklyn chose to minister to their African American, Hispanic, Indonesian, Korean, and Taiwanese neighbors, and all remain vibrant congregations today.

At the same time, many churches that are still mainly Anglo have very large ethnic populations. In this category, Marble Collegiate can claim the largest number of African Americans in the Classis of New York. While English is still the predominant tongue, in the Synod of New York the gospel is preached every Sunday in twelve languages.

The establishment of racial/ethnic councils—the Black Council (now the African-American Council) in 1968 and subsequently the Council for Hispanic Ministries and the Council for Pacific and Asian American Ministries—have done much to welcome people of many races and to provide leadership to sustain racially and ethnically diverse churches and their members in the Reformed Church. While the church's welcome of newcomers has hardly been a universal success, nonetheless its record is improving, and the inclusion of new and diverse members is doing much to sustain and enrich the ministry of the Reformed Church in America.

The Future

Success and vitality within the church can be seen in a variety of ways. On the most basic level, there is the vitality of the faith of the congregation and its individual members. The vitality of the congregation is expressed in its proclamation, nurture, and outreach. The vitality of a congregation and a denomination is also expressed in concern for the society in which the church lives. In the smallest congregations, which often are constricted by population change, vitality frequently is expressed in the continuance of lives of personal faith and maintaining ministry. In other congregations, often those in areas of growing population, growth into a megachurch with multiple programs represents vitality. In still other congregations, vitality is understood as stability, faithful preaching and nurture, ministry in the community, and generous contributions to denominational causes.

Statistical research done by sociologists Roger Nemeth and Donald Luidens[5] shows that the largest and smallest congregations are the ones that are, per capita, the most expensive to sustain. As a result, their giving to causes outside the congregation is often limited. On the other hand, congregations between three hundred and one thousand members are the most generous sustainers of the denomination and its mission.

Fortunately, there are Reformed congregations in every category, and there have been notable examples of small churches that have achieved new growth and vitality. It is to be hoped that as the megachurches stabilize, their passion will be directed increasingly to mission and to issues of social justice and inclusion. May those large, stable churches which now sustain the denomination, its missions, and its continuance of the Calvinistic tradition of ministering to all of society be aware of their context and be willing to be always reforming, and always Reformed.

One of Fifty—Out of Four Million

Allan Byron Ramirez Moncayo

"One of the fifty most powerful persons on Long Island." That was the description of the Reverend Allan Byron Ramirez Moncayo, graduate of Central College and Western Theological Seminary and pastor of the Brookville Reformed Church, at an honorary dinner sponsored by the *Long Island Press* on March 24, 2004.

Power comes in many forms. Ramirez was described as having power in part because of his persistent advocacy for the poor, especially for the exploited undocumented day laborers—advocacy that has challenged the wealthy at times, the police at times, and frequently ends up in the newspapers and courts.

Another form of power comes from the ability to bring together into a community of respect those whom the world regards as enemies. The Brookville congregation now plays host to two more congregations—one Jewish and one Muslim. These three religions, each remaining true to its own beliefs, nonetheless not only live in tolerance, but in increasing understanding and friendship. The occasion of Mel Gibson's movie, *The Passion of the Christ*, resulted in an invitation from the Jewish congregation for pastor Ramirez to explain the passion from his Christian perspective. At Passover, it has now become the custom for the rabbi to invite the Christian and Muslim congregants to the Passover feast. Similarly, the mullah invites Jews and Christians to the feasts of Ramadan.

If Allan Ramirez is one of the fifty most powerful men on Long Island, it is because his personal courage and integrity is augmented by a congregation that supports him in doing good.

The fellowship of believers, and the expression of faith in actions, will be sustained best on the basis of biblically, theologically, and liturgically informed congregations. At the beginning of the Reformation, the marks of a true church were defined as the right preaching of the Word and the administration of the sacraments. In a world of change, those marks still hold true, and they inform not only the Reformed understanding of Scripture and how we worship, but also how these practices fit together in a meaningful theological whole. This understanding of church also implies a welcoming fellowship of Christian love and support and social action that results from the right preaching of the Word and the administration of the sacraments. It is the continuing story of God's amazing grace.

Resources for Further Study

Clarity, Conscience, and Church Order: Reflections on the Book of Church Order, http://www.rca.org/images/aboutus/archives/bcoreflections.pdf

Constitutional Theology, by Allan J. Janssen. The Historical Series of the Reformed Church in America. Grand Rapids: Eerdmans, 2000.

Hands, Hearts, and Voices: Women Who Followed God's Call, by Una H. Ratmeyer. New York: Reformed Church Press, 1995.

History of Women's Involvement in the RCA, http://www.rca.org/lead/women/history.php

Patterns and Portraits: Women in the History of the Reformed Church in America, ed. Renée S. House and John W. Coakley. The Historical Series of the Reformed Church in America. Grand Rapids: Eerdmans, 1999.

[1] James Hart Brumm, ed., *Equipping the Saints, The Synod of New York, 1800-2000*. The Historical Series of the Reformed Church in America (Grand Rapids: Eerdmans, 2000), 89.
[2] Ibid., 89-90.
[3] Ibid., 91.
[4] Roger J. Nemeth and Donald A. Luidens, "Intra- and Intergenerational Transmission of Religious Practices in the Reformed Church in America: A Case for Individual-Level Secularization," in *Rethinking Secularization: Reformed Reaction to Modernity* (New York: Univ. Press of America, 1997), 247-63.
[5] Roger J. Nemeth and Donald A. Luidens, "Paying Peter and/or Paul: Church Finances and Congregational Vitality," in Donald A. Luidens, Corwin E. Smidt, and Hijime Stoffels, eds., *Reformed Vitality: Continuity and Change in the Face of Modernity* (New York: Univ. Press of America, 1998), 119-35.

By Grace Alone

Sometimes congregational church starts, like that of the denomination itself, seems totally dependent upon God's grace. The New Hope Community Church of Gilbert (Phoenix) Arizona, began inauspiciously. The congregation bounced from one rented location to another. Its pastor, Richard Koerselman, would load the digital organ and other church necessities onto a trailer behind his Nissan and it bounced from rented worship space to rented offices.

After such unstable beginnings, New Hope Community was able to purchase land in an excellent location next to a growing residential community. Its experience, as well as its message, was one of God's grace. By the turn of the century it had grown to 483 members and was seeking new ways to work out its mission of communicating God's grace.

Index

A

A.C. Van Raalte Church, Thule, S.D., 179
Abeel, David, 89, 90, 145
Academy Hall, 195
Adriance, Caroline E., 148
a'Lasco, John, 115
Albert, Bishop of Halberstadt, Magdeburg and Mainz, 7
Alcott, Gertrude (Whitenack), 146
Alexander, Robert, 28, 42
Alexander, Robert S., *Albany's First Church . . .* , 46
Algonquin Indians, 63
Allebach, Anne, 150
Alliance of Reformed Churches, 198, 200
Allison, Mary Bruins, *Doctor Mary in Arabia*, 98
American Board of Commissioners for Foreign Missions, 145
American Colonization Society, 102
Americanization, 136
Amity Press, 98
Amoy, China (now Xiamen), 90-98
Amoy Girls' School, 147
Amsterdam, 23
Anabaptists, 17
Anderson, Cornelia, 149
Anderson, Rufus, 145
Angola, Nicholas Manuel and Christina, 72, 73
Annville Institute, 151
Annville (Ky.) Reformed Church, 151
Antonides, Vincentius, 51
Anuak tribes, 100
Apache Indians, 68
Apostles' Creed, 14
Armerding, Paul L., *Doctors for the Kingdom*, 98
Asbury, Francis, 190, 191
Athanasian Creed, 14
Augustine, 5, 10, 11, 18
Auscherman, Charles, 162
Avignon, 6

B

Babb, Bernita, 146
Babylonian Captivity, 6
Bainton, Roland, *Here I Stand, A Life of Martin Luther*, 18
Baird, Donald R., *The McDowall Saga*, 178
Baptism, 23, 76, 77, 78, 94, 112, 113, 122, 124
Baptism, Eucharist and Ministry, 205
Baptists, 194
Barclay, Thomas, 44, 46
Bartholf, Guiliam, 49
Beardslee, Frances, 146
Beardslee, John W., III, "The Reformed Church in the American Revolution," 178
    Vision from the Hill . . . , 88,194
Beattie, John, 168, 169
Bechtel, Carol, 146
Bedminster Reformed Church, 145
Beeke, Joel R., ed., *Forerunner of the Great Awakening . . .* , 36, 58
Beidler, Fred P., 137
Beldman, Geertrui, 171
Belgic Confession, 14, 15, 58, 83, 128, 155
Beltman, Henry, 183
Benes, Louis, 172
Berenson, Murray J., 211

Bergan, John, 102, 103
Berry, J. Romeyn, 103
Bertholf, Guilliam, 44
Bethel Reformed Church, Passaic, N.J., 165
Bethesda Sanitarium, 183
Bethune, George Washington, 79, 80, 113
Bethune, Joanna, 145
Beys, Henricus, 51
Bianco of Siena, 7-8
Biblical preaching, 214
Bilkert, Henry, 96
Black Council (now African-American Council) 109, 216
Black Power, 109
Blauw, Jacob, 174
Board of Domestic Missions, 104, 105, 172, 173, 176
Board of Foreign Missions, 93
Boekhoven, Henry, 168, 175
Boel, Henricus, 48
Boersma, Jeanette, *Grace in the Gulf*, 98
Bogardus, Everardus, 26, 27, 60, 72, 75, 76, 77, 78, 80
Bons, Cor, 168, 175
Borgman, Joyce (de Velder), 146
Bottrell Reformed Church (Dog Pound), Alberta, 170
Bovendam, Henry, 182
Bovenkerk, Henry, 98
Bradley, Joseph, 162
Branch, Andrew, 107
Brewton, Ala., 105-107, 108
Broadhead, John Romeyn, 22
Broeffle, John, 168
Brookville Reformed Church, Long Island, N.Y., 217
Brouwer, Arie R., 156, 164, 165, 203
Brouwer, J. G., 182
Brown, Samuel, 94
Browne Street, Queens, N.Y., 216
Bruggers, Glenn and Phyllis, 98
Bruijn, L., 170, 172, 173
Bruins, Elton J., and Jeanne M. Jacobsen and Larry Wagonaar,
    Albertus C. Van Raalte, Dutch Leader & American Patriot, 134, 142
    and Robert P. Swierenga, *Family Quarrels . . .* , 124, 134, 142
    and Karen G. Schakel, Sara Fredrickson Simmons, and Marie N Zingle, *Albertus and Christina, The Van Raalte Family, Home, and Roots*, 134
Brumm, James Hart,
    Equipping the Saints . . . , 88, 218
    Singing the Lord's Song . . . , 36
Brummelkamp, Anthonie, 126, 127
Bucer, Martin, 9, 16, 17
Budde, D.A., 87
Bullen, Joseph, 67
Burlington, Iowa, 87
Burrell, David J., 161
Bussing Reformed Church, McKee, Ky., 151
Bussing, Emily M., (Mrs. John), 68, 148
Byrd, Manford Jr., 107, 109

C

Calvin, John, 1, 2, 9, 13, 16, 17, 18, 111, 115, 116, 118, 155
Canadian Reformed Churches, 167-178
Canons of Dort, 121, 122, 128
Cantine, James, 90, 91
Capitein, Jacobus Elisa Johannes, 74, 75

Carmichael, Stokley, 109
Carroll, John, 72
Cataraugus Indians, 67
Central College, 107, 184, 190
Chaat, Robert, 67
Chamberlain, Mary Eleanor Anable, *Fifty Years in Foreign Fields*, 152
Charavay, Florence, 58, 145
Charlemagne, 2, 4
Charter to Collegiate Church from William III, 36
Cheyenne Indians, 68
Chiapas, Mexico, 99
Chickasaw Indians, 67
Chippewa Indians, 67
Chiricahua Apache Indians, 65
Chittoor Female Seminary, Japan, 149
Christelijke Gereformeerde Kerk, 136, 142
Christian Action Commission, 163, 166
Christian Churches (Disciples of Christ), 194
Christian Reformed Church, 127, 132, 142, 170
Church World Service, 156, 159
Circuit rider, 191
Clarke, Angela, *Through the Changing Scenes of Life . . . Bahrain*, 98
Classis of Albany, 149, 152, 169
Classis of Amsterdam, 45, 51, 52, 54-56, 58, 61, 64, 75, 76, 77, 137
Classis of Brazil, 75
Classis of Brooklyn, 152
Classis of Grand Rapids, 172
Classis of Grand River, 141
Classis of Holland, 132, 141
Classis of Lake Erie, 151, 177
Classis of Middelstum, 124
Classis of Middleburg, 44
Classis of Montgomery, 149
Classis of New Brunswick, 103
Classis of New York, 104, 105
Classis of Ontario, 177
Classis of Philadelphia, 105, 106, 150
Classis of Queens, 215
Classis of Rockland-Westchester, 152
Classis of Schenectady, 160
Classis of Wisconsin, 141
Cleghorn, Mildred, 60, 69
Coakley, John, ed., *Concord Makes Strength . . .* , 202
Cobb, Henry E., 161
Coens, Henricus, 49
Coetus, 47, 49, 51-56
Coffin, Jose and Dona Luz, 99
Comforters of the Sick, 21, 23
Commanche Memorial Church, Lawton, Okla., 67, 68, 70
Committee on Education for World Peace, 158
Committee on Judicial Business, 152
Committee on Ministers' Fund, 160
Committee on Public Morals and Industrial Relations, 155, 156, 158
Common Lectionary, 205
Communion, *see* Lord's Supper
Communions, 137
Community Church, Cambria Heights, Brooklyn, N.Y., 216
Conciliarism, 6
Condict, Azubah C., 148
Conferentie, 47, 49, 51-56

Congregational, 113
Conscience Clause, 154
Conscientious objectors, 157
Consistory, 31
Constantine, 3
Constitution of the RCA, 85
Cooper, Stephen A., *Augustine for Armchair Theologians*, 18
Corinth Reformed Church, Byron Center, Mich., 165
Corona Community Church, Calif., 209
Couch, Sara M. 144, 153
Council for Hispanic Ministries, 216
Council for Pacific and Asian American Ministries, 216
Council of the Reformed Church in Canada, 177
Credo on Race Relations, 108, 109
Crystal Cathedral, Garden Grove, Calif., 187, 188
Cumming, William H., 95

D

Deacon, 14, 18, 150
de Bres, Guido, 15
De Cock, Hendrik, 121-124, 125, 126, 137
DeJong, Gerald F., *Dutch Reformed Church in the American Colonies*, 27, 70, 80, 98
    From Strength to Strength, 194
    Reformed Church in China, 98
Delaware Reformed Church, Lennox (Davis), S.D., 181
Dellius, Godfreidus, 60, 62, 64
De Moen, Christina Johanna (Van Raalte), 127
De Peyster, Sara, 144, 145
Deuteronomy 30:19
De Valois, John and Henriette, 97
de Velder, Joyce Borgman, 152
DeVos, Martin, 177
de Vries, David Pieterszoon, 26, 63
de Waard, D. Marc, 182
DeWitt Reformed Church, Manhattan, 107, 129, 216
De Witt, Thomas, 129
De Young, Benjamin, 151
Dirksen, Everett McKinley, 156, 162
Doleantie, 136, 142
Dooley, James, 102, 105, 106
Dorchester, S.S., 158
Doremus, Sara, 143, 145, 146, 148
Dort, Church Order of, 43, 44, 55
    Liturgy of, 113
    Synod of 111, 112, 119
Doty, Eleanor Ackley and Elihu, 144, 146, 147
Doty, Elihu, 90, 92, 96
Dragt, Gordon, 210, 211
Drayton Reformed Church, Drayton, Ont., 176
Drisius, Samuel, 60, 62, 76
Droog, Chester, 183, 186
DuBois, Catarina, 30, 35
DuBois, Gualtherus, 48, 51, 55
Dunnink, Arend, 172
Dunnink, Gerrit, 172
Duryee, Isaac G., 79
Dutch East India Company, 20, 21, 61

E

Early and medieval church history, 1-9
Educated ministry, 189-196
Ecumenical Creeds and Reformed Confessions, 18
Ecumenism, 93, 197-206
Edessa, Kingdom of, 168
Edinburgh, 1910, World Missionary Conference, 197, 204
Eelman, Neil, 173

Eighteenth Amendment, 156, 157
El Salvador, 165
Elder, 14, 18, 150
Elmendorf Reformed Church, Manhattan, 216
Elwood, Christopher, *Calvin for Armchair Theologians*, 18
Emmanuel Community Reformed Church, Alberta, 176
Emmanuel Reformed Church, Los Angeles, Calif., 185
English Presbyterian Church, 91, 96
Enlightenment, 140
Episcopal, 113, 114, 115
Erskine, Noel Leo, *Black People and the Reformed Church in America*, 80, 110
Esopus (later Kingston, Reformed), 45
Evangelical Lutheran Church in America, 200, 202
Excommunication, 13
Explanatory Articles, 81, 83

F

Fabend, Firth Haring, *A Dutch Family in the Middle Colonies*, 36
    Zion on the Hudson, Dutch New York . . ., 88
Fairview (Ill.) Reformed Church, 86
Faith and Order, 205
Falkenburg, Jan, 168, 175
Farel, Guilleume, 9, 13
Federal Council of Churches, 158, 159, 160, 198
Ferris Seminary, Yokohama, Japan, 149
Fieldmen, 176
Fikse, Al, 187
Fikse, Edward, 183
First Church, Albany, N.Y., 39, 42, 44, 48, 64
First Presbyterian Church, Cedar Grove, Wis., 137
First Reformed Church, Boyden, Iowa, 138
First Reformed Church, Cedar Grove, Wis., 137
First Reformed Church, Charles Mix, S.D., 181
First Reformed Church, Chatham, Ont., 174, 176
First Reformed Church, Denver, Colo., 183
First Reformed Church, Grand Rapids, Mich., 127
First Reformed Church, Jamaica, Queens, N.Y., 216
First Reformed Church, Lyndon, Wash., 182
First Reformed Church, New Brunswick, N.J., 57, 58, 101, 144, 145
First Reformed Church, Pella, Iowa, 136
First Reformed Church, Platte, S.D., 181
First Reformed Church, Saint Catharines, Ont., 177
First Reformed Church, Schnectady, N.Y., 158
Flypse, Vredryck, 53
Fordham Manor Reformed Church, Bronx, N.Y., 216
Foreman, Charles, 109
Formula of Agreement, 198, 200, 202, 204
Forrester, James, 129
Fort Nassau, 19, 20
Fort Sill, Okla., 65, 68, 69
Fort Washington Collegiate Church, N.Y., 160, 210
Foundation for Theological Education in Southeast Asia, 98
Fourth Corner Reformed Church, Bellingham, Wash., 182
Freeman, Bernardus, 64
Freemasonry, 136, 140, 141
Frelinghuysen, Frederick, 162
Frelinghuysen, Theodorus, 54
French and Indian War, 64
Freylinghuysen, Dina van Bergh, 71
Freylinghuysen, Johannes, 56, 57
Freylinghuysen, Theodorus Jacobus, 33, 48-51, 113
Fulton Street Prayer Meeting, 88
Fuqua International School of Christian Communication, 188

G

Garden Street Collegiate Church, N.Y., 35, 51
Gasero, Russell L., . . . *Changing Role of the Particular Synod*, 46
    Clarity, Conscience and Church Order . . ., 46
    Historical Directory, Reformed Church in America 1628-2000, 70
Gaut, Nora L., 151
Geertsma, Mrs. Martin, 171
General Synod, 91, 93
Geneva, 9, 13, 18
Gereformeerde Kerken, Nederlands, 170
Geronimo, 60, 69
Geyl, Pieter, *The Revolt in the Netherlands*, 17
Gorsuch, Judith Nelson, "Rev. Anne Jemima Allebach (1874-1918)" 154
Graafschaap Christian Reformed Church, 139
Grace Church, Orangeburg, 105
Gray Hawk Reformed Church, Ky., 151
Great Awakening, 49, 50
Great Schism, 6
Gronigen, University of, 121, 122, 124
Gronniger school of theology, 126
Gros, Jeffrey; Harding Meyer, and William G. Rusch, *Growth in Agreement . . .*, 206

H

Haan, Gijsbert, 139
Hageman, Howard G. 18, 109, 110, 117, 118, 215
    Our Reformed Church, 18
    Two Centuries Plus . . ., 88, 194
Hamilton, Ont., Canada, 172, 173
Han-chiong, Yap, 90
Hanhart, Karel, 175
Hardenbergh, Jacob Rutsen, 57
Harmelink, Herman, III, *Ecumenism and the Reformed Church*, 202
Harrison, Paul, 96
Hastings, Hugh, *Ecclesiastical Records of the State of New York*, 70
Heidelberg, 115
Heidelberg Catechism, 14, 15, 54, 128, 214,
Heideman, Eugene P., 161, 176, 178
    From Mission to Church . . . India, 98
Heldering, Johan, 168, 175
Hertzog, Ann, 145, 146
Hertzog Hall, 140
Hesselink, I. John, *On Being Reformed . . .*, 18
Hoekstra, Harvey and Lavina, 100
Hoff, Marvin D., "Fulton Street Prayer Meeting," 88
    Structures for Mission, 70, 98
Hoffman, Sam, 182
    and Helen, 99
Hondius, Jacobus, 74, 80
Honert, Jan van den, 75
Hope College, 125, 133, 134, 141, 157, 160, 187, 190
Hope Reformed Church, Los Angeles, Calif., 185
Hospers, Henry, 195
Hour of Power, 188
House, Renee S. and John W. Coakley, *Patterns and Portraits*...154, 164, 218
How, Samuel B. 72, 79, 80, 101, 208
Howard, William, 109, 203
Hudson, Henry, 19
Huizenga, Anna, 160
Humby, Peggy, *History of the Reformed Church in Canada*, 178
Hutton, Mancius Smedes, 115

Huygens, Jan, 23
Hymnal of the Reformed Church, 85
Hymnody, 214
Hymns, 113, 120, 122, 132, 138, 208, 214

I

Iglesia del Consolador, Chicago, Ill., 216
Iglesia La Senda, Corona, Calif., 209
Immigration and growth, 214, 215
Indigenous church, 94
Indulgences, 9, 10, 11
Institute of Successful Church Leadership, 188
International Missionary Conference, 204
Investiture conflict, 5
Irving, Washington, 53

J

Jackson County, Ky., 171
James, M. Stephen, 117
Jamison, Wallace N., 140
Janssen, Allan J., *Constitutional Theology*, 46, 154, 164, 218
Jesuits, 62
Jicarilla Apache Reformed Church, Dulce, N. Mex., 65, 69, 70
Jogues, Isaac, 38, 39
John 10:10, 166
Johnson, W. J., 102, 104, 105
Joint Declaration on Justification by Faith, 198, 205, 206
Joralmon, John S. 94
Jordan, Mark, 102
Justice issues, 155-166
Justification, 13, 18
Justinian, 2, 4

K

Kansfield, Mary,
    Letters to Hazel . . . , 154
    *Some Unique Contributions of RCA Women...*145, 146, 148
Kasper, Walter, 206
Kats, Wilma, 100
Kellogg Peace Pact, 157
Kempers, John and Mabel, 99
Kidder, Mary, 144, 146
Kieft, Willem, 26, 27, 39, 60, 63, 78
Kiel, Wesley, 182
King, Martin Luther, Jr., 109
Kinnamon, Michael, and Brian E. Cope, *The Ecumenical Movement . . .* , 202
Kleijn, H. G., 139
Klein, Corstian, 182
Knox, John, 18
Knox, Rebecca, 145, 146
Koerlin, E. F., 181
Koerselman, Richard, 218
Korver, Harold, 185
Krabbendam, Hans, *Dutch-American Experience . . .* , 88
Krol, Bastiaen Janszoon, 21, 23
Kuyper, Abraham, 136, 142
Kyle, Thomas, 84

L

Labagh, Peter, 84
Laidlie, Archibald, 30
Laman, Gordon, *Guido F. Verbeck . . .* , 95
Lap-Han-Chiong, 93
Lee, Hak Kwan, 213
Liberty Bell, New York, 52
Life and Work, 204

Lima Liturgy, 205
Liturgy, 15, 212
    of the church, 111, 116-117
Liturgy & Psalms, 1968, 115, 118
Liturgy and Psalms of the Reformed Church in America, 1906, 112
Livingston, John Henry, 55, 56, 81, 82, 83, 85, 8, 113, 134, 189, 191
London Mission Society, 91
Lord's Supper, 9, 15, 17, 18, 23, 24, 55, 62, 78, 112, 113, 117, 118, 132, 139, 208
Lubbers, Elaine, 146
Luidens, Donald, 217
    and Roger Nemeth, *Intra- and Intergenerational Transmission...*, 218; *Reformed Vitality...*, 218
Lull, Timothy F., *Luther for Armchair Theologians*, 18
Luther, Martin, 1, 2, 9, 10, 11, 12
Lutheran World Federation, 206
Lydius, Johannes, 64

M

Machinaw Indians, 67
Macy Reformed Church, Macy, Neb., 69
Marble Collegiate Church, N.Y., 161, 210, 216
Mast, Gregg A., *In Remembrance and Hope*, 18, 110, 118
Mayfair Community Church, Lakewood, Calif., 183
McDowell, Robert, 168, 169
Meeter, Daniel, *Meeting Each Other in Doctrine, Liturgy & Government*, 46
Megapolensis, Johannes, 25, 27, 28, 30, 39, 46, 60, 61, 62, 66
Mennonite, 111, 112, 113
Mescalero (N. Mex.) Reformed Church, 65
Methodists, 189, 190, 191, 193, 194
Meyerink, Paul and Dorothy, 99
Michaelius, Jonas, 21, 24, 25, 38, 60, 66, 75, 112, 207, 210, 211
Middle Collegiate Church, N.Y., 52, 156, 158, 207, 210, 211
Middle Dutch Church, N.Y., 34
Miller, Valerie De Marinus, 152
Minister of Word and sacrament, 150
Miraloma Community Church, San Francisco, Calif., 183
Miriam, Um, 91
Mission Gleaner, 148
Mission poultry farm, 97
Missionary activity of the Reformed Church in America, 89-100
Mohawk Indians, 23, 61, 63, 64
Molenaar, Gerrit, 168, 175
Monarch Reformed Church, Alberta, 167
Moore, Christopher, 73
    and Kim Baker, *Gathered from Many Nations . . .* , 27
    and Pamela Johnson, *Santa and Pete . . .* , 80
Motley, John Lathrop, *The Rise of the Dutch Republic*, 17
Mott Haven Reformed Church, Bronx, N.Y. 107, 216
Mullet, Michael, *Calvin*, 18
Murata, Wakasa, 90, 94
Muste, Abraham J., 160, 161, 165

N

Nagasaki, Japan, 153
Napoleonic Code, 123, 128
National Council of Churches of Christ, USA, 109, 164, 165, 198, 203
Native Americans, 59-70
Nederlands Hervormde Kerk, 170
Nemeth, Roger, 217
    and Donald A. Luidens, *Intra- and Intergenerational Transmission...*, 218; *Reformed Vitality...*, 218

New Brunswick Theological Seminary, 58, 83, 103, 105, 134, 139, 140, 189, 190, 192, 215
New Church of Greater New York, Roslyn Heights, N.Y., 213
New England Society for the Propagation of the Faith, 64
New Hope Community Church, Gilbert, Ariz., 218
New Lots Reformed, Brooklyn, N.Y., 107, 216
New Netherland Company, 19, 20
New Paltz, French Church, 33, 41
New York Missionary Society, 67
Nicene-Constinopolitan Creed, 2, 14
Nienhuis, Donald, 186
Noko, Ishmael, 206
Nooksack Valley Reformed Church, Nooksack, Wash., 182
North Church, Newark, N.J.. 215
Northern Missionary Society, 67
Northwestern College, 190, 195

O

Oggel House, 192
Oggel, Pieter J., 137
Old Dutch Church of Sleepy Hollow, 53
Old Mud Meeting House, 84, 114
Old Queen's, 83
Old Stone Church, 33
Omaha Indians, 68
Onondaga Indians, 64
Orthodoxy, 49
Osage Indians, 67
Osterhaven, M. Eugene, 139
Oudersluys, Richard C., 117
Our Song of Hope, 161

P

Particular Synod of Albany, 91, 93
Particular Synod of Chicago, 141
Patroon, 28, 74
Peace issues, 157
Peale, Norman Vincent, 196
Peale, Ruth Stafford, 148, 196
Penn, William, 72
Phelps, Frances (Otte), 146
Phelps, Phillip, 192
Phoenix, 137
Pietism, 47-52, 54
Pillar Church, 135, 142
Pioneer School, 195
Plan of Union, 81, 82, 85,
Pleasant Prairie Academy, 136, 190, 193
Polhemus, Johannes Theodorus, 40, 51
Poling, Clark V., 158
Pontier, Glenn, 166
Posthuma, Peter, 172
Presbyterian Church in the United States (Southern), 106
Presbyterian Church of Canada, 170
Presbyterian Church, USA, 201
Prone, 8
Psalm 31:15-18, 23-24, 55
Psalm 38:9-10, 17-22, 55
Psalms, 113, 120, 122
Pullain, Vallerand, 115

Q

Quakers, 73, 74
Queens College, New Brunswick, N.J., 57, 82, 83, 134

R

Ramirez, Allan, 217

Rancho Community Church, Temecula, Calif., 187
Rationalism, 140
Ratmeyer, Una H., *Hands, Hearts and Voices*, 154, 164, 218
Rebaptism, 73, 76, 200
Rebels, 47, 49
Redeker, Russell, 176
Reformation, 9-18
Reformed Church in the Netherlands, 119
Regional Synod of Canada, 177
Rensselaer, Kiliaen Van, 28, 46
Rensselaerswyck, 28, 61
Revelation 14:6-7, 89
Ridder, Herman J., 205
Roe, Mabel, 65
Roe, Walter C., 65
Roman Catholic Church, 206
Romero, Oscar, 165
Romeyn, Dirck, 67
Ronayne, Edmond, 141
Roosevelt, Theodore, 162
Runk, Mrs. Charles A., 68
Rutgers College, 83, 103
Rutgers University, 134

S

Sabbath observance, 157
Sanctification, 13
Schaff, Philip, 138
Schieffelin, Samuel, 133
Schism, 142
Scholte Club, 126, 127
Scholte, H. P., 122, 123, 125, 126, 127, 128, 136, 137
Schuller, Robert H., 187,188
    My Journey From an Iowa Farm to a Cathedral of Dreams,
    188
Schwarz, Diebold, 9
Scudder, Ida S., 146, 147
Scudder, John and Harriet Waterbury, 144, 148
Scudder, Lewis R., III, *The Arabian Mission's Story*, 96, 98
Scudder, Sara, 144
Scudder, Sarah Tracy (Mrs. Ezekiel), 147
Secession, 121, 123, 124
Second Dutch Reformed Church, Albany, N.Y., 130
Second Reformed Church, Artesia, Calif., 184
Second Reformed Church, New Brunswick, N.J., 103
Secularism, 212
Selyns, Henry, 76
Seneca Indians, 67
Serrano, Andres, 209
Shin Kwang Church, Bayside, Long Island, N.Y., 215
Simmons, D. B., 94
Six Mile Run Reformed Church, 33
Slavery, 71-80
Smith, Cora A., 151
Smith, George N. and Arvilla A., 131
Social security, 156, 159-161
Society for Foreign Missions, 67
Society for Propagation of the Gospel in Foreign Parts, 64
Sommerville, Reformed Church in, 57
Southern Normal School, 106, 107, 109, 110
Soviet Union, 164, 188
St. Nicholas (Stone church in the Fort), N.Y., 26, 73
St. Nicholas Collegiate Church, N.Y., 67, 114
St. Thomas, Reformed Church, Virgin Islands, 43
Stedge, Joyce, 152
Stellingwerff, Johan, *Iowa Letters: Dutch Immigrants on the
    American Frontier*, 87, 88

Stewart, Sonja, 146
Stobbelaar, H., 138
Strasbourg, 9
Struikmans, Steve, 187
Stuyvesant, Peter, 29, 40, 74, 78, 80
Sudan, Africa, 100
Suffrage, 149
Sunday school, oldest, 144
Sunnyside Reformed Church, Queens, N.Y., 150
Swart, Morrell F., *Call of Africa*, 98
Swart, Robert and Morrell, 100
Swierenga, Robert P., *Dutch Chicago . . .*, 88
Synod, 31
Synod of Dort, 15, 37
Synod of New York, 215
Synod of North Holland, 55, 56, 82
Synod of South Holland, 35, 198, 199, 201

T

Tai-hoey, 89, 93
Talmadge, Abby F. Woodruff, 149
Talmage, John Van Nest, 93, 95, 96
Tarrytown, Reformed Church in, 53
Temperance, 149, 156
ten Zythoff, Gerrit J., 176, 178
    Sources of Secession . . ., 124, 134
Tesschenmacker, Peter, 38, 45
Theology, 214
Thomas à Kempis, 8
Thomas, Felicia, 210
Thomas, Sally, 144, 145
Thunderbird, Mary, 68
Tories, 47, 49, 57, 58
Torrance, Thomas F., 214
Tuscaora Indians, 67
Twain, Mark, 207
Twin Falls (Idaho) Reformed Church, 186

U

Ulrum, 121, 124
Union with Christ, 18
United Church of Canada, 170, 172, 173
United Foreign Missionary Society, 67
United Presbyterian Church, 100

V

van Alstine, Peter, 168
van Beaumont, Adrian 76
van Bergh, Dina, 54-57, 71
Van Bunschooten, Elias, 85
Van Buren, Martin, 162
Van Cleef, Amelia Lent, 149
Van den Berg, Richard, 173
Vander Lugt, Gerrit T., 117, 118
Van der Meulen, Cornelius, 130
Van der Meulen, Jacob, 138
VanderMey, Albert, *To All Our Children . . .*, 171-175, 177, 178
Vander Schuut, K., 137
Van Doren, Sara, 143
Van Driessen, Peter, 64, 66
Van Dyke, Albert, 183
Van Dyke, Gerard, 57
    Diary of Dina van Bergh, 58
Van Dyke, John, 72, 79, 80
Van Elderen, Marlin, and Martin Conway, *Introducing the World
    Council of Churches*, 202
Van Engen, Garold and Ruth, 99
Van Ess, Dorothy, *Pioneers in the Arab World*, 96, 98

Van Ess, John 90, 96
Van Hoeven, James W., *Piety and Patriotism*, 58, 178
    Word and World: Reformed Theology in America, 142, 164
Van Kleek, R. D., 103
van Kuiken, Jellie, 168, 175
Van Liewen, William, 137
Van Lummel, A. J., 141
Van Nieuwenhuysen, Wilhelmus, 44
Van Peursem, Josephine, 91
Van Raalte, Albertus (senior), 121
Van Raalte, Albertus Christiaan, 125-134, 135, 136, 139, 190, 192
Van Santvoord, C., 103
Van Staalduinen, C., 172
Van Velzen, Simon, 126, 127
Van Vleck Hall, 133
Van Vorst, Julia, 106
Van Wylen, Gordon J., *Vision for a Christian College*, 134,194
Venema, Janny, *Deacons Accounts . . .*, 36
Verbeck, Guido, 94
Vietnamese conflict, 163, 166
Voorhees, Elizabeth, 145
Votum, 15, 112
Vriesman, Brian, 187?
Vrooman, Barent, 41

W

Walden, Islay, 102, 103
War of 1812, 169, 170
Waring, Hart, 127
West End Collegiate Church, 26, 73, 161, 210
West India Company, 20, 25, 34, 37, 38, 72, 74, 75
Westdale Reformed Church, Hamilton, Ont., 177
Western Theological Seminary, 58, 106, 107, 109, 110, 125, 133,
    134, 165, 185?, 190, 192
Whitefield, George, 75
Wiley, Charles, 103
Wilkes, Amy (Mrs. Samuel Zwemer), 148
William I, 120, 121, 129, 138
William of Orange (the Silent), 16
Williams, Samuel, 107
Winnebago (Neb.) Reformed Church, 70
Woman's Board of Foreign Missions, 145, 148
Women deacons and elders in South Fukian Synod, 97
Women's Board of Domestic Mission, 151
Women's Executive Committee, Board of Domestic Missions, 65
Women's ordination to church offices, 149, 150-153
Woolman, John, 72, 75, 80
World Council of Churches, 159, 164 170, 198, 199, 204, 205
World War I, 170
World War II, 170
Worship, 111-118
Worship, Reformation, 8, 9
Wright, Frank Hall, 60, 68
Wyckoff, Isaac Newton, 79, 80, 130

Y

Young, George, 127
Ypma, Martin A., 130

Z

Zabriskie, F. N., 104
Zegerius, Harri, 172, 173, 174, 177
Zonne, Pieter, 136, 137
Zurich, 12
Zwemer, James, 195
Zwemer, Samuel, 90, 91
Zwingli, Ulrich, 1, 2, 8, 9, 12, 115